King and Cultus
in Chronicles

Worship and the
Reinterpretation of History

William Riley

Journal for the Study of the Old Testament
Supplement Series 160

JOURNAL FOR THE STUDY OF THE OLD TESTAMENT SUPPLEMENT SERIES
160

JSOT Press
Sheffield

Copyright © 1993 Sheffield Academic Press

Published by JSOT Press
JSOT Press is an imprint of
Sheffield Academic Press Ltd
343 Fulwood Road
Sheffield S10 3BP
England

Typeset by Sheffield Academic Press
and
Printed on acid-free paper in Great Britain
by Biddles Ltd
Guildford

British Library Cataloguing in Publication Data

Riley, William
    King and Cultus in Chronicles: Worship
    and the Reinterpretation of History.—
    (JSOT Supplement Series, ISSN 0309-0787;
    No. 160)
    I. Title II. Series
    222

    ISBN 1-85075-397-0

CONTENTS

ACKNOWLEDGMENTS

The present study represents a revised and edited version of a dissertation presented to the Pontifical University of St Thomas in Rome in October 1990. I wish, therefore, to register my debt of gratitude to the Reverend Professor Joseph Agius, OP, who acted as moderator of the work and who improved this study greatly by his kind and wise suggestions and by his remarkable generosity with both personal interest and time. Qualities such as kindness, wisdom and generosity, which everyone preparing a dissertation might hope for in a moderator, inspire the most sincere gratitude in the candidate who actually benefits from them. Thanks are also due to other members of the faculty, in particular the Reverend Professor Emeritus P.P. Zerafa, OP, the Reverend Professor Bernardo G. Boschi, OP, and the Reverend Professor Albert Paretsky, OP, all of whom offered helpful and insightful comments on the work.

I must also express my gratitude to the late Archbishop Kevin McNamara of Dublin who asked me to begin work on this dissertation and who provided me with the time and resources to undertake it, and to Archbishop Desmond Connell who has shown sincere interest in this work since his elevation to the See of Dublin in 1988. Thanks are also due to the Reverend Dr Dermot Lane, Director of the Mater Dei Institute of Education, to Teresita Durkan, former President of Our Lady of Mercy College of Education (now lamentably no longer in existence as a college of education), and to my colleagues and former colleagues in both colleges who accommodated my periods of study leave, at times not without some inconvenience to themselves. I express my debt of gratitude also to my friends Father Shán Ó Cuív and Dr Carmel McCarthy, RSM, who read portions of this work (both in its former state and in its present reincarnation) and who offered invaluable and encouraging comments. I am also greatly indebted to the editors of the *Journal for the Study of the Old Testament* for the inclusion of this work in their Supplement Series and to the staff of

Sheffield Academic Press for their assistance in preparing it for publication.

Finally, I record my gratitude to my parents, James and Genevieve Riley, who first taught me to value the things of God. To them this work is dedicated.

William Riley
Mater Dei Institute
Dublin
1 May 1992

ABBREVIATIONS

AB	Anchor Bible
AJSL	*The American Journal of Semitic Languages and Literatures*
ANET	J.B. Pritchard (ed.), *Ancient Near Eastern Texts*
AsSeign	*Assemblées du Seigneur*
ATD	Das Alte Testament Deutsch
BA	*The Biblical Archaeologist*
BDB	F. Brown, S.R. Driver and C.A. Briggs, *Hebrew and English Lexicon of the Old Testament*
BEATAJ	Beiträge zur Erforschung des alten Testaments und des antiken Judentums
BHS	*Biblia hebraica stuttgartensia*
Bib	*Biblica*
BKAT	Biblischer Kommentar: Altes Testament
BO	*Bibbia e Oriente*
BTB	*Biblical Theology Bulletin*
BWANT	Beiträge zur Wissenschaft vom Alten und Neuen Testament
BZ	*Biblische Zeitschrift*
CAB	Cahiers d'Archéologie Biblique
CAT	Commentaire de l'Ancien Testament
CB	The Century Bible
CBC	The Cambridge Bible Commentary on the New English Bible
CBQ	*Catholic Biblical Quarterly*
CBSC	The Cambridge Bible for Schools and Colleges
CTM	*Concordia Theological Monthly*
DSB	The Daily Study Bible
EncJud	*Encyclopaedia Judaica*
ETL	*Ephemerides theologicae lovanienses*
Expos	*The Expositor*
FOTL	The Forms of the Old Testament Literature
FRLANT	Forschungen zur Religion und Literatur des Alten und Neuen Testaments
FTS	Freiburger theologische Studien
GBSOT	Guides to Biblical Scholarship: Old Testament Series
GKC	*Gesenius' Hebrew Grammar*, ed. E. Kautzsch, trans. A.E. Cowley
GPT	Growing Points in Theology
HAT	Handbuch zum Alten Testament

HBT	*Horizons in Biblical Theology*
HSM	Harvard Semitic Monographs
HTR	*Harvard Theological Review*
ICC	International Critical Commentary
IDB	G.A. Buttrick (ed.), *The Interpreter's Dictionary of the Bible*
IDBSup	*IDB*, Supplementary Volume
Im	*Immanuel*
Int	*Interpretation*
JBL	*Journal of Biblical Literature*
JETS	*Journal of the Evangelical Theological Society*
JSOT	*Journal for the Study of the Old Testament*
JSOTSup	*Journal for the Study of the Old Testament*, Supplement Series
JSS	*Journal of Semitic Studies*
JTS	*Journal of Theological Studies*
LD	Lectio divina
LS	*Louvain Studies*
MBS	Message of Biblical Spirituality
NCB	The New Century Bible
NEchtB	Die Neue Echter Bibel
NERT	W. Beyerlin (ed.), *Near Eastern Religious Texts Relating to the Old Testament*
NVB	Nuovissima Versione della Bibbia
OLP	Orientalia lovanensia periodica
Or	*Orientalia*
OTG	Old Testament Guides
OTL	Old Testament Library
OTM	Old Testament Message
OTS	Old Testament Studies
OTWSA	Oud-Testamentiese Werkgemeenskap in Suid-Africa
PEGLMBS	*Proceedings, Eastern Great Lakes and Midwest Bible Societies*
PIBA	*Proceedings of the Irish Biblical Association*
PTMS	Pittsburgh Theological Monograph Series
RB	*Revue biblique*
RivB	*Rivista Biblica*
RTP	*Revue de théologie et de philosophie*
SB	La Sainte Bible
SBA	Studies in Biblical Archaeology
SBB	Soncino Books of the Bible
SBibbia	La Sacra Bibbia
SBLDS	Society of Biblical Literature Dissertation Series
SBLMS	Society of Biblical Literature Monograph Series
SBS	Stuttgarter Bibelstudien
SBT	Studies in Biblical Theology
SD	*Sacra Doctrina*

SJT	*Scottish Journal of Theology*
SNTSMS	Society for New Testament Studies Monograph Series
VTSup	*Vetus Testamentum*, Supplements
TBC	Torch Bible Commentaries
TDOT	*Theological Dictionary of the Old Testament*
THAT	E. Jenni and C. Westemann (eds.), *Theologisches Handwörterbuch zum Alten Testament*
TLZ	*Theologische Literaturzeitung*
TQ	*Theologische Quartalschrift*
TrinJ	*Trinity Journal*
TTh	*The Theologian*
TynBul	*Tyndale Bulletin*
VD	*Verbum domini*
VT	*Vetus Testamentum*
WBC	Word Biblical Commentary
WMANT	Wissenschaftliche Monographien zum Alten und Neuen Testament
WTJ	*The Westminster Theological Journal*
ZAW	*Zeitschrift für die alttestamentliche Wissenschaft*

INTRODUCTION

Even the uninitiated reader can perceive that the books of Chronicles display a striking interest in the cultus of Israel. Readers of Chronicles who are familiar with the older presentation of Israel's monarchical history in the books of Samuel and Kings will also notice that the Jerusalem kings are portrayed with greater attention paid to their cultic activities in the Chronicler's history than is evident in the earlier work. This study explores the relationship that the Chronicler has portrayed between the Jerusalem kings and the cultus and investigates the liturgical focus that the Chronicler has given to his history.

The consideration of any biblical work must first situate that work against its immediate background. In an attempt to establish the context from which the books of Chronicles emerge, the first chapter of this book takes into account some of the recent scholarly investigation of Chronicles and states the position taken on such introductory questions as the extent and unity of the Chronicler's work, the sources employed by him in its composition and the identification of the author and his time. This initial chapter also considers the possible need which the author perceived and which led him to construct his history.

Recent literary study of biblical narratives has emphasized the necessity of the synchronic consideration of canonical texts in addition to the diachronic investigations which have characterized much of biblical scholarship in the twentieth century. The second chapter pursues an investigation of the relationship between king and cultus by means of a final form study of the Chronicler's monarchical narratives. This study also pays particular attention to the emergence of the Chronicler's approach to the dynastic promise in the unfolding of his history.

The investigation undertaken in the final form study allows for various aspects of the Chronicler's thought to emerge. The final chapter attempts to draw together some of these into a synthesis of the

Chronicler's message concentrating on the nature of the kingly vocation in the Chronicler's outlook, the fulfilment of the Davidic promise, and the identification of the Davidic heritage in the Chronicler's post-exilic world.

Among the various investigations and considerations presented in this work, the reader is asked to notice in particular how the ancient Near Eastern temple ideology has exerted its influence upon the Chronicler. Indeed, that influence has been exerted in both directions, for not only has the Chronicler used the ideology (which he had inherited in its specifically Israelite expression in Israel's cultic and historical traditions), but through his use of the ideology, he has transformed it, making it a means of viewing both the rise and the fall of the Davidic dynasty. The Chronicler's application of that ideology to both the monarchical story and his contemporary situation gave the Chronistic History much of its subtlety and artistry and enabled the Chronicler to express his conviction of the undiminished continuation of God's faithfulness towards the divinely chosen nation, even in the face of apparent discontinuity. By doing so, the Chronicler has also captured an aspect of the divine relationship with humanity that is still worthy of the pondering and celebrating found in the Chronicler's own narrative of the interaction between God and the nation of Israel.

Chapter 1

SITUATING THE WORK OF THE CHRONICLER

Introduction

Theologians—both ancient and modern—form their insights and express them within a manifold environment. The ideological presuppositions within that environment might provide a supportive framework for these insights at times, while at other times they represent misconceptions which the theologian wishes to dispel. Political and economic conditions will lend urgency to some aspects of the human relationship with the divine, while other aspects temporarily receive a lesser emphasis. Religious symbols and expressions of another time and circumstance are often made to speak with new vigour, new clarity, and sometimes new meaning.

Those who investigate the theologies of the biblical authors immediately encounter the necessity of seeing these theologies in their proper linguistic, social, historical and ideological contexts, since these differ so markedly from the contexts of the investigators. The identification of the original contexts can never be comprehensive since the background information available to the modern investigator is limited both by its scope and by its own need for contextualization; the fact that any national community at a given time contains not one but several combinations of linguistic, social and ideological factors further limits the possibility of exactitude in identifying a precise set of factors as the context for a biblical work or its theology. Yet the quest to situate the canonical writings within their proper environments is the only way of liberating them from slavery to modern ideologies.

The very existence of the books of Chronicles raises the question of the complex relationship between theology and environment; the narratives contained in these books are largely extant in older canonical works, most notably in the Deuteronomistic History. Why, then, should the books of Chronicles be composed at all? The name given to this work in the Septuagint, Παραλειπόμενα, itself seems to represent an attempt to answer this question; the material contained in Chronicles is intended to supplement the narrative of the Deuteronomistic History.[1] However, the attempted answer fails, for it misrepresents the Chronicler's method:[2] material from the Deuteronomistic History is not simply repeated with supplementary material, but reworked in its re-presentation. The new context of the Chronicler has also necessitated a reworking of many of the characters and symbols he has inherited in the narrative that provides the skeleton of his work; among these are the king and cultus at the centre of the present study.

This chapter attempts to identify the environment in which the Chronicler's work was written. The first section outlines the position taken in the present investigation on some introductory questions. The Chronicler's need to re-present the monarchical history—an issue which bears directly upon his purpose and theological method and which has special significance for this study—is considered separately in the second section of this chapter.

A Consideration of Some Introductory Questions

The past century of scholarly investigation of the Chronistic History and the issues concerning it have produced a range of conclusions which seem to span the full spectrum of possible options. Perhaps the greatest effect that these scholarly efforts have had is the replacement of former certainties and presuppositions with caution and an awareness of the need to investigate carefully the questions relating to Chronicles from the internal evidence afforded by the Chronicler's work. The careful work and detailed investigations of recent scholars allows the proposal of working hypotheses on some introductory questions against which the present study of king and cultus in Chronicles is undertaken.

---

1. W. Rudolph, *Chronikbücher*, p. iii.
2. H.G.M. Williamson, *1 and 2 Chronicles*, p. 4, indicates the misrepresentation of the nature and purpose of the Books of Chronicles implicit in the Greek name and expresses the opinion that 'the influence of this misnomer in the Septuagint and Vulgate on the Christian church has contributed significantly to the undervaluing and consequent neglect of these books until comparatively recent times'.

The Extent and Unity of the Chronicler's Work

Until recently, the extent of the Chronicler's work was seen to encompass the present biblical books of First and Second Chronicles, Ezra and Nehemiah. This position might well have been taken to be one of the sure results of modern biblical scholarship and, as such, is often proposed or assumed both in standard works of Old Testament introduction[1] and in specialist studies of Chronicles[2] alike.

Appeal is sometimes made to the Babylonian Talmud to demonstrate the essential unity of Chronicles with Ezra–Nehemiah. Leaving aside the question of the value of such witness for the composition of the biblical books, it must be noted that the reference to Chronicles in the Babylonian Talmud does not, in fact, unify the said books; instead, it states that there were two stages in the composition of Chronicles, one by Ezra and the other by Nehemiah.[3] There is no more evident intention to see Chronicles and Ezra–Nehemiah as a unified work than there is to attribute such unity to the books of Jeremiah and Kings, to which the Babylonian Talmud also applies a common authorship.[4]

The unity of Chronicles with Ezra-Nehemiah began to be examined afresh as a result of the linguisitic arguments for separation of these biblical works proposed by Japhet[5] and developed by Williamson.[6] Theological investigations produced further indications that

---

1. For example S.R. Driver, *An Introduction to the Literature of the Old Testament*, pp. 535-40; O. Eissfeldt, *The Old Testament: An Introduction*, pp. 530-31; A. Robert and A. Feuillet, *Introduction to the Old Testament*, pp. 485, 495.

2. Among the many scholars who have worked on Chronicles and who have deemed it to be part of a larger work with Ezra and Nehemiah we might mention: J. Wellhausen, *Prolegomena to the History of Ancient Israel*, p. 171; E.L. Curtis and A.A. Madsen, *A Critical and Exegetical Commentary on the Books of Chronicles*, pp. 27-36; F. Michaeli, *Les livres des Chroniques, d'Esdras et de Néhémie*, pp. 32-35; J.M. Myers, *I Chronicles*, p. xviii; L. Randellini, *Il libro delle Cronache*, pp. 25-26; R. Mosis, *Untersuchungen zur Theologie des chronistischen Geschichtswerkes*, pp. 205-207; F.M. Cross, 'A Reconstruction of the Judean Restoration', pp. 4-5; S.L. McKenzie, *The Chronicler's Use of the Deuteronomistic History*, pp. 17-23; A.M. Solomon, 'The Structure of the Chronicler's History: A Key to the Organization of the Pentateuch', pp. 51-64.

3. *b. B. Bat.* 15a.

4. *b. B. Bat.* 15a.

5. 'The Supposed Common Authorship of Chronicles and Ezra–Nehemiah Investigated Anew', pp. 330-71.

6. *Israel in the Books of Chronicles*, pp. 5-70.

Chronicles existed as a separate work from Ezra–Nehemiah.[1] Although the arguments put forward for seeing Chronicles and Ezra–Nehemiah as separate compositions did not win immediate support from those working in the field, the question had been successfully reopened and new possibilities could be considered to account for both the similarities and the differences; these possibilities include the composition of separate works by the same author or school,[2] the sharing of common tradition by separate authors composing separate works[3] and a unity which arises not from their genesis but from the biblical presentation of these works.[4] Among the various possibilities, a single author (or school of authors) composing one grand work running from the present First Chronicles to the end of the book of Nehemiah now seems more and more unlikely.

Problems of extent also arise in relation to the books of Chronicles themselves, particularly with respect to the genealogies of 1 Chronicles 1–9 which are often seen as a later addition to the work.[5] However, Johnson,[6] Williamson[7] and Dillard[8] have discovered some of the same theological concerns in the genealogies as in the

1. Cf. J.D. Newsome, 'Toward a New Understanding of the Chronicler and his Purposes', pp. 201-17; D.J. McCarthy, 'Covenant and Law in Chronicles–Nehemiah', pp. 25-44; M.A. Throntveit, *When Kings Speak: Royal Speech and Royal Prayer in Chronicles*, pp. 1-9. Throntveit had earlier expressed the judgment that the arguments of Japhet and Williamson had not forced a conclusion of separate authorship for Chronicles and Ezra–Nehemiah, although they had succeeded in shifting the burden of proof; see M.A. Throntveit, 'Linguistic Analysis and the Question of Authorship in Chronicles, Ezra and Nehemiah', pp. 201-16.

2. T. Willi, *Die Chronik als Auslegung*, pp. 176-82; P. Welten, *Geschichte und Geschichtsdarstellung in den Chronikbüchern*, p. 4; P.R. Ackroyd, 'The Historical Literature', p. 307.

3. W.J. Dumbrell, 'The Purpose of the Books of Chronicles', pp. 257-58; R.L. Braun, 'Chronicles, Ezra, and Nehemiah: Theology and Literary History', pp. 52-64; *idem, 1 Chronicles*, p. xx.

4. P.R. Ackroyd, 'Chronicles–Ezra–Nehemiah: The Concept of Unity', pp. 199-201.

5. For example, see Wellhausen, *Prolegomena to the History of Ancient Israel*, p. 211; M. Noth, *The Chronicler's History*, p. 69; Newsome, 'Toward a New Understanding of the Chronicler and his Purposes', p. 215.

6. *The Purpose of the Biblical Genealogies*, pp. 47-55.

7. *Israel in the Books of Chronicles*, pp. 81-82.

8. 'Reward and Punishment in Chronicles: The Theology of Immediate Retribution', pp. 169-70.

remainder of Chronicles; while not denying that the books might contain later additions either in the genealogies or elsewhere, these scholars show the possibility that there might be a theological cohesion and a literary unity present in Chronicles.[1]

The intended relationship of Chronicles to Samuel–Kings presents a different problem, although it has not occupied the time of investigators to the degree that questions of unity and extent have. Willi proposes that Chronicles was intended to illuminate the text of Samuel–Kings and to bring a new understanding to the former work.[2] Dillard suggests that the Chronicler's narrative presumes in his audience a high level of familiarity with Samuel–Kings.[3] Such a thesis is difficult to establish in the light of the alterations which the Chronicler makes to the narrative of his *Vorlage*. The positive end to the story of Manasseh,[4] to take but one example, hardly admits of a facile harmonization in the audience's mind with their supposed thorough knowledge of the negative Deuteronomistic account. Rather, the Chronicler's liberties with his sources and simple transformation of the story identified by Brunet[5] point to his intention in producing a new work, which may presume a general knowledge of Israel's historical heritage but which does not expect that the audience engage in a detailed synoptic study of this production alongside its *Vorlage*.[6]

There therefore exists some considerable justification in recent scholarship for seeing Chronicles as a distinct literary whole which is independent of Ezra–Nehemiah and which does not presume detailed familiarity or comparison with Samuel–Kings for its meaningful reception. While allowing that the text of Chronicles has not necessarily remained static since the day of its first literary crystallization, the present study will follow the synchronic approach and examine the work as it has been received canonically. This approach has the

1. For a study which argues for the unity of Chronicles with regard to another passage often cited as a later addition, cf. J.W. Wright, 'The Legacy of David in Chronicles: The Narrative Function of 1 Chronicles 23–27', pp. 229-42.

2. *Die Chronik als Auslegung*, pp. 66 and 233.

3. 'The Reign of Asa (2 Chronicles 14–16): An Example of the Chronicler's Theological Method', p. 214.

4. 2 Chron. 33.10-20; compare 2 Kgs 21.10-18.

5. 'Le Chroniste et ses sources', p. 497.

6. R.K. Duke, *The Persuasive Appeal of the Chronicler: A Rhetorical Analysis*, pp. 36-37, 111-12.

advantage of respecting an essential feature of the nature of Chronicles as a written narrative[1] and of viewing the message of the work within the literary unity as it now exists rather than through hypothetical former stages of redaction.[2]

The Sources Used by the Chronicler
The question of the sources used by the Chronicler is raised by the text itself and the many references that it seems to make to other documents.[3] For many authors, the question of sources is also bound up with the issue of the historical worth of Chronicles. Wellhausen,[4] for instance, concludes with undisguised disdain that any sources used by the Chronicler apart from the other canonical books were worthless; the only likely coherent source was an apocryphal expansion of the books of Kings, and the Chronicler's genealogies were largely post-exilic in origin.

Even the relationship of Chronicles to the other canonical books, especially to Samuel and Kings, has not proved to be a straightforward matter.[5] Most authors would agree with the observation of Brunet[6] that the Chronicler used the redacted forms of the canonical books and not their traditions—a position also adopted in this study. Yet misgivings about the Chronicler's simple dependency on a *Vorlage* identical with the Masoretic Text of the Deuteronomistic History are voiced by Curtis and Madsen[7] on the basis of 'the occasional fuller text of 𝕲, which implies an earlier fuller Heb. text', by Mowinckel[8] because of his theory of a continuing oral tradition, and by van den Busshe[9] on the basis of supposed later corruptions in

---

1. C. McCarthy and W. Riley, *The Old Testament Short Story*, pp. 30-35.

2. Cf. J.R. Porter, 'Old Testament Historiography', p. 155.

3. Cf. 1 Chron. 9.1; 29.29; 2 Chron. 9.29; 12.15; 13.22; 16.11; 20.34; 24.27; 25.26; 26.22; 27.7; 28.26; 33.18,19; 35.25, 27, 32; 36.8.

4. *Prolegomena to the History of Ancient Israel*, pp. 211-27.

5. P. Vannutelli, *Libri Synoptici Veteris Testamenti seu Librorum Regum et Chronicorum Loci Paralleli*, has set out the parallels between Chronicles and the canonical books for both the MT and LXX, and A. Bendavid, *Parallels in the Bible*, has performed the same task (somewhat more analytically) for the MT alone.

6. 'Le Chroniste et ses sources', p. 481.

7. *A Critical and Exegetical Commentary on the Books of Chronicles*, p. 22.

8. 'Erwägungen zum chronistischen Geschichtswerk', cols. 4-5.

9. 'Le Texte de la prophétie de Nathan sur la Dynastie Davidique (II Sam.,VII–I Chron., XVII)', pp. 388-91.

Samuel–Kings. Lemke[1] confirms the suspicion expressed by Curtis and Madsen by utilizing evidence from 4QSam[a] which preserves a fuller reading also found in 2 Chron. 21.16. The work of comparing the Masoretic Text of Chronicles with the Septuagintal and Qumran manuscript evidence for a Palestinian text type for Samuel–Kings is extended considerably by Klein[2] and McKenzie.[3]

Many authors suggest that the Chronicler availed himself of an expanded version of Kings, sometimes identified with מדרש ספר המלכים referred to in 2 Chron. 24.27. Thus Wellhausen[4] concludes that the various citations in Chronicles all refer to a non-historical midrashic treatment of Kings. Curtis and Madsen[5] also suggest that the lack of abundant historical information in Chronicles' treatment of the period covered by Kings might indicate that the basic source was a midrash on Kings. Eissfeldt[6] concurs on the use of a midrashic form of Kings, but allows that it might contain material of historical worth. Driver[7] proposes a more complex relationship of common sources behind both the canonical Kings and a post-exilic 'Book of the Kings of Israel and Judah', and suggests that these two subsequent works both served as sources for the Chronicler. Harvey-Jellie[8] finds that the Chronicler has used three major sources: a fuller version of the monarchical history, a midrash written upon it and Proto-Isaiah. More recently, Rudolph[9] and Japhet,[10] among others, also accept a fuller version of Kings as a source for the Chronicler.

The question of sources unrelated to canonical works provides more room for speculation. Some commentators allow for a variety of written and oral sources available to the Chronicler,[11] and studies of

1. 'The Synoptic Problem in the Chronicler's History', pp. 355-57.
2. *Textual Criticism of the Old Testament: The Septuagint after Qumran.*
3. *The Chronicler's Use of the Deuteronomistic History.*
4. *Prolegomena to the History of Ancient Israel*, pp. 225-27.
5. *A Critical and Exegetical Commentary on the Books of Chronicles*, p. 22.
6. *The Old Testament: An Introduction*, pp. 532-35.
7. *An Introduction to the Literature of the Old Testament*, pp. 531-32.
8. *Chronicles*, pp. 14-15.
9. *Chronikbücher*, pp. xi-xiii.
10. 'Chronicles, Book of', cols. 527-28.
11. Cf. W.E. Barnes, *The Books of Chronicles*, pp. xviii-xxi; Michaeli, *Les livres des Chroniques, d'Esdras et de Néhémie*, pp. 11-12; Myers, *I Chronicles*, pp. xlvi-xlvii; S. Japhet, *The Ideology of the Book of Chronicles and its Place in Biblical Thought*, pp. 8-9.

the source-formulae and genealogies in particular indicate the presence of underlying sources, many of which seem to be pre-exilic.[1] Considerations of the historical worth of material absent from Samuel–Kings but present in Chronicles control much of the discussion of sources for the Chronicler's narrative. Thus many scholars postulate sources on the grounds of the historically valid material conceded to be unique to the Chronicler.[2] Although North once held to a similar opinion,[3] he later expresses the contrary view that there was no extrabiblical source involved and that 'any information communicated to us only by the Chronicler may be due in every case to his own legitimate theological inference or paraphrase from the canonical Scriptures'.[4] For the Chronicler's narrative of the Judaean kings, North may have shown that there is no additional historical material present that necessitates the Chronicler's use of an extrabiblical source;[5] this, however, does not exclude the use of sources which—like the often postulated Midrash on the History of Israel—would themselves fail to satisfy North's historical canons.[6] The characteristic way in which the Chronicler shapes his material may make the quest for sources in Chronicles rather like judging 'the difference between the sculpture and the block',[7] yet the evidence present in the genealogies should indicate that some sources, of whatever nature and how

1. Johnson, *The Purpose of the Biblical Genealogies*, pp. 63-66; J.P. Weinberg, 'Das Eigengut in den Chronikbüchern', p. 181; *idem*, 'Das Wegen und die funktionelle Bestimmung der Listen in I Chr 1–9', pp. 91-114; D. Edelman, 'The Manassite Genealology in 1 Chronicles 7:14-19: Form and Source', pp. 179-201; N. Na'aman, 'Sources and Redaction in the Chronicler's Genealogies of Asher and Ephraim', pp. 99-111; W.M. Schniedewind, 'The Source Citations of Manasseh: King Manasseh in History and Homily', pp. 450-61.

2. For example A. Bea, 'Neuere Arbeiten zum Problem der biblischen Chronikbücher', pp. 46-58; Noth, *The Chronicler's History*, pp. 57-58; Brunet, 'Le Chroniste et ses sources', pp. 376-86; G.J. Botterweck, 'Zur Eigenart der chronistischen Davidsgeschichte', p. 404; Welten, *Geschichte und Geschichtsdarstellung in den Chronikbüchern*, pp. 191-94.

3. R. North, 'The Chronicler: 1–2 Chronicles, Ezra, Nehemiah' [1968], pp. 403-404.

4. R. North, 'Does Archeology Prove Chronicles' Sources', p. 392.

5. North, 'Does Archaeology Prove Chronicles' Sources', pp. 375-401.

6. North himself seems to reflect this same viewpoint in 'The Chronicler: 1–2 Chronicles, Ezra, Nehemiah' [1989], p. 363.

7. B. Halpern, 'Sacred History and Ideology: Chronicles' Thematic Structure—Indications of an Earlier Source', p. 36.

ever used, were available to the Chronicler beyond the canonical books.

However, before moving beyond the question of sources, the possibility of one further biblical source for the Chronicler should be considered. It is commonly granted by those who judge Chronicles to be part of a larger work which incorporated Ezra–Nehemiah that 2 Chron. 36.22-23 is taken from Ezra 1.1-3;[1] this already points to the fact that the canonical form of Chronicles used Ezra–Nehemiah as a source. However, this can only be of limited significance if the passage is seen as a later addendum rather than an integral part of the literary whole. Recent scholarship suggests that Ezra–Nehemiah pre-dates Chronicles and that there is evidence that the Chronicler has used Ezra–Nehemiah apart from the quotation in 2 Chron. 36.22-23,[2] and this increases the likelihood that the ending verses of Chronicles may constitute an original and deliberate conclusion to the Chronicler's work. This possibility will be investigated in the second chapter of this work.

1. As examples of this common opinion, cf. Curtis and Madsen, *A Critical and Exegetical Commentary on the Books of Chronicles*, p. 525; Rudolph, *Chronikbücher*, p. 338; F. Michaeli, *Les livres des Chroniques, d'Esdras et de Néhémie*, p. 250.

2. Johnson, *The Purpose of the Biblical Genealogies*, pp. 37-38, 42, judges Neh. 11.3-24 to be prior to 1 Chron. 9.2-34 and Ezra 3.8 to be prior to the Chronicler's attribution of cultic arrangements to David. Although Brunet, 'Le Chroniste et ses sources', p. 484, sees Ezra–Nehemiah as part of the Chronicler's work, he makes a similar observation about the relationship of Neh. 11.3-24 to 1 Chron. 9.2-34. M.P. Graham, 'A Connection Proposed between II Chr 24,26 and Ezra 9–10', pp. 256-58, suggests that the information concerning Joash's assassins in 2 Chron. 24.26 is an adaptation of data taken from Ezra 9–10. W. Johnstone, 'Guilt and Atonement: The Theme of 1 and 2 Chronicles', pp. 114-15, appeals to 1 Chron. 9.2-17 and, to a lesser degree, to 2 Chron. 36.22-23 as indications of the Chronicler's use of Ezra–Nehemiah. Although making no judgments concerning the possible utilization of the earlier work as a source, Japhet also finds indications in her philological investigations that Chronicles is a later work than Ezra–Nehemiah; see Japhet, 'The Supposed Common Authorship of Chronicles and Ezra–Nehemiah Investigated Anew', pp. 343-44, 346, 371. T.C. Eskenazi, 'The Chronicler and the Composition of 1 Esdras', pp. 39-61, postulates that the Chronicler used Ezra–Nehemiah as a source, but in the composition of 1 Esdras, not of Chronicles. In the end, it is such indicators as these that should be examined; the chronology of the narratives related in the two works under consideration should not prejudge the chronology of their composition.

Apart from the comparison of Chronicles with the new textual evidence available for Samuel–Kings, the question of sources used by the Chronicler is so thoroughly complicated by varying approaches to the problem of historicity (as well as considerations of levels of redaction and later additions to the text) that it is unlikely that a verifiable hypothesis or clear consensus on this point will ever emerge. However, the interpreter of Chronicles would do well to heed a final point in relation to the matter of sources made by Friedman:[1] it is the text that we read, not the sources, for a text which utilizes sources is far more than the sum of its parts. The comparison of the final product to its sources will help to illumine the author's purpose and message, but in the end only an integrated reading of the text does justice to what the sacred writer has actually produced.

Author and Date

The Mishnah records the tradition that Chronicles was one of the works read to the high priest during the night before the ceremonies of Yom Kippur.[2] There could be many reasons for this practice: it has been taken as an engrossing narrative which would help to pass the sleepless night; various themes, such as retribution and seeking Yahweh, may have been found particularly appropriate to the feast; the Chronicler's story of worship under the kings might have served to instil the proper attitude in the high priest as he prepared to exercise his most sacred function. But there might also be in this practice a shadow of the Chronicles' original purpose: a cultic history written by cultic functionaries especially for the use of cult personnel.[3]

---

1. 'Sacred History/Sacred Literature', p. 1.
2. *M. Yom.* 1.6.
3. The fact that the author of Chronicles belonged to the cultic personnel is generally conceded, and further refinements of this position are not lacking. For an identification of the Chronicler as a Levitical singer, cf. Driver, *An Introduction to the Literature of the Old Testament*, pp. 518-19; Harvey-Jellie, *Chronicles*, p. 10; W.F. Stinespring, 'Eschatology in Chronicles', p. 201. North, 'The Chronicler: 1–2 Chronicles, Ezra, Nehemiah' [1989], pp. 364, 367, even suggests that the Chronistic genealogies contain the Chronicler's own genealogy as a Levitical cantor. North at first identifies 1 Chron. 3.19-24 as the relevant genealogy, but this is an obvious error since it occurs within the Davidic genealogy; within the body of his commentary, he identifies 1 Chron. 6.31-48 (according to the English version versification, which is 1 Chron. 6.16-33 in MT) as the pertinent text. For the identification of the author as a Levitical preacher, cf. G. von Rad, 'The Levitical

Although the identification of authorship must remain an exercise in conjecture, it is a useful way of summarizing various aspects perceived in a work and of associating these aspects with their probable situation. In the case of Chronicles, the situation is complex; that the Chronicler used sources is known by the survival of at least some as canonical writings, but what proportion of the remainder is attributable to sources and what proportion to the Chronicler? Did the Chronicler, as Wellhausen[1] suggests, simply continue the type of thinking which was already before him in a document or documents now lost? The material now contained in Chronicles does exhibit signs of a particular outlook, but commingled with inconsistencies. The various suggestions for different levels of redaction[2] and later additions[3] might be better visualized in terms of a school of tradition, a member or members of which gave the final shapes to the canonical work.[4] The priestly and Levitical concerns of the work lead the hypothesis towards Porter's suggestion of the Temple as the locus for the school,[5] and the interest shown in the traditions which legitimate the Temple and its cultus opens the possibility that Chronicles might

Sermon in I & II Chronicles', pp. 278-80; P.R. Ackroyd, 'History and Theology in the Writings of the Chronicler', p. 511.

1.   *Prolegomena to the History of Ancient Israel*, pp. 224-27.

2.   A.C. Welch, *The Work of the Chronicler: Its Purpose and Date*, pp. 149-157, and K. Galling, *Die Bücher der Chronik, Esra, Nehemiah*, pp. 6-16, both suggest two major strands of composition (although identifying the two strands differently). A threefold stratification of Chronicles–Esra–Nehemia is set forth by Cross, 'A Reconstruction of the Judean Restoration', pp. 7-14; Cross's proposal is a refinement of an earlier proposal by D.N. Freedman, 'The Chronicler's Purpose', pp. 439-42, and has been followed by D.L. Petersen, *Late Israelite Prophecy: Studies in Deutero-Prophetic Literature and in Chronicles*, pp. 58-60, and by McKenzie, *The Chronicler's Use of the Deuteronomistic History*, pp. 25-26. Willi, *Die Chronik als Auslegung*, pp. 195-96, attributes the Levitical concern evident in Chronicles to a later redactor of the work.

3.   For example, cf. Barnes, *The Books of Chronicles*, p. x; W. Rudolph, 'Problems of the Books of Chronicles', p. 402; Randellini, *Il libro delle Cronache*, pp. 27-31; S.J. De Vries, *1 and 2 Chronicles*, p. 13.

4.   The possible existence of such a unified and continuing shaping of the tradition in Chronicles has been suggested in different ways by Barnes, *The Books of Chronicles*, p. x, by Mowinckel, 'Erwägungen zum chronistischen Geschichtswerk', cols. 4-5, and by Ackroyd, 'History and Theology in the Writings of the Chronicler', pp. 503-504.

5.   'Old Testament Historiography', p. 157.

represent an official or semi-official document which preserves a portrait of the Temple as the central institution of the people of God.

Although the date is also a matter of conjecture, one must take seriously the observations made by Albright[1] and Williamson[2] to the effect that, while there are clear signs which bring the work into the fourth century BCE, there are no indications that the author was aware of anything peculiar to the Hellenistic period. This latter point is especially surprising given the Chronicler's lack of embarrassment over anachronisms. If it is correct, as suggested above, that Chronicles was written after Ezra–Nehemiah which served as one of its sources, then the basic redaction of Chronicles should be placed in the late Persian period, as the genealogy contained in 1 Chron. 3.19-24 implies.

The Chronicler's Need to Re-Present the Royal History

The Historical Nature of the Chronicler's Work

Historiographical production which is the result of purely antiquarian interest finds its own justification for existing; simple curiosity concerning what really happened in the past can provide a great motivation to the enquiring mind. However, the modern reader of Chronicles soon observes that purely antiquarian interest would not have produced the work under consideration, just as it is apparent that the author has adopted a method quite different from those which might be employed today. Insight into the nature of the Chronicler's historiography should throw light onto the task which he set himself as a historian; this, in turn, will begin to open the deeper question of why he felt it necessary to act as historian to Jerusalem's ancient monarchs despite the existence of the work of the Deuteronomistic Historian.

Investigators of Chronicles differ considerably on the question of the historical nature and worth of the work,[3] and various attempts

1. 'The Judicial Reform of Jehoshaphat', pp. 62-67, 71-72.
2. *1 and 2 Chronicles*, pp. 15-16.
3. For example, Wellhausen, *Prolegomena to the History of Ancient Israel*, p. 215, states of Chronicles: 'One might as well try to hear the grass growing as attempt to derive from such a source as this a historical knowledge of the conditions of ancient Israel'. C.C. Torrey, *The Chronicler's History*, pp. xxv-xxix, proposes that the Chronicler was responsible for inventing the story of the return from exile

have been made to categorize Chronicles as a true historical production while respecting the difference between the Chronicler's historiographical method and methods appropriate to modern historians.[1] Perhaps the most useful suggestion is made by Goldingay,[2] who proposes that the Chronicler's work is truly history, but a precritical history which incorporates artistic, ethical, etiological and apologetic features.

The writing of histories, whether critical or precritical, displays the belief that the past is meaningful for the present and can yield perennial lessons. In this regard, the observations of Lévi-Strauss are a useful starting-point in the consideration of the Chronicler's activity. Speaking in an age which presumes that history is critical, he says:

> When we try to do scientific history, do we really do something scientific, or do we too remain astride our own mythology in what we are trying to make as pure history?... I am not far from believing that, in our own societies, history has replaced mythology and fulfils the same function, that for societies without writing and without archives the aim of mythology is to ensure that as closely as possible—complete closeness is obviously impossible—the future will remain faithful to the present and to the past.[3]

The past does not change, but the age of the historian does, necessitating that new lessons be gleaned and new perspectives be taken and new histories be written.

---

and that he had even interpolated supporting passages in older canonical writings. On the more positive side of the argument, W.E. Barnes, 'The Religious Standpoint of the Chronicler', p. 19, finds no bias so strongly present in Chronicles that it should exclude the work from constituting an authority for Israel's history; and S. Japhet, 'The Historical Reliability of Chronicles: The History of the Problem and its Place in Biblical Research', p. 99, concludes that the negative evaluation of the historical reliability of Chronicles will not be the final verdict on the book.

1. W.A.L. Elmslie, *The Books of Chronicles*, pp. ix-xv, suggests a didactic type of history which concentrates on drawing the religious and moral lessons inherent in the historical material. Galling, *Die Bücher der Chronik, Esra, Nehemia*, p. 5, characterizes the work as a Church History of Jerusalem. Japhet, *The Ideology of the Book of Chronicles and its Place in Biblical Thought*, p. 11, suggests that the work could be termed ' "theocentric historiography", in which every sphere of life derives its significance and ultimate reality from its relationship to God'.

2. 'The Chronicler as a Theologian', pp. 108-110.

3. *Myth and Meaning*, pp. 41-43.

Modern authors agree that such was the concern that brought Chronicles into being. Von Rad[1] observes that the shift in circumstances required a new orientation to the traditional historical materials; Myers[2] speaks of the Chronicler trying to bring history to bear on the religious problems of his day; Japhet[3] sees Chronicles as a response to a new generation's need to live the religious experience contained in history as the arena of God's way with humanity; Johnstone[4] describes the activity of the Chronicler as a hermeneutical exercise, receiving the tradition and seeing its application in new circumstances; Duke[5] identifies the Chronicler's self-imposed task as a creative use of historical narrative for instructive and apologetic purposes. Implicit in all of these opinions is that the Chronicler is as much theologian as historian[6] and that his concern is more with his contemporary community than with establishing what actually happened in the past.[7] These insights into the historical task that the Chronicler has set himself should lead to the conclusion that his worth is not to be judged solely on the historical veracity of his work, as would be involved in the evaluation of modern historical writing.[8]

The difference between the Chronistic historiography and modern ideas of history leads many scholars to describe the Chronicler's method by employing non-historical categories. Among the categories invoked are midrash,[9] homily[10] and polemic.[11] Unless the first two

1. *Das Geschichtsbild des chronistischen Werkes*, pp. 120-21.
2. 'The Kerygma of the Chronicler: History and Theology in the Service of Religion', p. 273.
3. 'Conquest and Settlement in Chronicles', p. 205; cf. also Japhet, *The Ideology of the Book of Chronicles and its Place in Biblical Thought*, p. 516.
4. 'Reactivating the Chronicles Analogy in Pentateuchal Studies, with Special Reference to the Sinai Pericope in Exodus', p. 17.
5. *The Persuasive Appeal of the Chronicler: A Rhetorical Analysis*, p. 49.
6. Cf. also H. Cazelles, *Les livres des Chroniques*, pp. 15, 22; J.N. Schumacher, 'The Chronicler's Theology of History', pp. 12-13; R.J. Coggins, *The First and Second Books of the Chronicles*, pp. 5-6.
7. Von Rad, *Das Geschichtsbild des chronistischen Werkes*, p. 133; L. Randellini, 'Il libro delle Cronache nel decennio 1950–1960', pp. 144-45.
8. On this latter point, cf. also Japhet, 'The Ideology of the Book of Chronicles and its Place in Biblical Thought'; S.B. Berg, 'After the Exile: God and History in the Book of Chronicles and Esther', p. 109; R.L. Braun, *1 Chronicles*, p. xxiii.
9. Cf. Wellhausen, *Prolegomena to the History of Ancient Israel*, p. 227; W.E. Barnes, 'The Midrashic Element in Chronicles', pp. 426-39; I.W. Slotki, *Chronicles*, p. xii; C. Mangan, *1–2 Chronicles, Ezra, Nehemiah*, p. 3. One should

categories are taken as descriptions of the total reality of Chronicles or unless they distract the modern reader from the authentic historical endeavour which the Chronicler has undertaken, they are useful in describing some of the ways in which the author's theological aim can take shape in his text. However, since the supposed polemical nature of Chronicles is largely the result of the reading of Chronicles as part of a larger work incorporating Ezra–Nehemiah, the arguments which show Chronicles to be a distinct literary production simultaneously render invalid the categorization of Chronicles as an anti-Samaritan polemic.[1]

The Chronicler's historical interest, therefore, has two foci: the events of the past and his contemporary community. The precritical historical task that he has set for himself is to tell past events in such a way that he is actually speaking equally about the present. The Chronicler's historiographical method involves bringing the two foci of his interest into close theological dialogue, not just to bring out isolated lessons from the past, but to discover the identity and the destiny of the post-exilic community through the lens of pre-exilic history. The problems with which the Chronicler has concerned himself are not primarily the problems connected with discovery of past events and personages; instead his historical writing is dominated by the problems of his own contemporaries and the history of his nation is told in such a way that history's lessons can illuminate such problems.

The Problem of the Davidic Tradition

The Chronicler's work exhibits a high degree of interest in the promise to David, which is asserted and alluded to several times in the

note in particular Barnes's conclusion that Chronicles displays too many points of contact with history for the work to be considered totally as a midrash, although Chronicles contains much haggadah.

10. Von Rad, 'The Levitical Sermon in I & II Chronicles', pp. 267-80; Noth, *The Chronicler's History*, p. 80; P.R. Ackroyd, *The Age of the Chronicler*, p. 45; Myers, *I Chronicles*, p. xviii.

11. Elmslie, *The Books of Chronicles*, pp. xxxviii-xl; Rudolph, *Chronikbücher*, p. ix; O. Plöger, *Theocracy and Eschatology*, p. 40; J. Becker, *I Chronik*, p. 10.

1. Cf. R.L. Braun, 'The Message of Chronicles: Rally 'Round the Temple', pp. 502-14; *idem*, 'Solomon, the Chosen Temple Builder: The Significance of 1 Chronicles 22, 28, and 29 for the Theology of Chronicles', p. 581.

narrative.[1] Given the fact that Chronicles was composed well after the collapse of the Davidic dynasty, the modern reader is led by these references and by the royal focus of the narrative to see that the lack of a Davidide upon the throne constituted a real problem for the Chronicler and his audience and possibly provided a considerable part of the motivation for his historiographical endeavour. The repeated reference to the Davidic promise also indicates that the Chronicler hoped to shed light upon this problem by retelling Israel's monarchical history. Any success which the Chronicler may have had in this regard has not extended unequivocally to his modern interpreters who differ radically on issues such as the eschatology and messianism present in the work.

Saebø[2] claims that part of the difficulty in interpreting the Davidic promise in Chronicles lies in the confused manner in which the term 'messianism' is used by scholars; while some use the term to connote the tradition of the Christian church which looks to the Psalms and prophetic literature for its basis, others use it in terms of ancient Near Eastern royal ideology and still others use it as a near synonym for eschatology. Saebø's incisive observation, together with the nature of the opinions expressed by modern authors, helps to categorize modern views according to four possibilities: the first possibility is that Chronicles possesses an eschatology which involves the hope for Davidic restoration;[3] the second, that Chronicles is basically non-eschatological and non-messianic;[4] the third, that Chronicles expresses

---

1. Cf. 1 Chron. 17.10-14, 17, 23-27; 22.6-10; 28.2-7; 2 Chron. 1.8-9; 6.4-10, 15-17, 42; 7.17-18; 13.5, 8; 21.7; 23.3.

2. 'Messianism in Chronicles? Some Remarks to the Old Testament Background of the New Testament Christology', p. 87.

3. Von Rad, *Das Geschichtsbild des chronistischen Werkes*, p. 134; A. Noordtzij, 'Les intentions du Chroniste', p. 163; Noth, *The Chronicler's History*, p. 105; R. de Vaux, review of *Chronikbücher*, by W. Rudolph, p. 280; Brunet, 'Le Chroniste et ses sources', p. 508; cf. A.-M. Brunet, 'La théologie du chroniste: théocratie et messianisme', pp. 386-90, 397; Botterweck, 'Zur Eigenart der chronistischen Davidsgeschichte', pp. 422-23, 433; Stinespring, 'Eschatology in Chronicles', p. 211; Randellini, 'Il libro delle Cronache nel decennio 1950–1960', pp. 144, 154; R. North, 'Theology of the Chronicler', pp. 376-81; S. Virgulin, *Libri delle Cronache*, p. 49; H.G.M. Williamson, 'Eschatology in Chronicles', pp. 129, 147-49; Saebø, 'Messianism in Chronicles? Some Remarks to the Old Testament Background of the New Testament Christology', p. 90.

4. Wellhausen, *Prolegomena to the History of Ancient Israel*, pp. 419-25;

hopes of a Davidic restoration which can hardly be termed 'messianic';[1] and finally some interpreters suggest that Chronicles shows a true eschatology which does not involve monarchic restoration.[2] Since the range of possibilities is so wide and presumptions concerning messianism are so easily made, the reason for the Chronicler's apparent concern with the Davidic dynasty must be considered afresh with a new emphasis both on the Chronicler's situation and on his use of the royal figures in his narrative.

Turning firstly to the author's use of Israel's royal figures, the reader is soon struck by the Chronistic idealization of David and Solomon;[3] this idealization establishes these figures as a type of normative past for the Chronicler's narrative. Whether the intensity of that normative status is of the author's own creation or whether it had already fully blossomed in the tradition to which he had fallen heir is of little importance for present considerations. The normative status of the figure of David was already present in the Deuteronomistic History, as is evidenced by its use of David as the canon by which other kings are evaluated.[4]

It is clear that the Chronicler has brought his concept of the normative status of David to bear on his revision of the picture of Israel's

Rudolph, 'Problems of the Books of Chronicles', pp. 404, 408; *idem, Chronikbücher*, pp. viii-ix, xxiii; Plöger, *Theocracy and Eschatology*, pp. 38-44; Petersen, *Late Israelite Prophecy: Studies in Deutero-Prophetic Literature and in Chronicles*, pp. 56, 98.

1.   Freedman, 'The Chronicler's Purpose', pp. 437-40; Porter, 'Old Testament Historiography', p. 159. North's later work removes the eschatological stress and speaks of the restoration of the Davidic dynasty according to its pre-exilic form; see 'The Chronicler: 1–2 Chronicles, Ezra, Nehemiah' [1989], p. 363.

2.   Schumacher, 'The Chronicler's Theology of History', pp. 19-21; A. Caquot, 'Peut-on parler de messianisme dans l'oeuvre du Chroniste?', pp. 118-19; Ackroyd, 'History and Theology in the Writings of the Chronicler', pp. 514-15; P.R. Ackroyd, 'The Chronicler as Exegete', pp. 3-4; J. Coppens, *Le messianisme royal*, pp. 107-10; Goldingay, 'The Chronicler as a Theologian', pp. 114-16; Mosis, *Untersuchungen zur Theologie des chronistischen Geschichtswerkes*, pp. 164-69, 211-14; Dumbrell, 'The Purpose of the Books of Chronicles', pp. 261-66; Becker, *1 Chronik*, pp. 8-9; De Vries, *1 and 2 Chronicles*, p. 20.

3.   The primary idealization in Chronicles pertains to David. However, the Chronicler's omission of the faults of Solomon and his theological responsibility for the Northern schism from his *Vorlage* (1 Kgs 11) indicates that a lesser idealization has also taken place for Solomon.

4.   Cf. 1 Kgs 9.4; 11.4, 6, 33, 38; 14.8; 15.3, 11; 2 Kgs 14.3; 16.2; 18.3; 22.2.

golden age in the United Monarchy, emphasizing in particular those
aspects of David which constitute the standard by which other
monarchs are to be measured;[1] it is also evident that the normative
status of David has had a greater influence on the Chronicler's Davidic
narrative than was the case with his Deuteronomistic forebear. The
terms of the Chronicler's idealization of David, and therefore the
aspect of David which is most emphasized by the acknowledgment of
his normative status, emerge with a clear and unambiguous emphasis
from the work, as Wellhausen has expressed with extreme
disapproval:

> See what Chronicles has made out of David! The founder of the kingdom
> has become the founder of the temple and the public worship, the king
> and hero at the head of his companions in arms has become the singer and
> master of ceremonies at the head of a swarm of priests and Levites; his
> clearly cut figure has become a feeble holy picture, seen through a cloud
> of incense.[2]

The nature of the idealized picture indicates that the primary function
of David (and Solomon) for the Chronicler is now to be sought in the
area of the cultus.

Although it would be impossible to disentangle completely the
theological and political concerns in biblical Israel, these were the two
poles on the axis of Israel's national identity. As Ackroyd suggests, it
might be that the political picture of David had become less feasible
for the age of the Chronicler and that this necessitated a
reinterpretation which veered toward the theological end of the axis.[3]

The theological reinterpretation was facilitated by the way in which
the Davidic tradition was preserved in the community. The dynastic
promise to David not only lived on in the historical memory and literature of the post-exilic community; it also lived on in the cultus, as
is evidenced by Psalm 89 and Psalm 132. The continuation of this
tradition in the liturgical life of Israel explains why it could not easily
be forgotten or dismissed once the Davidic throne was empty; it also

---

1. Examples of the normative use of David may be found in 2 Chron. 7.17
(|| 1 Kgs 9.4); 17.3; 28.1 (|| 2 Kgs 16.2); 29.2 (|| 2 Kgs 18.3); 34.2 (|| 2 Kgs 22.2).
Although most of these explicit statements of comparison rely upon the
Deuteronomistic *Vorlage*, the portrait to which they refer in Chronicles is, of course,
the Chronistic and not the Deuteronomistic portrayal of David.
2. *Prolegomena to the History of Ancient Israel*, p. 182.
3. 'History and Theology in the Writings of the Chronicler', p. 512.

explains why the Chronicler, as one involved with the Temple liturgy, might have felt a particular need to reinterpret the dynasty which the cultus continued to celebrate even though its reign had apparently come to a final end. The continued presence of the dynastic promise in the absence of a Davidic regent demanded reinterpretation, either in terms of a Davidic restoration or otherwise. I would suggest that the Chronicler attempted such a reinterpretation of the Davidic promise, prompted largely by the cultic commemoration, and that he accomplished it through a re-presentation of the royal history.

In his reinterpretation of the history of the House of David, the Chronicler's cultic interests are not only evident in his emphasis on the Temple and its worship and cultic personnel; they also manifest themselves in his method and vocabulary. Thus the liturgical aspect of accession scenes is heightened in his work,[1] battles sometimes become divine victories accompanied by cultic action,[2] and such terms as דרש, מעל כנע, נוח and שמח have been imbued with a cultic flavour in their Chronistic use.[3]

Several authors have noted the influence of the Psalms and their language on the Chronicler's work. Von Rad[4] sees that Psalm 89 and Psalm 132 had been drawn upon in the Chronicler's narrative of David and Solomon; Ackroyd[5] suggests that the Chronicler, who belonged to the same community that framed the Psalter, used the

1. Cf. 1 Chron. 29.20-22; 2 Chron. 23.1-16.
2. This is especially evident in 2 Chron. 13.13-18 and 20.20-28.
3. The Chronicler's use of דרש and מעל is discussed in Chapter 2. The cultic associations of נוח fit into the association of rest and divine dwelling place found elsewhere in the ancient Near East; cf. H. Brunner, 'Egyptian Texts: Precepts for Life', p. 48, and H. Frankfort, *Kingship and the Gods*, p. 272. A similar association of נוח and the Jerusalem cultus may be discerned through the use of the verb in its *qal* and *hiphil A* forms in 1 Chron. 22.9, 18; 23.25; 2 Chron. 6.41; 14.5, 6; 15.15; 20.30. The Chronicler provides 16 of the 25 occurrences of the *niphal* of כנע in the Hebrew Bible, and all but two of the occurrences in Chronicles refer to a cultic act; cf. 1 Chron. 20.4 (a non-cultic use); 2 Chron. 7.14; 12.6, 7 (twice), 12; 13.18 (a non-cultic use); 30.11; 32.26; 33.12, 19, 23 (twice); 34.27 (twice); 36.12. The cultic overtones in the Chronicler's use of שמח derive from earlier usage, as may be seen in the Psalms and Deuteronomy—and the Chronicler derives two uses of the verb from his quotations from the Psalms; cf. 1 Chron. 16.10 (ǁ Ps. 105.3) and 16.31 (ǁ Ps. 96.11). For examples of the Chronistic association of the word with Temple worship see 1 Chron. 29.9; 2 Chron. 6.41; 15.15; 29.36; 30.24-26.
4. *Das Geschichtsbild des chronistischen Werkes*, pp. 126-28.
5. *The Age of the Chronicler*, pp. 9, 17.

Psalms and prophetic writings to aid his presentation of events; Virgulin[1] perceives from Chronicles that the Chronicler had a great intimacy with the Psalms; Goldingay[2] stresses the need to compare Chronicles with the Psalms and the Priestly tradition as much as with Samuel–Kings; Williamson[3] notes the dependence of the Chronicler on the Psalms for features of his characteristic vocabulary; the importance of the Psalms in the study of Chronicles is emphasized by Welten[4] who views the Chronistic David–Solomon narrative as largely an expansion of Ps. 132.1. The greatest argument for the influence of the Psalms upon the Chronicler is his own unmistakable use of verses from the Psalter, especially in the events which surround the establishment of the Temple.[5]

The Psalms themselves contain elements which have a potential for reinterpreting the place of David and for allowing the cultic aspect of the founder of the dynasty to blossom; chief among these must be the fact that Yahweh's choice of David is explicitly linked to his choice of Zion in the Psalms.[6] As Cazelles has noted,[7] many psalms also reflect a piety centred on the Temple which was characteristic of the Chronicler's epoch and which is evident in his work. Saebø[8] also adverts to the fact that the new emphasis that Chronicles gives to the kingship of Yahweh over Israel, the theocracy theme noted by most authors, is itself a development of a theme already present in the Psalms. If the Chronicler's thought does not benefit directly from the Psalms—and it would seem most likely that it does—then the least that can be said is that developments evident in Chronicles are akin to elements which were already to be found in this cultic poetry of the post-exilic community.[9]

1. *Libri delle Cronache*, p. 19.
2. 'The Chronicler as a Theologian', p. 118.
3. *Israel in the Books of Chronicles*, pp. 47, 53, 54.
4. 'Lade–Tempel–Jerusalem: Zur Theologie der Chronikbücher', pp. 180-83.
5. 1 Chron. 16.8-36; 2 Chron. 6.41-42; 7.3, 6.
6. Ps. 78.68-72; Ps. 132.11-18.
7. *Les livres des Chroniques*, pp. 9-10.
8. 'Messianism in Chronicles? Some Remarks to the Old Testament Background of the New Testament Christology', pp. 100-101.
9. Apart from the specific influence that the Psalms may have had upon the composition of Chronicles, there seems to be a more general influence exerted by the cult on Israel's concept and formulation of history which should not be overlooked. This is evident from several texts which, though obviously liturgical in character,

When the Chronicler's political situation (the continuing absence of a Davidic regent) and liturgical situation (the continued celebration of the Davidic covenant) are taken together, the Chronicler's portrayal of David and his house in cultic terms may be seen as an emphasis on the religious contribution that the dynasty has made and as a disavowal of the necessity for a post-exilic Davidic successor to the throne of Israel. In this way, the Chronicler has justified the continued liturgical celebration of David which is undiminished by its lack of political expression through a dynasty. Various authors have perceived such a shift away from the realm of political rule and expressed it in different ways: Plöger[1] points to the Temple as the symbol of religious continuity; Caquot[2] suggests that, for the Chronicler, David continues his soteriological function through the Temple; Ackroyd[3] sees that the Chronicler's hope no longer centres on a Davidic restoration so much as on the Temple and its congregation; Mosis[4] observes that the Chronicler's only real interest in David and Solomon lies in their function of constructing the Temple; Williamson[5] (who sees hopes of a Davidic restoration in Chronicles) also notes that the second Temple is an embodiment of the Davidic promise for the Chronicler; Brueggemann[6] categorizes the Chronicler's perception of David's truth as a liturgical rather than a political truth.

---

take the actions of Yahweh in Israel's historical traditions as their subject (e.g., Exod. 15.1-22; Pss. 77, 78, 105, 106, 136), as well as the historical rationale proposed for the agricultural feasts of Passover and Weeks (cf. Exod. 12.1–13.9; 23.42-43). G.E. Wright, 'Cult and History: A Study of a Current Problem in Old Testament Interpretation', pp. 3-20, examines (with particular reference to the Pentateuch) how cult and history were intertwined in Israel, each exerting a formative influence upon the other. G.W. Trompf, 'Notions of Historical Recurrence in Classical Hebrew Historiography', pp. 214-16, postulates that the patterned perception and presentation of history in Israel was due ultimately to the use of historical material and re-enactment in the Israelite cultus; more particularly he suggests that the built–destroyed–rebuilt story of the Temple may have supplied the Chronicler with his own particular pattern of recurrence.

1. *Theocracy and Eschatology*, p. 38.
2. 'Peut-on parler de messianisme dans l'oeuvre du Chroniste?', pp. 118-19.
3. *The Age of the Chronicler*, p. 50.
4. *Untersuchungen zur Theologie des chronistischen Geschichtswerkes*, pp. 162-63.
5. *1 and 2 Chronicles*, p. 29.
6. *David's Truth in Israel's Imagination and Memory*, p. 108.

In emphasizing the Temple-building role of David and Solomon and in applying the cultic theme to the post-Solomonic monarchs, the Chronicler has concentrated a theme present elsewhere in the Hebrew Bible and given it its clearest expression.[1] This study will show that, in highlighting the relationship between king and temple in Israel, and in the direct and indirect utilization of cultic materials from the royal psalms, the Chronicler has invoked elements which were originally rooted in a wider ancient Near Eastern ideology which embraced deity, king and temple. In this way the Chronicler could attempt to restate the importance of David and his dynasty for the post-exilic community and, through his narrative, demonstrate the validity of ancient promise for his contemporary reality, indicating the many lessons to be learnt along the way.

Conclusion

The Chronicler, who is to be identified as a member or school of members of the personnel serving the cultus of the post-exilic community, has set forth his theology in a narrative expression largely coterminous with the canonical books of Chronicles. Although matters related to introductory questions remain disputed by exegetes, the evidence seems to indicate that Chronicles is an independent production of a single literary composer (whether an individual or a school) working in the late Persian period and utilizing sources, prime among which is the Deuteronomistic History. In his reconsideration of the monarchical history he has been influenced both by the continuance of the Davidic promise in the cultus and the absence of a Davidic monarch; however, the cultus itself and its monarchical origins also provide a major focus of interest for the Chronistic Historian. As a result, the Chronicler's History is, in effect, a re-presentation of the formative monarchical period of Israel's history as viewed especially through the cultic lens.

---

1.   N. Poulssen, 'Rex et Templum in Israel', pp. 268-69.

Chapter 2

THE CHRONICLER'S CULTIC PORTRAYAL OF KINGS:
A FINAL FORM STUDY

Introduction

The obvious subject matter of the bulk of the Chronicler's narrative is the Judaean monarchy; the kings in Jerusalem are the main characters in most of the episodes, each king is treated in turn, and the beginning and end of the Chronicler's narrative corresponds roughly with the termini of the Judaean monarchy. Yet, if this obvious subject matter is confused with the main concern of the composition, then the Chronicler's work loses its vital distinction from the books of Samuel and Kings in the eyes of its audience; this type of verdict seems to be reflected in the Septuagintal title Παραλειπόμενα.

The Chronicler's real concerns are not to be discovered simply by considering this one aspect of his narrative in isolation, albeit an obvious and central aspect. Given that he has written his work in the presence of an already extant monarchical history, and one that he even uses as a source, the Chronicler's concerns only become evident when the shadings and emphases that he brings out in his own monarchical narrative are considered.

The fact that the Chronicler has linked his interest in the monarchy with an interest in the Temple and its worship cannot be ignored in this context. Through this linkage, the Chronicler has been able to forge a new interpretation of the monarchical period in the light of the relationship between the monarchs and the cultus. King and cultus had already been joined in an ideology found in different forms throughout the ancient Near East where the king was held responsible for the building and maintenance of the national temples,[1] a

---

1. Among the many texts that testify to this role of the ancient Near Eastern king might be mentioned the following examples which are readily accessible:

responsibility that passed from native regents to conquerors and their successors in the Persian and Hellenistic periods.[1] The ideology not only placed a cultic responsibility on the king; it also emphasized his divine election[2] and promised him divine blessings of stable rule, victory and fertility in return for the king's cultic faithfulness.[3] However, the royal ideology had undergone two important changes before it was reflected in the Chronicler's work: first, it had been integrated into the unique belief-system of Yahwism; secondly, it survived after a period of separation from the Jerusalem Temple and in the continued absence of a Davidic king. These factors ensure that neither the specifically Israelite forms of the royal ideology in existence during the Davidic monarchy nor the post-exilic

A.L. Oppenheim: 'Gudea, Ensi of Lagash', pp. 268-69; *idem*, 'Tiglath-pileser I (1114–1076): Expeditions to Syria, the Lebanon and the Mediterranean Sea', p. 275; *idem*, 'Ashurnasirpal II (883–859): Expedition to Carchemish and the Lebanon'; *idem*, 'Adad-Nirari III (810–783): Expedition to Palestine', p. 281; *idem*, 'Nabonidus (555–539): Nabonidus' Rise to Power', p. 310; *idem*, 'The Dedication of the Shamash Temple by Yahdun-Lim', p. 556; A. Sachs, 'Temple Program for the New Year's Festivals at Babylon', p. 334; A. Goetze, 'Ritual for the Erection of a House', p. 356-57; *idem*, 'Daily Prayer of the King', pp. 396-97; J.A. Wilson, 'From Amen-hotep III's Building Inscription', p. 375; H. Schmökel, 'Mesopotamian Texts: Hymns, Prayers and Lamentations', pp. 112-13.

1. This is evident in A.L. Oppenheim, 'Cyrus (557–529)', pp. 315-16; *idem*, 'Antiochus Soter (280–262/1)', p. 317.

2. This can be seen most clearly in texts which speak of the king as having come to power precisely through the god's desire to build or repair the temple. See S.N. Kramer, 'Ur-Nammu Hymn: Building of the Ekur and Blessing by Enlil', pp. 583-84; Oppenheim, 'Nabonidus (555–539): Nabonidus' Rise to Power', pp. 308-11; *idem*, 'Cyrus (557–529)', p. 315. The Egyptian perspective is slightly different and tends to see divine legitimation as providing the basis for the king's temple-building activity; cf. J.A. Wilson, 'The Divine Nomination of Thut-mose III', pp. 446-47, and H. Brunner, 'Egyptian Texts: Royal Texts', pp. 27-29.

3. For example, cf. S.N. Kramer, 'Gilgamesh and Agga', p. 46; *idem*, 'Ur-Nammu Hymn: Building of the Ekur and Blessing by Enlil', pp. 583-84; J.A. Wilson, 'The Hymn of Victory of Thut-mose III', pp. 373-75; *idem*, 'From Amen-hotep III's Building Inscription', pp. 375-76; A. Goetze, 'The Telepinus Myth', p. 128; *idem*, 'Ritual for the Erection of a House', p. 356; S.N. Kramer, 'Inanna and the King', p. 641. The divine blessings were especially connected with the king's participation in the sacred marriage; cf. H. Ringgren, *Religions of the Ancient Near East*, pp. 25-30, 85, 88-89, 163-64; H. Frankfort, *Kingship and the Gods*, pp. 188-90, 297-98.

continuation of elements of that ideology correspond point for point with the royal ideology as it is found elsewhere in the ancient Near East;[1] but those ways of viewing king and Temple continue to be perpetuated, albeit in new forms to meet new needs, in the Chronicler's narrative presentation of the relationship between king and cultus.

This chapter considers the Chronicler's monarchical material in a fivefold division of the narrative: Saul, David, Solomon, the post-Solomonic kings to Josiah, and the post-Josian kings to the Edict of Cyrus. Although the focus of the study lies in the material contained in 1 Chronicles 10–2 Chronicles 36, occasional reference is also made to the genealogical material contained in the first nine chapters of the Chronicler's work.

The investigation undertaken in this chapter is a final form study of the text; that is, this investigation considers the work primarily in the completed canonical form in which the work presents itself to the audience. However, the synchronic emphasis of this chapter cannot ignore the value and even necessity of diachronic study. Occasional diachronic considerations, especially the comparisons of the Chronicler's narrative to its Deuteronomistic source, are not designed to weaken the synchronic nature of this investigation but rather to clarify the Chronicler's particular concerns as he tells once again the story of the Judaean kings.

Saul, the Non-Cultic King

The Chronicler limits his concern with the story of Israel's first king to the account of his death, an account largely dependent upon the Chronicler's Deuteronomistic *Vorlage*;[2] other mentions of Saul also occur in the work, but none within the context of a connected narrative of Saul's reign.[3]

The narrative of 1 Chronicles 10 presents the reader with an enigma, as enunciated by Ackroyd:

---

1. R.E. Clements, *God and Temple*, p. 130.
2. 1 Chron. 10.1-14 (‖ 1 Sam. 31.1-13).
3. 1 Chron. 5.10; 8.33 (twice); 9.39 (twice); 11.2; 12.1, 2, 20 (twice), 24, 30; 13.3; 15.29; 26.28.

We might have expected the Chronicler, to whom clearly the kingship of
David was the only valid kingship, to omit any mention of Saul. He could
leave unmentioned most of the kings of the north—they appear only as
opponents of Judah or as involving Judah in sin. He could equally have
ignored Saul and passed straight into the anointing of David.[1]

Given that the Chronicler has decided to include Saul in his history, a
further aspect of the enigma emerges: why is the story of Saul
restricted to this final episode? By such restriction, the Chronicler has
sacrificed material from the *Vorlage* which might be regarded as
germane to the Chronicler's pro-Davidic stance, such as the anointing
of David by Samuel, or David's triumph over Goliath. The Chronicler
has even decided to forgo an opportunity to portray David's pious
loyalty by omitting all reference to David's actions consequent upon
Saul's death, including his lament for Saul and Jonathan.

The common solution to this enigma proposed by commentators lies
in the contrast between the black tragedy of Saul and the bright triumph of David, so that (in the often quoted words of Rudolph) 'Out
of the darkness into which Saul lapses, the Star of David goes forth
beaming'.[2] The effect of this solution upon the interpretation of
Chronicles is that the Chronicler's Saul narrative has come to be
widely viewed as simply a minor part of the Davidic material, even
though David is only mentioned in the final phrase of the passage.[3]

While agreeing that the Chronicler's Saul stands in antithesis to his
David, Mosis[4] proposes a wider significance for the Saul narrative.

---

1. *The Age of the Chronicler*, p. 48. Ackroyd's assertion that David's kingship
was the only valid kingship for the Chronicler is not necessarily as self-evident as
this quotation implies.
2. 'Aus dem Dunkel, in dem Saul versinkt, geht strahlend der Stern Davids';
Chronikbücher, p. 96. The function of the Saul narrative in Chronicles is similarly
viewed by, among others, von Rad, *Das Geschichtsbild des chronistischen Werkes*,
p. 79; Galling, *Die Bücher der Chronik, Esra, Nehemia*, p. 41; Michaeli, *Les livres
des Chroniques, d'Esdras et de Néhémie*, p. 76; Virgulin, *Libri delle Cronache*,
p. 133; and Halpern, 'Sacred History and Ideology: Chronicles' Thematic
Structure—Indications of an Earlier Source', pp. 36-37.
3. Thus, for example, Galling, *Die Bücher der Chronik, Esra, Nehemia*, p. 40,
identifies the Davidic material as 1 Chron. 10.1–29.30. Similar headings and titles
can be found in many commentaries, including Randellini, *Il libro delle Cronache*,
p. 145; P.R. Ackroyd, *I & II Chronicles, Ezra, Nehemiah*, p. 48; and Myers, *I
Chronicles*, pp. 75-77.
4. *Untersuchungen zur Theologie des chronistischen Geschichtswerkes*, p. 28.

According to Mosis, the Saul narrative forms, together with the narrative of David and Solomon, a threefold paradigm which moves from the situation of the lack of salvation to the fulfilment of salvation and in terms of which the post-Solomonic kings are portrayed;[1] this proposal is also largely accepted by Ackroyd[2] and Becker.[3] Other paradigmatic possibilities are also suggested: Mangan[4] suggests a two-fold paradigm, Saul standing for what a king should not be and David for what a king should be; Coggins[5] states that Saul's story in Chronicles stands as a paradigm for the whole history of Israel to the restoration of Judah.

Those commentators who view 1 Chronicles 10 as paradigmatic see that Saul is a real force in the Chronicler's narrative, albeit a largely negative one. While this consideration of the Chronistic Saul material as a key element of the work seems justified, there is no consensus as to how the Chronicler intended the paradigm to be applied, even though many agree on the paradigmatic nature of the material. The shedding of further light upon the terms and intended application of the Saul paradigm would aid in the discovery of the Chronicler's intention and purpose in re-presenting the monarchical history.

In examining the enigma of the Chronicler's Saul material, the following investigation begins from a number of premises: that the position of this episode at the beginning of the Chronicler's narrative material is significant;[6] that the identification of the paradigmatic nature of this material by recent scholars is correct;[7] that at least some

1. *Untersuchungen zur Theologie des chronistischen Geschichtswerkes*, pp. 164-69.

2. 'The Chronicler as Exegete', pp. 3-4.

3. *1 Chronik*, pp. 8-9.

4. *1–2 Chronicles, Ezra, Nehemiah*, p. 27.

5. *The First and Second Books of the Chronicles*, p. 64. Similar views are expressed by Willi, *Die Chronik als Auslegung*, pp. 9-12, and Williamson, *1 and 2 Chronicles*, p. 93.

6. There seems to be general agreement on this point. The only noteworthy distinction seems to be between those who see the importance of the position of the Saul material primarily in relation to the Davidic material alone (and therefore as a contrasting, non-paradigmatic narrative) or in relationship to both Davidic and post-Davidic material (and therefore as paradigmatic). In either view, the presence, choice and placing of the Saul material is seen by most commentators as more than the effect of a chronological imperative.

7. This is especially indicated by the Chronicler's conclusion to the Saul

of the changes and additions made by the Chronicler to his *Vorlage* reflect his paradigmatic intention;[1] that the narrative of 1 Chronicles 10 should have resonance with at least some of the more fragmentary Saul material in the Chronicler's work;[2] and that the cultic concern evidenced elsewhere in the Chronicler's work might also have application to his portrayal of Saul.[3]

The Chronicler's greatest alteration to his *Vorlage* in this episode is the addition of a summary passage:

> And Saul died because of his treachery (במעלו) in which he acted treacherously (מעל) against Yahweh contrary to the word of Yahweh which he did not keep, even to asking a ghost for seeking. But he did not seek Yahweh, and he killed him and he caused the kingship to turn to David, son of Jesse (1 Chron. 10.13-14).

This addition has great importance since it bears the Chronicler's explicit judgment upon Saul; it gives the cause in v. 13 for the tragic scene of 1 Chron. 10.1-12 and then further explicates both cause and effect in v. 14.

The cause of Saul's tragedy is here identified as his מעל. The importance of this term (in both noun and verb forms) in the Chronicler's narrative has been identified by commentators,[4] and its

---

narrative in 1 Chron. 10.13-14 and the presence of terms such as מעל and דרש in that passage; cf. Mosis, *Untersuchungen zur Theologie des chronistischen Geschichtswerkes*, pp. 28-43; Willi, *Die Chronik als Auslegung*, p. 169.

1. In particular, the changes made at 1 Chron. 10.6 and 10.10, as well as the concluding passage of 1 Chron. 10.13-14. Although the possibility that the Chronicler has used a Palestinian text type of his *Vorlage* no longer directly available to us diminishes the certainty of any evaluation of such minor changes as those noted for vv. 6 and 10, there is no Septuagintal evidence for Samuel which indicates that the Chronicler's wording here derives from his *Vorlage* and the Qumran evidence is lacking. Cf. Klein, *Textual Criticism of the Old Testament: The Septuagint after Qumran*, pp. 70-71; McKenzie, *The Chronicler's Use of the Deuteronomistic History*, pp. 58-60.

2. In particular, the genealogical material and the references to Saul in 1 Chron. 13.3 and 1 Chron. 15.29 are investigated.

3. It is also assumed that, in the original situation in which Chronicles was written and read, the meaning of Saul in the story would not be as enigmatic as it is to the modern interpreter; this assumption, however, does not have the same bearing upon the analysis of the Saul material as the premises listed in the text above.

4. For example Johnstone, 'Guilt and Atonement: The Theme of 1 and 2 Chronicles', pp. 113-38; Mosis, *Untersuchungen zur Theologie des chronistischen*

strong presence in v. 13 strengthens the impression that the Chronistic Saul narrative is intended to act as a paradigm in the Chronistic history. Elsewhere in the Hebrew Bible the root מעל is linked negatively with habitation of the land;[1] the Chronicler has retained this association in his usage[2] and also used both noun and verb to indicate cultic offences elsewhere in his work.[3] The probability is that the term is meant to have the same associations in the Chronicler's judgment on Saul.[4] The cultic overtone of this term is significant, since it immediately brings into this paradigmatic passage that vision which was common to the ancient Near East of the king as one who had responsibility and accountability in relation to the cultus.

Saul's cultic offence is not only implied by the use of the term מעל, but also by the statement ולא־דרש ביהוה, for the seeking of Yahweh in the Chronicler's eyes has largely become a matter of concern for, and involvement in, the official cultus—as a consideration of the term דרש in Chronicles reveals.[5] The negative use of דרש here indicates that the

Geschichtswerkes, pp. 29-31; S.D. Walters, 'Saul of Gibeon', pp. 64-67.

1. Thus Moses may not enter the land of Canaan because of his unfaithful action at Meribath-Kadesh (Deut. 32.51); the treachery of Achan becomes known when the attempt to take Ai fails (Josh. 7.1-10); exiled Israel must confess its treachery in order to be restored to the land (Lev. 26.40); exile is caused by treachery (Ezek. 39.23) and restoration means that Israel will put treachery behind them (Ezek. 39.26).

2. Cf. 1 Chron. 5.25-26; 9.1; 2 Chron. 12.3-4, 8; 28.17-19; 30.6-8; 36.14-20.

3. Cf. 1 Chron. 5.25; 2 Chron. 26.16, 18; 28.22-25; 29.6; 30.7; 36.14.

4. Given the nature of the Chronicler's use of מעל, the statement of Welten, 'Lade–Tempel–Jerusalem: Zur Theologie der Chronikbücher', p. 171, to the effect that the Chronicler sees the death of Saul as 'die Folge der nicht weiter spezifizierten Untreue, daß er sich nicht an Gott gehalten hat' could be misleading. The Chronicler's failure to define the מעל of Saul in very specific terms invokes the wider picture, allowing the offence to assume an archetypal quality and the judgment to apply to the whole of Saul's reign; cf. Braun, *1 Chronicles*, p. 151.

5. The cultic roots of the seeking of Yahweh can be seen in its use for the mantic consultation of the Deity (as in Gen. 25.22), a usage found in Chronicles, sometimes bringing this implication from the Deuteronomistic *Vorlage*; cf. 1 Chron. 21.30; 2 Chron. 18.4, 6, 7 (‖ 1 Kgs 22.5, 7, 8); 34.21, 26 (‖ 2 Kgs 22.13, 18); although less clear, 1 Chron. 10.13, 14 and 2 Chron. 1.5 might be added to this list. The Chronicler has invested the expression of seeking Yahweh with a connection to the Jerusalem cultus—a perception that is similar to the use of the term in Deut. 12.5. Thus, the Tent which is later to be incorporated into the Temple is the proper place where Yahweh is to be sought (1 Chron. 21.30; 2 Chron. 22.19); the building of the

cultic offence should be seen as one of omission. Saul's failure to seek Yahweh is also indicated by the preceding phrase וגם־לשאול באוב לדרוש; here the Chronicler uses a wordplay upon the name of Saul[1] which has the effect of emphasizing the depth of Saul's failure.[2] The phrase על־דבר יהוה may also give a cultic overtone to Saul's offence since reference to the word of Yahweh generally relates to matters of either cultus or legitimate kingship in the Chronicler's Davidic and Solomonic narratives.[3]

The Chronicler has indicated that Saul has failed in relation to the cultus elsewhere in the work, most notably at 1 Chron. 13.3; there

Temple depends on the setting of the leaders' hearts to seek Yahweh (1 Chron. 22.19); those who come to Jerusalem for Hezekiah's Passover are involved in seeking Yahweh (2 Chron. 30.19), a term that also describes Hezekiah's efforts on behalf of the Temple cultus (2 Chron. 31.21).

1. שָׁאוּל/שָׁאוּל. The paronomasia clearly sees Saul's name as the *qal* passive participle of שׁאל; cf. BDB, p. 982; Duke, *The Persuasive Appeal of the Chronicler: A Rhetorical Analysis*, pp. 97-98. This would be highly significant if the suggestion of a reciprocal relationship of seeking between king and Deity made by J.G. McConville, 'I Chronicles 28:9: Yahweh "Seeks Out' Solomon", pp. 105-108, is correct; in that case, the Chronicler would certainly be emphasizing Saul's divine election in the midst of its tragic failure.

2. Willi, *Die Chronik als Auslegung*, p. 170. The Chronicler's fondness for exploring the meaning of names in his narrative is evident elsewhere; Willi, *Die Chronik als Auslegung*, p. 185, also points to the use of the root שׁלם in material related to Solomon; Wellhausen, *Prolegomena to the History of Ancient Israel*, p. 191, notes the nominal connection in the appointment of judges by Jehoshaphat; Halpern, 'Sacred History and Ideology: Chronicles' Thematic Structure—Indications of an Earlier Source', p. 49, considers but rejects a connection between the Chronicler's use of the root חזק and the name of Hezekiah. Recognition of the Saul paronomasia demonstrates that the sequence of events in 1 Sam. 28.6-7 (wherein Saul inquires of Yahweh and looks for the witch of Endor only after Yahweh does not answer) poses no problem for the reading of 1 Chron. 10.13-14; the Chronicler has not limited Saul's failure to seek Yahweh to this one incident, but applies it to the whole of Saul's reign; cf. C.T. Begg, '"Seeking Yahweh" and the Purpose of Chronicles', pp. 131-132. For an interesting consideration of paronomasia in the Deuteronomistic History, see M. Garsiel, 'Puns upon Names as a Literary Device in 1 Kings 1-2', pp. 379-86.

3. Cf. 1 Chron. 11.3, 10; 15.15; 17.3, 6, 23; 22.8; 2 Chron. 1.9; 6.10, 17. This connotation is not as noticeable in the post-Solomonic narratives, but it is not entirely lacking; cf. 2 Chron. 10.15; 19.11; 30.12; 35.6. The phrase בדברי יהוה in 2 Chron. 29.15 also refers to cultic matters.

David's concern with the Ark is contrasted with Saul's neglect, using the verb דרש once again in a pejorative reference to the reign of Saul: ‎ונסבה את־ארון אלהינו אלינו כי־לא דרשנהו בימי שאול‎.[1] A similarly negative relationship between Saul and the Ark is implied in the disapproval of Saul's daughter Michal of David's cultic dance before the Ark in 1 Chron. 15.29.[2] Thus the general picture of Saul implied in 1 Chron. 10.13-14 and confirmed more explicitly in 1 Chron. 13.3 and 1 Chron. 15.29 is of a monarch who has failed to be concerned for the cultus of Yahweh.[3]

Saul's lack of concern for the Ark may be symbolically represented through a change which the Chronicler introduces at 1 Chron. 10.10; whereas 1 Sam. 31.10 tells of Saul's body being fastened to the wall of Beth-shan, 1 Chron. 10.10 reads ‎ואת־גלגלתו תקעו בית דגון‎. By altering ‎בית שן‎ to ‎בית דגון‎, the Chronicler may be alluding to the Philistine attempt to house the Ark in the temple of Dagon,[4] and giving an ironic manifestation of the failure of Saul in the very place where the Ark of Yahweh had shown its strength,[5] a strength which would have been available to Israel had Saul shown proper concern for the Ark. The struggle with the Philistines is thus shown as a type of cultic war which Saul has lost due to his cultic failure.

As has been noted, the Chronicler's use of ‎מעל‎ often has the consequence that Israel's security in the land is endangered or destroyed;

---

1. The *hiphil* of ‎סבב‎ provides a further verbal link between this verse and 1 Chron. 10.13-14.

2. Becker, *1 Chronik*, p. 52, notes that, by omitting reference to the marital dispute narrated in 2 Sam. 6.20-23, the Chronicler has placed even greater emphasis upon the tension between the house of Saul and the cultus.

3. 1 Chron. 26.28 seems to be the exception to this general picture. Here Saul is listed with non-monarchic leaders of Israel who have dedicated material for cultic use. The strong contrast between this verse and the rest of the Chronicler's portrayal of Saul leads many commentators to ascribe this verse to a later hand; in any event, this mention of Saul amounts to a minor aberration from the general picture rather than a complete contradiction. Cf. Rudolph, *Chronikbücher*, p. 177; Ackroyd, *I & II Chronicles, Ezra, Nehemiah*, p. 86; Braun, *1 Chronicles*, p. 253.

4. 1 Sam. 5.2-7; cf. Williamson, *1 and 2 Chronicles*, p. 94; Becker, *1 Chronik*, p. 52. The suggestion sometimes made that this alteration springs from a different text of the *Vorlage* is possible, but is made without textual attestation; cf. Rudolph, *Chronikbücher*, pp. 92, 95; Myers, *I Chronicles*, p. 81; McKenzie, *The Chronicler's Use of the Deuteronomistic History*, p. 59.

5. Ackroyd, 'The Chronicler as Exegete', p. 6.

this is clearly the case in 1 Chronicles 10. The chapter begins with the rout of Israel (1 Chron. 10.1) and continues with the loss of cities to the Philistines (1 Chron. 10.7). It is possible that this element is part of the paradigmatic picture constructed by the Chronicler on the basis of material drawn from the *Vorlage*: Becker[1] sees a parallel to the events of the exile in the abandonment of Israel's cities and their habitation by non-Israelites; Mosis[2] finds an implicit connection between the Saul narrative and the exile in the Chronicler's statement that Saul did not keep the word of Yahweh, for this link between שמר and דבר יהוה is only found in one other place in the Chronicler's work, and that occurs in the context of impending exile (2 Chron. 34.21).

The Chronicler indicates a further effect of Saul's מעל in 1 Chron. 10.6, wherein reference in the *Vorlage* to the death of Saul's armour-bearers and men (1 Sam. 31.6) is replaced by the phrase וכל־ביתו יחדו מתו. Although the Chronistic nature of this variant is generally acknowledged, it is not always conceded that its presence is significant.[3] Some commentators, evidently interpreting וכל־ביתו as primarily signifying 'and all his family', see the phrase as an indication that the genealogies, which trace the descendants of Saul (1 Chron. 8.33-40; 9.39-44), belong to a different outlook than that of the Chronicler.[4]

Given the general context in which it occurs, it seems that the most reasonable rendering of וכל־ביתו would be 'and all his dynasty', and the phrase is understood to bear this significance by several

---

1.   *1 Chronik*, p. 52. Becker here seems to be following the suggestion of Mosis, *Untersuchungen zur Theologie des chronistischen Geschichtswerkes*, p. 23, that the elimination of some geographical references in 1 Chronicles 10 implies the flight of the whole people, a suggestion heavily criticized by Ackroyd, 'The Chronicler as Exegete', p. 5.

2.   *Untersuchungen zur Theologie des chronistischen Geschichtswerkes*, p. 36.

3.   Thus Curtis and Madsen, *A Critical and Exegetical Commentary on the Books of Chronicles*, p. 181, judge the phrase to be a careless abridgment by the Chronicler of the Deuteronomistic *Vorlage*; McKenzie, *The Chronicler's Use of the Deuteronomistic History*, pp. 58-59, considers the phrase an expansion upon a text shorter than that which survives in the MT of 1 Samuel 31 (the LXX at 1 Kgdms 31.6 reads simply καὶ ἀπέθανεν Σαουλ καὶ οἱ τρεῖς υἱοὶ αὐτοῦ καὶ ὁ αἴρων τὰ σκεύη αὐτοῦ ἐν τῇ ἡμέρᾳ ἐκείνῃ κατὰ τὸ αὐτό), and argues against a specific significance of the phrase for the Chronicler's thought.

4.   Rudolph, *Chronikbücher*, p. 95; Randellini, *Il libro delle Cronache*, p. 146.

commentators;[1] that בית can have this meaning in Chronicles is indicated by other occurrences of the word in the work.[2]

The Chronicler's Deuteronomistic *Vorlage* explicitly states that Saul could have been the founder of a divinely appointed dynasty if only he had been obedient to Yahweh,[3] and there is no evidence in Chronicles that its author's outlook differed in this regard from that of the *Vorlage*. However, the Chronicler seems to presume upon this dynastic possibility, rather than state it, as he portrays its frustration. In this context, it is noteworthy that two of the Chronicler's alterations in his Saul narrative introduce into this negative passage the same dual significance of the term בית which provides the focus of Nathan's oracle.[4] By this usage, the Chronicler contrasts the concern of David with the Temple and the consequent granting of a dynasty to him with Saul's neglect of the cultus, symbolized in part by the humiliation of his head as a trophy in the temple of Dagon, and the death of both Saul and his dynastic hope through Yahweh's judgment. The connection between Nathan's oracle and the Saul narrative is evident in the text of the oracle itself, as Yahweh promises not to remove his חסד from Solomon, as he had מאשר היה לפניך.[5] It would seem that, by his use of the term בית, the Chronicler has strengthened the relationship between the story of Saul and Nathan's oracle which was already present in his *Vorlage*, demonstrating that Saul's house was disqualified from being Yahweh's chosen dynasty because of Saul's lack of attention to his cultic responsibilities.

Such a dynastic interpretation of בית indicates that, for the Chronicler, one of the effects of kingly מעל is the endangerment of dynasty, an effect to which Yahweh's action in turning the kingdom to David in v. 14 also bears witness.[6] This verse may also be

---

1. For example Ackroyd, *I & II Chronicles, Ezra, Nehemiah*, p. 50; Michaeli, *Les livres des Chroniques, d'Esdras et de Néhémie*, pp. 76-77; Virgulin, *Libri delle Cronache*, p. 134; Williamson, *1 and 2 Chronicles*, p. 93; Braun, *1 Chronicles*, p. 149-50; S. Zalewski, 'The Purpose of the Story of the Death of Saul in 1 Chronicles X', p. 462.

2. Cf. especially 1 Chron. 17.10, 24-25 and 2 Chron. 21.7.

3. 1 Sam. 13.13. Cf. Braun, *1 Chronicles*, p. 152; S.J. De Vries, 'The Schema of Dynastic Endangerment in Chronicles', p. 61.

4. 1 Chron. 17.1-15 (‖ 2 Sam. 7.1-17).

5. 1 Chron. 17.13 (‖ 2 Sam. 7.15).

6. Williamson, *1 and 2 Chronicles*, p. 94, notes that this verse forms an

acknowledging the royal status of Saul in stating of his death ולא־דרש
ביהוה וימיתהו, making it clear that Saul's demise (and that of his
dynasty) was not simply an act of war, but a divinely willed event.[1] In
so doing, the Chronicler shows his respect for the humanly inviolable
person of the king, a respect which the *Vorlage* has demonstrated
before him.[2] Thus, just as a king and his dynasty can only be established by divine action, so they can only be disposed of by decision of
the divine will; and, in the case of Saul, royal מעל has provoked such a
decision.

A final form reading of the Chronistic material relating to Saul
demands that the narrative of 1 Chron. 10.1-14 be seen in the context
of the genealogical material related to Saul in 1 Chron. 8.29-40 and 1
Chron. 9.35-44; the second inclusion of the Saul genealogy[3] immediately before the narrative of his death indicates that either the
Chronicler or a later redactor intended that the genealogical material
and the story of Saul's death should be viewed in the light of each
other.[4]

The very literary form of the Chronicler's genealogies seems
opaque to modern interpreters,[5] with the result that interpretative

---

inclusio with v. 6.

1. Welch, *The Work of the Chronicler: Its Purpose and Date*, p. 12.

2. 1 Sam. 24.7, 21; 26.9, 11, 23; 2 Sam. 1.14, 16. See E. Galbiati, 'Il carattere
sacro della regalità nell'antico Israele', p. 97; Zalewski, 'The Purpose of the Story
of the Death of Saul in 1 Chronicles X', p. 463.

3. The singular is used here and elsewhere; the differences between 1 Chron. 8.
29-40 and 1 Chron. 9.35-44 are not great enough to warrant considering them as
separate genealogies. Cf. Rudolph, *Chronikbücher*, pp. 92-93.

4. Ackroyd, *I & II Chronicles, Ezra, Nehemiah*, p. 47; Williamson, *1 and 2
Chronicles*, pp. 91-92. J.W. Flanagan, *David's Social Drama: A Hologram of
Israel's Early Iron Age*, p. 211, suggests that the effect of the duplication is to bind
Saul's death to all of the genealogical material, thus making the death of Saul a judg-
ment on all of pre-Davidic Israel; the amount of post-Davidic material in the genealo-
gies does not allow such an interpretation.

5. While Noth, *The Chronicler's History*, p. 42, observes 'The great bulk of
that which is now found in 1 Chron. 2-9 is a confused and secondary mass of rank
textual growth', Harvey-Jellie, *Chronicles*, p. 85, is probably closer to the truth
when he states, 'Reviewing the genealogical records as a whole, one is struck by the
fact that almost everywhere there are signs of an underlying greater symmetry of
plan, once prominent, but now no longer recoverable'. In any event, few would
argue with the remark of Michaeli, *Les livres des Chroniques, d'Esdras et de*

comments on the significance of isolated sections of these genealogies are necessarily highly tentative. Nevertheless, study of the genealogies in 1 Chronicles 1–9 has revealed their overall harmony with the concerns of the whole work and justifies an integrative approach to their interpretation, even in a diachronic study.[1] More specifically, although the reference to the death of the בית of Saul in 1 Chron. 10.6 has been seen by some as indicating a contradiction with the genealogical material (which is thereby judged to be a later addition to the work),[2] the dynastic understanding of בית in this passage as advocated above eliminates the apparent contradiction.[3]

The apparent contradiction, however, does indicate an aspect of the Saul genealogy which is worthy of consideration: that, despite the tension created with 1 Chron. 10.6, the line of Saul is recorded down to the time of the exile.[4] The genealogy might have its roots in the continuing prominence of Saul's family, at least locally,[5] or perhaps even in a level of support for Saul's line which has been generally lacking in the biblical record due to the more widespread concern in the canonical books with Davidic legitimacy.[6]

The origin of the Saul genealogy does not necessarily shed light on its purpose in the work. Although it has often been argued that the purpose of the Chronicler's genealogies is to give legitimacy to the

---

Néhémie, p. 74: 'Nous avons sans doute perdu aujourd'hui ce sens spirituel des généalogies'.

1. 'The result to which we are led is to consider chapters 1-9 of I Chronicles an integral part of the Chronicler's work, although the hand of later editors is to be admitted at several points. At the least, the weight of the evidence puts the burden of proof on those who would consider the entire genealogical introduction to Chronicles a later addition' (Johnson, *The Purpose of the Biblical Genealogies*, p. 55); however, Johnson admits that the Saul genealogy in 1 Chronicles 8 is a particularly difficult one to analyse: 'Attempts to apply the principles of literary criticism to these Benjaminite lists have resulted only in a further demonstration of the impossibility of doing so' (*The Purpose of the Biblical Genealogies*, p. 51).

2. Rudolph, *Chronikbücher*, p. 95; Randellini, *Il libro delle Cronache*, p. 146.

3. Williamson, *1 and 2 Chronicles*, p. 93.

4. Curtis and Madsen, *A Critical and Exegetical Commentary on the Books of Chronicles*, pp. 166-67; Harvey-Jellie, *Chronicles*, p. 79; Braun, *1 Chronicles*, p. 127.

5. Coggins, *The First and Second Books of the Chronicles*, p. 55.

6. Ackroyd, *I & II Chronicles, Ezra, Nehemiah*, p. 42.

post-exilic community,[1] this suggestion is too generically stated to have much validity or usefulness; as Johnson has pointed out:

> The legitimacy principle—perhaps given too high an importance by the commentators—appears to have been crucial only with regard to cultic functions and this above all with regard to the priesthood.[2]

It would seem, therefore, that the genealogical material in 1 Chronicles 1–9 should be viewed as serving a function within the terms of the work, rather than having a purpose which existed apart from the work, such as providing pedigrees for the members of the post-exilic community.[3]

Considered in the wider context of the first chapters of Chronicles, the Saul genealogy finds a corresponding royal genealogy in the list of David's descendants in 1 Chron. 3.1-24. Although those who find in the Chronicler a hope for Davidic restoration sometimes point to this Davidic genealogy as a sound indicator of the Chronicler's hope,[4] there is nothing in the structure of 1 Chronicles 3 itself which indicates an expectation of the restoration of David's line any more than there is such an indicator in the genealogy of Saul. The only indication that a dynasty is involved comes in 1 Chron. 3.10-16 wherein the genealogy is limited to those of the Davidic line who reigned as kings in Jerusalem.[5] After this list, that is, after the dynasty has ceased to function, the genealogy shows a concern with tracing a limited horizontal and vertical lineage of David in much the same way as the descendants of Saul are traced. The presence of the Saul genealogy, therefore, makes it impossible to point to the David genealogy in

---

1. See for example North, 'Theology of the Chronicler', pp. 369-71; Virgulin, *Libri delle Cronache*, pp. 67-68; Weinberg, 'Das Wegen und die funktionelle Bestimmung der Listen in I Chr 1–9', pp. 91-114.

2. *The Purpose of the Biblical Genealogies*, p. 79.

3. This last mentioned purpose could not apply to all of the genealogical material in any event; note the inclusion of Reuben in 1 Chron. 5.1-10 and Simeon in 1 Chron. 4.24-43.

4. For example Stinespring, 'Eschatology in Chronicles', p. 210; Williamson, 'Eschatology in Chronicles', p. 129; *idem, 1 and 2 Chronicles*, pp. 49-50.

5. The sole exception to this is Johanan who is identified as Josiah's firstborn son in v. 15; Braun, *1 Chronicles*, p. 51, discusses the problems connected with this otherwise unknown royal person. Zedekiah is mentioned twice (vv. 15-16) to indicate both his line of descent and his place as regent in the dynasty; Virgulin, *Libri delle Cronache*, pp. 87-88.

1 Chronicles 3 as a proof of the Chronicler's interest in a Davidic restoration; since the Saul genealogy traces a royal בית which according to the Chronicler has been made ineffective by the action of Yahweh (1 Chron. 10.6, 14), the Davidic genealogy itself offers no guarantee that the Chronicler has not given a similar account of another dynasty which will never function again to the best of his knowledge.[1]

The very first royal material to be contained in the Chronistic genealogies also indicates that the modification or elimination of the hope of Davidic restoration may have been one of the very reasons for the inclusion of the Saul genealogy. The most striking feature of the list of kings of Edom in the opening chapter of the work[2] is the complete lack of dynasty, as is made explicit both by the naming of the father of each king[3] (a feature which the Chronicler derived from his *Vorlage*) and also by the ending of the list with the death of the last king without a successor (the Chronicler's only noteworthy alteration to his *Vorlage*). Unless the Chronicler is incorporating an implicit statement about kingship in this list, it is difficult to postulate what his purpose may have been in including this list of foreign monarchs.[4]

One feature of the Saul genealogy provides an interesting connection with the narrative material of Chronicles, and that is the location

---

1.   Cazelles, *Les livres des Chroniques*, p. 63, suggests that the longer genealogy afforded David in comparison with that of Saul demonstrates 'la pérennité de la dynastie davidique'; this argument would seem to require more substantiation than Cazelles give it.

2.   1 Chron. 1.43-51 (‖ Gen. 36.31-39).

3.   The only exception to this is Hadad in 1 Chron. 1.50 whose father is unnamed.

4.   J.R. Bartlett, 'The Edomite King-List of Genesis XXXVI.31-39 and I Chron. I.43-50', pp. 301-14, provides a thorough study of this material but makes no real suggestion as to the purpose of the list's inclusion in Chronicles. Ackroyd, *I & II Chronicles, Ezra, Nehemiah*, p. 32, admitting that the Chronicler has momentarily abandoned his concern with the true line of Israel, makes the suggestion that the Chronicler is reminding his readers 'that physical descent is not everything, and also that their neighbours are not unrelated to them'. Becker, *1 Chronik*, p. 16, considers that the Edomite kings are included as predecessors of David as rulers over Edom. Williamson, *1 and 2 Chronicles*, p. 44, admits that the reason for inclusion is not evident and suggests that the Chronicler may be exhibiting a desire for completeness which he does not follow consistently.

of his family in Gibeon (1 Chron. 8.29; 9.35). This location for the Chronicler was primarily the place where the Tent remained until it was brought to Jerusalem by Solomon,[1] and commentators suggest that in this locative reference the Chronicler has made a deliberate connection between the house of Saul and the sanctuary.[2] Just as such a reference emphasizes the connection between king and sanctuary, so too it serves to underscore the cultic failure of Israel's first king.

Although the tentative nature of the interpretation of the genealogical material here presented must be admitted, it is consistent with what is present in the Chronicler's portrayal of Saul. The end of dynasty and the failure to be concerned with the cultus are both important aspects of the Chronistic treatment generally, and both are enhanced by the allusions to them in the genealogical material.

The paradigm presented by the Chronicler through his portrayal of Saul can be expressed thus: he is a king whose failure to seek Yahweh in the cultus amounts to מעל; the effect of this cultic מעל is to endanger Israel's security in the land and to provoke the anger of Yahweh; in turn, Saul and his dynasty are terminated and the kingship is turned elsewhere. This paradigm fits well (even if in a negative way) into the ancient Near Eastern understanding of king and temple, for the Chronicler has presented in his picture of Saul the very antithesis of the ideal king who bears responsibility for the temple, whose kingship depends upon his fulfilment of that responsibility, and who ensures blessings for the land through his cultic concern.

The range of application that the Chronicler intended for this paradigm is more problematic. Although those who judge the story of Saul to be paradigmatic have no difficulty in seeing that it applies to

1.   Cf. 1 Chron. 21.29; 2 Chron. 1.3; 5.5.
2.   For example Curtis and Madsen, *A Critical and Exegetical Commentary on the Books of Chronicles*, p. 164; Cazelles, *Les livres des Chroniques*, pp. 62-63; Ackroyd, *I & II Chronicles, Ezra, Nehemiah*, p. 47. Walters, 'Saul of Gibeon', pp. 70-72, proposes a different hypothesis. According to Walters, Saul is linked to the Canaanite cultic site of Gibeon rather than placed in genealogical relationship to a tribe in Israel; by doing this, the Chronicler has signalled that Saul is unfit to reign as king in Israel. The Chronicler's identification of Gibeon as an authentic cultic site for Israel before the construction of the Temple poses great difficulties for Walters' hypothesis and leads the audience to see the connection between Saul and Gibeon as one with positive potential, even though this potential becomes frustrated in the person of Saul.

individual post-Solomonic kings,[1] some go further and see the paradigm applying to the whole panorama of the nation's history to the exile.[2]

A third application might be added to the above: the Chronicler has not only formed a paradigm for individual unsatisfactory monarchs, but for dynasties as well. The Chronicler obviously records the end of Saul's dynasty with the death of the king and his sons; however, he also includes allusions to Saul's dynastic potential through the genealogy and the use of בית in 1 Chron. 10.6.[3] It could therefore be significant that the Chronicler's historical narrative, in which he records the story of David's dynasty from its beginning to its effective end, begins with a paradigm that demonstrates that dynasties can fail.

David, Founder of Cultus and Dynasty

A concern with David shows itself throughout the Chronistic history. If the occurrence of the name דויד may be taken as a rough indication of the extent of the Chronicler's concern with David, then an investigation reveals that, apart from the Chronicler's narrative of David's reign (1 Chron. 11–29) and his Davidic genealogical material,[4] the text contains 76 additional occurrences of the name placed throughout the work.[5] There are several contexts in which the name occurs, including: as part of an identifying temporal, geographical or

---

1. For example Mosis, *Untersuchungen zur Theologie des chronistischen Geschichtswerkes*, pp. 200-204; Ackroyd, 'The Chronicler as Exegete', p. 9; C. Mangan, *1–2 Chronicles, Ezra, Nehemiah*, p. 27.

2. See Mosis, *Untersuchungen zur Theologie des chronistischen Geschichtswerkes*, pp. 41-42; Coggins, *The First and Second Books of the Chronicles*, p. 64; Becker, *1 Chronik*, pp. 51-52. Interestingly enough, Coggins traces this paradigm into the genealogies and finds hope for the survival of Israel in the continuing line of Saul after his downfall.

3. Perhaps another allusion to Saul's dynastic potential is to be found in the phrase ויסב את־המלוכה לדויד בן־ישי in 1 Chron. 10.14; the turning of kingship is not only from Saul, but from his dynastic heirs.

4. 1 Chron. 2.9-17; 3.1-24.

5. 1 Chron. 4.31; 6.16; 9.22; 10.14; 2 Chron. 1.1, 4 (twice), 8, 9; 2.2, 6, 11, 13, 16; 3.1 (twice); 5.1, 2; 6.4, 6, 7, 8, 10, 15, 16, 17, 42; 7.6 (twice), 10, 17, 18; 8.11 (twice), 14 (twice); 9.31; 10.16 (twice), 19; 11.17, 18; 12.16; 13.5, 6, 8, 23; 16.14; 17.3; 21.1, 7 (twice), 20; 23.3, 9, 18 (twice); 24.16, 25; 27.9; 28.1; 29.2, 25, 26, 27, 30; 30.26; 32.5, 30, 33; 33.7, 14; 34.2; 35.3, 4, 15.

patronymic phrase;[1] as one who was concerned with the cultus and who prepared for it and provided for its arrangements;[2] as the one who received the kingship and dynasty;[3] and as a term of comparison for subsequent monarchs.[4] In this section I will be primarily concerned with the narrative picture of David's reign given in Chronicles, to which many of the secondary occurrences of דויד noted above obviously refer in the Chronistic text.[5]

The Nature of the Chronicler's Davidic Picture

The Chronicler's Davidic narrative constitutes a chronologically disproportionate amount of his total narrative: 19 chapters out of a total of 56. In other words, approximately a third of the space that the Chronicler allows for the 450-year story of Israel from the reign of Saul to the Edict of Cyrus is allocated to the 33-year reign of David over Israel and Judah.

Despite the amount of material concerned with the reign of David, some scholars have observed an underlying unity between the Chronicler's Davidic and Solomonic material which indicates that the Davidic narrative cannot be taken in isolation from the Chronistic presentation of Solomon. Braun, for instance, concludes 'that the Chronicler wished to portray the reigns of David and Solomon as a single unit centring in the construction of the Jerusalem temple'.[6] Welten makes a similar observation when he states that 'One can get the impression that the entire narrative of David and Solomon

---

1. For example, cf. the phrases עד־מלך דויד (1 Chron. 4.31), בן־דויד (2 Chron. 1.1; 11.18; 13.6; 30.26; 35.3), עיר דויד (2 Chron. 5.2; 8.11; 9.31; 12.16; 13.23; 16.14; 21.1, 20; 24.16, 25; 27.9; 32.5, 30; 33.14).

2. Cf. 1 Chron. 6.16; 9.22; 2 Chron. 1.4; 2.6; 3.1; 5.1; 6.7, 42; 7.6; 23.9, 18; 29.25, 26, 27, 30; 33.7; 35.4, 15.

3. Cf. 1 Chron. 10.14; 2 Chron. 1.8, 9; 2.11; 6.4, 6, 10, 15, 16, 17; 7.18; 8.11, 14; 10.16, 19; 13.5, 8; 21.7; 23.3.

4. Cf. 2 Chron. 7.17; 17.3; 28.1; 29.2; 34.2.

5. This is particularly true of those passages in which David is presented either in his cultic concern, in his capacity as founder of the dynasty or in comparison with other kings. Even though this last category depends upon the Deuteronomistic *Vorlage* in four of its five occurrences (2 Chron. 7.17 ‖ 1 Kgs 9.4; 2 Chron. 28.1 ‖ 2 Kgs 16.1; 2 Chron. 29.2 ‖ 2 Kgs 18.3; 2 Chron. 34.2 ‖ 2 Kgs 22.2), it is the Chronistic David who constitutes the term of comparison in the Chronicler's work.

6. 'Solomon, the Chosen Temple Builder: The Significance of 1 Chronicles 22, 28, and 29 for the Theology of Chronicles', p. 581.

represents nothing but one vast expansion of the first verse of Ps. 132'.[1] The basic unity of these two narratives has also been indicated by others, including Brunet,[2] Runnalls,[3] Throntveit[4] and Allen.[5] In allowing this underlying unity, J.W. Flanagan gives the caveat that the union is far from equal; the overwhelming amount of text concerned with David reveals the Chronicler's prime concern.[6] The length of the Davidic narrative alone justifies a consideration of this material in the present study with a measure of isolation from the Solomonic material; however, such a procedure does not deny that the Davidic material is incomplete in itself and forces the audience onward into the story of Solomon—and beyond. My consideration in this section of the Davidic material will therefore be complemented by a consideration of the Chronistic presentation of Solomon in the next section.

It is clear to all that the Chronicler is strongly concerned with David; the nature of that concern, however, remains a matter of debate. Some scholars interpret the Davidic narrative as providing a paradigm or part of a paradigm for the Chronicler.[7] The etiological character of much of the Davidic narrative in Chronicles, and even the very length of the material, shows that the Davidic narrative cannot function paradigmatically in the same way that the Saul narrative does. Even though it is clear that David serves as a standard of comparison for later kings,[8] the term 'paradigm' could be misleading when applied to the Chronistic David if it implies anything more than the fact that David has been portrayed as an idealized king of Israel.

Many exegetes find that the Chronicler has portrayed David explicitly in terms of an eschatological hope for a Davidic

1. 'Lade–Tempel–Jerusalem: Zur Theologie der Chronikbücher', p. 181.
2. 'La théologie du chroniste: théocratie et messianisme', p. 387.
3. 'The King as Temple Builder: A Messianic Typology', p. 24.
4. *When Kings Speak: Royal Speech and Royal Prayer in Chronicles*, p. 114.
5. 'Kerygmatic Units in 1 & 2 Chronicles', pp. 23-24.
6. *David's Social Drama: A Hologram of Israel's Early Iron Age*, p. 211.
7. Cf. Mosis, *Untersuchungen zur Theologie des chronistischen Geschichtswerkes*, pp. 164-69; Ackroyd, 'The Chronicler as Exegete', pp. 3-4; Becker, *1 Chronik*, pp. 8-9; Mangan, *1–2 Chronicles, Ezra, Nehemiah*, p. 27; Duke, *The Persuasive Appeal of the Chronicler: A Rhetorical Analysis*, pp. 56-66.
8. 2 Chron. 7.17; 17.3; 28.1; 29.2; 34.2. It should be noted that David is not the only king to provide a term of comparison with a later king; cf. 2 Chron. 26.4; 27.2.

restoration;[1] others find in Chronicles a messianism which is somewhat hidden but yet detectable.[2] For such scholars, the Chronistic picture of David has been primarily constructed with a view to the Davidide who will rule Israel in fulfilment of the divine promise.

Those who do not find a hope for Davidic restoration in Chronicles interpret the nature of the Davidic picture differently, often in terms of a post-exilic theocracy centred around the Jerusalem Temple. Thus, for example, Rudolph suggests that the Chronicler has attempted to portray the realization of theocracy in Israel and the creation of the ordinances which governed the worship of the post-exilic community.[3] The Temple is emphasized by Caquot as the Davidic heritage which is central to the Chronistic portrayal.[4] Michaeli sees the Chronicler's Davidic concern producing an ideal picture of the theocracy in which Yahweh is the true regent.[5] Mosis observes that the Chronicler's interest in David (and Solomon) lies chiefly in the task of building the Temple,[6] an opinion in which Dumbrell concurs.[7]

Although the eschatological interpretation of the Chronicler's Davidic concern and the view that interprets the Chronicler as a proponent of post-exilic theocracy are sometimes seen as opposite and mutually exclusive positions,[8] such need not be the case. Thus Brunet views the Chronistic picture of David as a model for a future messianic and theocratic king;[9] Botterweck observes the Chronicler

1. The following may serve as examples: von Rad, *Das Geschichtsbild des chronistischen Werkes*, pp. 127 and 135; Stinespring, 'Eschatology in Chronicles', pp. 210-11; Poulssen, 'Rex et Templum in Israel', pp. 268-69; Saebø, 'Messianism in Chronicles? Some Remarks to the Old Testament Background of the New Testament Christology', pp. 97-102; Brueggemann, *David's Truth in Israel's Imagination and Memory*, pp. 101-102.

2. Cf. Noth, *The Chronicler's History*, p. 105; Virgulin, *Libri delle Cronache*, p. 49.

3. 'Problems of the Books of Chronicles', pp. 404 and 409.

4. 'Peut-on parler de messianisme dans l'oeuvre du Chroniste?', pp. 114-20.

5. *Les livres des Chroniques, d'Esdras et de Néhémie*, p. 32.

6. *Untersuchungen zur Theologie des chronistischen Geschichtswerkes*, pp. 162-63.

7. 'The Purpose of the Books of Chronicles', p. 264.

8. This polarization is particularly evident in the writings of Plöger; see *Theocracy and Eschatology*, pp. 34-44; *idem*, 'Reden und Gebete im deuteronomistichen und chronistischen Geschichtswerk', p. 57.

9. 'Le Chroniste et ses sources', p. 508.

legitimizing the institutions of post-exilic Judah in expectation of a Davidic restoration,[1] as does Freedman in a somewhat less messianic way;[2] Saebø holds to an interpretation which is expressly both theocratic and messianic.[3]

I have already indicated my view that the Chronicler has reinterpreted the Davidic promise in terms of the cultus in which the promise continued to be enunciated. However, this or any other position regarding the Chronicler's concern with the dynastic aspect of David can only be satisfactorily established through a consideration of the full story of the dynasty which unfolds in the Chronistic history; therefore, the observations made in regard to the Davidic narration must, of necessity, be verified by tracing the theme through the remainder of the Chronistic narrative in subsequent sections.

Perhaps the most useful way of characterizing the Chronistic portrayal of David has been proposed by De Vries when he states that the 'idealized figure of David in 1–2 Chronicles belongs therefore not to the eschaton but to the *Urzeit*'.[4] In the words of Goldingay, the Chronicler has portrayed his David 'not as hope for the future but as a past reality which is constitutive of what it means to be Israel now'.[5] What often seems to be a tendency of the Chronicler towards simple idealization and anachronism might be more accurately viewed as a type of etiology narrated in the *Urzeit* of the Chronicler's Israel.[6] This *Urzeit* portrayal of David accounts for many of the features of the Chronistic narrative: David's function as a founder of the cultus,[7] the impression the Chronicler gives that David has communicated directly with Yahweh,[8] the domestic peace which characterizes

---

1. 'Zur Eigenart der chronistischen Davidsgeschichte', pp. 433-35.

2. 'The Chronicler's Purpose', pp. 436-42.

3. 'Messianism in Chronicles? Some Remarks to the Old Testament Background of the New Testament Christology', pp. 101-102.

4. S.J. De Vries, 'Moses and David as Cult Founders in Chronicles', p. 639.

5. 'The Chronicler as a Theologian', p. 113.

6. 'A new mode of viewing the past history of his nation began to prevail. . . the past, in a word, was *idealised*, and its history, where necessary, rewritten accordingly. Thus the institutions of the present, which, in fact, had been developed gradually, are represented as organized in their completeness by David' (Driver, *An Introduction to the Literature of the Old Testament*, p. 533).

7. For example 1 Chronicles 13, 15–16; 21.18–22.5; 23–26.

8. For example 1 Chron. 14.10, 14-16; 22.8-10; 28.3, 6-7, 11-19. With the

David's reign over Israel[1] and the near sinlessness of his personal response to God.[2] The idealized picture of David and his reign indicates both the pedigree and the potential of the cultus which, for the Chronicler, stands at the centre of Israel's greatness; the portrayal of the Davidic *Urzeit* also locates the height from which Israel's history was soon to descend.

The Cultic Role of David

The sacral character of the ancient Near Eastern monarch manifested itself in the priestly functions of the king. As Keel observes:

> Throughout the entire ancient Near East, but especially in ancient Sumer, cultic responsibilities devolve upon the king. The ancient Sumerian Ensi was as much priest as prince. He resides in the temple and is responsible for the welfare of the city god... As late as the Neo-Sumerian period, Ur-Nammu appears not only as temple builder but also in a priestly capacity. Iconographic evidence for the priestly functions of Mesopotamian kings are extant well into the latest Assyrian epoch.[3]

The reference to king as כהן in Ps. 110.4 testifies to the survival of this aspect of kingship in Israel,[4] even though the priestly nature of Israelite kingship remains ambiguous in some Old Testament texts.[5]

---

exception of 1 Chron. 28.11-19, the Chronicler may have intended his audience to understand that David has communicated with Yahweh through more usual channels, such as through the prophets who are portrayed as active elsewhere in the Chronicler's story of David (cf. 1 Chron. 17; 21.9-13).

1. Note in particular the absence of the struggle with Ish-baal (2 Sam. 2.8-4.12), the lack of mention of Absalom's revolt (2 Sam. 15.1–19.1) and the smooth transition to the reign of Solomon (compared to 1 Kgs 1.5-53).

2. David is only portrayed as sinful in the story of the census in 1 Chronicles 21; most noticeably absent is the story of David and Bathsheba (2 Sam. 11–12).

3. O. Keel, *The Symbolism of the Biblical World*, pp. 278-79. Cf. also P.P. Zerafa, 'Il sacerdozio nell'antico Testamento', pp. 625-26.

4. H. Gunkel, *Die Psalmen*, p. 483; A. Weiser, *The Psalms*, p. 695; Galbiati, 'Il carattere sacro della regalità nell'antico Israele', p. 94.

5. Indeed, passages such as 1 Sam. 13.8-14 and 2 Chron. 26.16-20 seem to condemn kings who take it upon themselves to exercise a priestly function. However, the biblical author may not have placed the emphasis in 1 Sam. 13.8-14 on the cultic action as it appears at first glance. Cultic activity was not incompatible with military or tribal leadership in pre-monarchical Israel, as can be seen from Judg. 6.24-26 or from the figure of Samuel himself. H.W. Hertzberg, *I & II Samuel*, p. 106, interprets the sin of Saul as having no patience and allowing 'the disturbing

One does not have to search far in the Chronicler's narrative to discover a priestly portrayal of a king, for the telling of the successful
transport of the Ark to Jerusalem in 1 Chron. 15.1–16.43 already
contains such a portrayal. The cultic nature of David's own role was
already manifest in the Chronicler's *Vorlage* and remains evident in
Chronicles itself at 1 Chron. 15.25-28, though not without change;
thus, for example, the sacrificing of offerings attributed to David in 2
Sam. 6.13 becomes an act of the Levites in 1 Chron. 15.26. On the
other hand, the Chronicler heightens the liturgical portrayal of the
king when he states that David was vested in the fine linen robe (as are
the other cultic functionaries) in 1 Chron. 15.27, most probably
reflecting the liturgical apparel familiar to the Chronicler.[1] The linen
ephod mentioned in the same verse was probably understood by the
Chronicler as a priestly garment,[2] an understanding not necessarily
intended by the mention of the ephod in the Deuteronomistic
Vorlage;[3] similarly, the Chronicler may have understood David's act
of blessing the people בשם יהוה in 1 Chron. 16.2 as the exercise of
what would otherwise be a priestly prerogative.[4] In thus retaining the
priestly portrayal of David, the Chronicler has shown David to participate in a cultic role as would have been normal for any ancient Near
Eastern monarch.[5]

situation to be the most important factor in his decision'. Such an interpretation,
which takes the emphasis from the cultic nature of Saul's impatient action, also resonates with the demand of the holy war that fear be excluded since the nation
depends utterly on the victorious presence of Yahweh (cf. Deut. 20.3-4, 8).
Similarly, it is possible that the condemnation of Uzziah's action in 2 Chron. 26.16-
20 may not be a statement against the priestly nature of kingship so much as the
delineation of a priestly action not permitted to kings in the later Priestly legal tradition (Exod. 30.7-10; Num. 16.40); cf. Rudolph, *Chronikbücher*, p. 286; J. Becker,
2 Chronik, p. 87. The Chronicler might even here be addressing a specific cultic
problem of the illicit offering of incense, given the large number of incense altars
excavated from Persian period Palestine (including over two hundred at Lachish
alone); cf. A. Rolla, 'La Palestina Postesilica alla luce dell'archeologia', pp. 117-18.
    1.   Harvey-Jellie, *Chronicles*, p. 116; Galling, *Die Bücher der Chronik, Esra,
Nehemia*, p. 49.
    2.   Cf. Exod. 28.4-5; Lev. 8.7.
    3.   2 Sam. 6.14. Cf. Williamson, *1 and 2 Chronicles*, p. 126.
    4.   Harvey-Jellie, *Chronicles*, p. 117.
    5.   Cf. also Throntveit, *When Kings Speak: Royal Speech and Royal Prayer in
Chronicles*, p. 102.

The Chronicler has also portrayed David in the light of the ancient Near Eastern expectation that the king was the one responsible for building the national temples. The traditional history of the monarchy (as exemplified by the Chronicler's *Vorlage*) unambiguously stated in 2 Sam. 7.1-17 that David's desire to build the Temple went unfulfilled and that the actual task of temple-building fell to Solomon. In portraying David in accordance with the cultic picture of the ancient Near Eastern king, the Chronicler worked within the framework of this tradition; however, he heightened the Davidic role in the Temple's genesis in several ways: David declares the authenticity of the site which is revealed to him as the chosen place for the Temple;[1] David makes material preparations for the Temple,[2] as well as various arrangements for the cultic personnel;[3] David explicitly commissions his son Solomon and the assembly to build the Temple;[4] most importantly, David has received the תבנית for the Temple from the hand of Yahweh.[5]

In his consideration of historical and mythical accounts of temple origins in the ancient Near East, Kapelrud summarizes the stories of temple-building as follows:

> In the cases where a king is the actual temple builder the following elements are most often found: 1. Some indication that a temple has to be built; 2. The king visits a temple overnight; 3. A god tells him what to do, indicates plans; 4. The king announces his intention to build a temple; 5. Master builder is engaged, cedars from Lebanon, building-stones, gold, silver, etc. procured for the task; 6. The temple finished according to plan; 7. Offerings and dedication, fixing of norms; 8. Assembly of the people; 9. The god comes to his new house; 10. The king is blessed and promised everlasting domination.[6]

1. 1 Chron. 21.18–22.1.
2. 1 Chron. 22.2-5, 14-16; 29.2-9, 17 (cf. also 1 Chron. 18.8, 10-11).
3. 1 Chron. 15.2-24; 16.4-7, 37-42; 23.2–26.32; 28.13, 21.
4. 1 Chron. 22.6-19; 28.1-10, 20-21; 29.19.
5. 1 Chron. 28.11-19.
6. A.S. Kapelrud 'Temple Building, a Task for Gods and Kings', p. 62. Kapelrud makes extensive use of texts related to Gudea of Lagash. On the designation *ensi* (the title of the temple-building Gudea of Lagash), cf. Frankfort, *Kingship and the Gods*, pp. 226-28. Frankfort holds that the difference between the titles *lugal* ('king') and *ensi* ('governor') had been obliterated by the Early Dynastic Sumerian period and that the difference lay chiefly in the size of the territory that was ruled.

When the Chronicler's augmentation of David's role in the origins of the Jerusalem Temple is viewed against Kapelrud's summary, it becomes clear that the Chronicler has taken the role of temple-builder (which the Deuteronomistic Historian had given to Solomon)[1] and divides it between David for its inauguration and Solomon for its completion. Thus David is the one who perceives the need for the Temple,[2] who receives the plan for the Temple,[3] who announces the intention to build the Temple,[4] who provides raw materials— including the all-important cedar wood—for its construction,[5] who fixes norms for its cultic personnel,[6] and who is promised everlasting domination;[7] each of these aspects of the Chronistic David corresponds to one or other of the common elements of royal temple-building in the ancient Near East, as identified by Kapelrud.

Viewing the Chronistic portrayal of David against the more general pattern of kingly temple-builders also shows the inadequacy of characterizing the Chronicler's David as 'a patron of the religious establishment, and administrator'.[8] Instead, the reader senses that it was important to the Chronicler 'to trace back the temple-building fundamentally to David'.[9] As Clements observes of the Chronistic narrative, 'David, the founder of the dynasty, is regarded as the true cult-founder, rather than Solomon who merely carried out his father's instructions'.[10]

Yet the Chronicler and his audience know of Moses as a cult founder who preceded David. The Chronicler acknowledges the cult-founding role of Moses both within the Davidic narrative[11] and

---

1   Kapelrud, 'Temple Building, A Task for Gods and Kings,' pp. 59-62.
2.   1 Chron. 17.1.
3.   1 Chron. 28.11-19.
4.   1 Chron. 22.1, 7-10; 28.1-6.
5.   1 Chron. 22.2-5.
6.   1 Chron. 23.2–26.32.
7.   1 Chron. 17.10-14, 23-27. This promise, of course, applies to David's House rather than to David personally.
8.   As characterized by D.L. Petersen, 'Portraits of David, Canonical and Otherwise', p. 141.
9.   Von Rad, *Das Geschichtsbild des chronistischen Werkes*, p. 130.
10.   *God and Temple*, p. 129.
11.   1 Chron. 15.15; 21.29; 22.13.

elsewhere in his work;[1] the role of Moses is also acknowledged
indirectly in the portrayal of David as a second Moses, as perceived
by many scholars.[2] On the one hand, David is shown as one who is
careful to implement the Law given through Moses;[3] on the other,
David is portrayed as one who is also a receiver of revelation and
therefore entitled to introduce authoritatively new elements into the
religious life of Israel. David is, therefore, a faithful observer of the
Mosaic Law; he is also, according to the Chronicler, a cultic legislator
and founder in his own right.[4]

David's right to introduce new cultic elements can be seen in the
conclusion to the narrative of the erection of the altar of holocaust on
the threshing-floor of Ornan.[5] The Chronicler notes Yahweh's acceptance of David's sacrifice with fire upon his altar of holocaust, a sign
that was taken from the Mosaic picture at the end of Aaron's conse-
cration.[6] After leaving no doubt in the mind of his audience as to the
legitimacy of the new altar of holocaust in Jerusalem, the Chronicler
reminds his audience that the Mosaic altar of holocaust is still in
Gibeon with the Tent (1 Chron. 21.29). Even though both seem to be
legitimate altars of sacrifice, the Chronicler gives the precedence to
the Jerusalem altar through David's statement: זה הוא בית יהוה האלהים
וזה־מזבח לעלה לישראל (1 Chron. 22.1); that David's confident and
solemn pronouncement is neither an empty boast nor the mere result
of fear[7] is amply demonstrated by the subsequent construction of the
Temple on David's site (2 Chron. 3.1).

1. 1 Chron. 6.34; 2 Chron. 1.3; 5.10.
2. For example Poulssen, 'Rex et Templum in Israel', p. 268; Cazelles, *Les
livres des Chroniques*, p 123; Myers, 'The Kerygma of the Chronicler: History and
Theology in the Service of Religion', pp. 268-69; Virgulin, *Libri delle Cronache*,
p. 46.
3. 1 Chron. 15.11-15; 22.12-13.
4. The fact that David's foundational legislation in Chronicles is restricted to
cultic matters—many of which touch directly upon the future Temple—supports the
suggestion of Myers that the portrayal of David as new Moses is fundamentally
linked with the concept of the Davidic covenant; Myers, 'The Kerygma of the
Chronicler: History and Theology in the Service of Religion', p. 269.
5. 1 Chron. 21.26–22.1. This ending replaces the less dramatic ending of the
Vorlage (2 Sam. 24.25) which simply notes that David built the altar, offered
sacrifices, and that Yahweh removed the pestilence.
6. 1 Chron. 21.26; Lev. 9.24.
7. Cf. 1 Chron. 21.30.

The most striking way in which the Chronicler portrays David as a law-giver like Moses is in the giving of the תבנית;[1] even the word itself reminds the audience of the תבנית for the Tent which was shown to Moses.[2] However, the תבנית of David is by no means restricted to the ground-plan of the Temple; it also includes provisions for the priestly and Levitical courses as well as all the work of the Temple service.[3]

By showing David as a cultic founder, the Chronicler is acknowledging that the Temple was a religious innovation in Israel, even though it also stood in a continuing relationship to the Tent and the Ark which it was to encompass.[4] As innovation, the Temple requires a new revelation to regulate its construction and service. The Temple not only houses the Ark and the Tent, it inherits their Mosaic traditions and regulations;[5] as innovation, however, the Temple is directed by Davidic regulations, looking back to the divinely inspired authority behind its foundation.

In relationship to the Temple, therefore, the Chronicler has truly constructed an *Urzeit* in his portrayal of David, a period in which the institution of the Temple receives its validation through the revelation given to David as the divinely appointed authority. Especially in the Davidic narrative, but also elsewhere in his history, the Chronicler has retained the importance awarded the king in the ancient Near East as the one who establishes the Temple and its cultus.[6]

Given the reality in which the Chronistic History was composed, this authenticating revelation to David is far more important for the Chronicler and his audience than the actual construction of the Temple

1. 1 Chron. 28.11-19. Cf. von Rad, *Das Geschichtsbild des chronistischen Werkes*, pp. 130-31; De Vries, 'Moses and David as Cult Founders in Chronicles', pp. 626 and 630.

2. Exod. 25.9, 40.

3. 1 Chron. 28.13. The phrase ולכל־מלאכת עבדת בית־יהוה is intriguing; given the significance of עבדה elsewhere in Chronicles (e.g., 1 Chron. 24.3, 19; 25.1; 2 Chron. 35.10), it is possible that the Chronicler here portrays David's תבנית as regulating the entire Temple liturgy. Cf. Japhet, *The Ideology of the Book of Chronicles and its Place in Biblical Thought*, p. 230.

4. 2 Chron. 5.2-10.

5. As one example, Joash collects the tax for the Tent in 2 Chron. 24.6-9 and applies it to the repair of the Temple.

6. Cf. Newsome, 'Toward a New Understanding of the Chronicler and his Purposes', p. 215.

under Solomon, for the Chronicler's concern with the cultus in his
non-story world was not with Solomon's Temple as such; he records
that the Babylonians had already destroyed that initial structure by the
time of his composition in 2 Chron. 36.19. The Temple known to the
Chronicler had to be built anew according to 2 Chron. 36.23, and
looked to the Davidic *Urzeit* for its legitimacy, just as the Solomonic
Temple had done before. However, as shall be seen, the Solomonic
Temple held a unique importance for the Chronicler as the perfect
realization of the Davidic תבנית to which the Second Temple must also
be faithful.

Some elements in the Chronicler's Davidic narrative, such as the
arrangements for the cultic personnel and the giving of the תבנית,
unequivocally belong to the foundational time of the Temple in the
Chronistic History. Several authors view other major elements of this
narrative in ways that conform to the pattern of the cultic *Urzeit*, at
least in broad terms if not in every detail. Welten notes that the effect
of the rearrangement of the *Vorlage* in 1 Chronicles 11–16 is to join
more closely the anointing of David with the Ark narrative and to
present them in a single narrative flow.[1] Plöger states that the
Chronicler treats the Ark narrative as an 'Introit' to his temple-
building theme.[2] Welch identifies the Chronicler's treatment of the
story of David's census as a transformation into 'the ἱερὸς λόγος of
the temple',[3] a transformation also perceived by Noth.[4]

The narratives of David's wars merit special attention. The
Chronicler's text makes it clear that his involvement in these wars has
meant that David himself was disqualified from being the actual
temple-builder.[5] However, the Chronicler also includes an explicitly
positive dimension to these campaigns, in that from them were gained
materials which would later be used in the Temple cultus.[6]

The narratives of David's wars also stand as a contrast to the theme
of rest which is often associated firstly with the Ark and then with the

---

1. 'Lade–Tempel–Jerusalem: Zur Theologie der Chronikbücher', p. 172.
2. 'Reden und Gebete im deuteronomistichen und chronistischen
Geschichtswerk', pp. 56-57.
3. *The Work of the Chronicler: Its Purpose and Date*, pp. 23.
4. *The Chronicler's History*, p. 34.
5. 1 Chron. 22.8; 28.3.
6. 1 Chron. 18.8, 10-11.

Temple.[1] There was also a certain association between the presence of Yahweh in his cultic habitation and the resting (מנוחה) of the people.[2] The association of the dwelling of the deity with the concept of rest is to be found elsewhere in the ancient Near East, indicating that this association of concepts is not indigenous to Israel.[3]

In the books of Chronicles an association of rest with the cultic place is also evident.[4] The Chronicler especially makes it clear, particularly in the royal speeches, that rest is a prerequisite for the cultic act of building the Temple;[5] hence David is debarred from fulfilling his wish to construct the House of God. Yet the wars, while blocking David's way to building the Temple, have the effect of satisfying the prerequisite, making it possible for his successor to carry out the construction in peace (1 Chron. 22.18-19). Thus the campaigns which

---

1. It is hardly surprising that ordinary words for rest should become terms to describe the temporary or permanent stationing of the Ark. The *qal* infinitive of נוח is so used in Num. 10.36. Psalm 132 uses מנוחה twice to describe the permanent home of the Ark (Ps. 132.8, 14). It is probably a development from this usage that Trito-Isaiah could use מנוחה as a reference to the earthly habitation of Yahweh, albeit in a negative sense, in Isa. 66.1. An identification of the Temple with the מנוח of the soul may be contained in Ps. 116.7; cf. Weiser, *The Psalms*, p. 720, and F. Stolz, 'נוח *nûaḥ* ruhen', col. 45.

2. Thus in Num. 10.33 the Ark goes before the people to search out a resting-place for them and, according to Deut. 12.5-11, only when Israel has come to its permanent resting-place can they make recourse to the place where Yahweh makes his name to dwell.

3. For example, a reference in the 14th-century Teaching of Ani contrasts the temple as resting-place of the deity with human tumult, showing a need for a peaceful attitude in the temple; see Brunner, 'Egyptian Texts: Precepts for Life', p. 48. The same association of divine rest and human peace centred on the temple is evident in the Gudea texts as well; see Frankfort, *Kingship and the Gods*, p. 272.

4. In the first instance, this rest pertains to the permanent station of the Ark: in 1 Chron. 6.16 and 28.2 the place of rest (מנוח in 6.16, מנוחה in 28.2) for the Ark is identified as the Temple; Solomon calls upon Yahweh to ascend with his Ark to take his rest in 2 Chron. 6.41. 1 Chron. 17.9 and 22.18 link the rest afforded to the whole people of Israel with the construction of the Temple; 1 Chron. 23.25 associates the rest given to Israel with the eternal dwelling of Yahweh in Jerusalem.

5. 1 Chron. 22.8-9, 18-19; 28.2-3; cf. Throntveit, *When Kings Speak: Royal Speech and Royal Prayer in Chronicles*, p. 87. The description of Solomon as איש מנוחה in 1 Chron. 22.9 together with the clear association of his name with שלם in the same passage shows that the Chronicler understood human rest to be an essential quality in the one who would undertake the construction of the divine resting-place.

precede the coming of the Ark to Jerusalem[1] serve to allow the triumphant entrance of the Ark into the city;[2] the triumphs which follow the Ark narrative[3] serve to show Yahweh's blessings upon David as well as the establishment of the national rest required for the future construction of the Temple.[4] David's wars also can be seen as a historicized equivalent to the victories and the act of establishing order which normally preceded temple-building in the ancient Near East.[5]

The Chronicler's portrayal of David, therefore, shows different cultic dimensions of this *Urzeit* king: David, the priestly king, David, the cult founder, and David, who progresses the cultus even when he wages war and (reprehensibly) takes a census.[6]

From Cultus to Dynasty

The Saul narrative of 1 Chronicles 10 has been analysed in the previous section of this chapter as a paradigm containing certain elements: the king fails to seek Yahweh in the cultus with the result that Israel's security in the land is endangered; the unfaithful king's dynasty is thus terminated.

The Chronicler establishes the comparison between Saul as non-cultic king and David in his cultic concern from the beginning of the Ark narrative. In 1 Chron. 13.2-3, David exhorts the קהל ישראל to retrieve the Ark, noting its neglect in the days of Saul; thus David's concern is shown as a type of rectification of Saul's מעל.[7] A further negative

---

1. 1 Chron. 11.4-8 and 1 Chron. 14.8-16; 1 Chron. 11.15-19 is simply an illustration of the exploits of David's heroes.

2. Welten, 'Lade–Tempel–Jerusalem: Zur Theologie der Chronikbücher', p. 175.

3. 1 Chron. 18.1-13; 19.1–20.8.

4. Cazelles, *Les livres des Chroniques*, p. 93; Williamson, *1 and 2 Chronicles*, pp. 137-38; Allen, 'Kerygmatic Units in 1 & 2 Chronicles', pp. 24-25.

5. The pattern that places the building of the temple after conquest and the establishment of order can be seen clearly in the *enuma elish* and in the Ugaritic Baal epic. See H.L. Ginsberg, 'Poems about Baal and Anath', pp. 129-42; E.A. Speiser, 'The Creation Epic', pp. 60-72; A.K. Grayson, 'The Creation Epic: Additions to Tablets V-VII', pp. 501-503.

6. The story of the census, recounted in 1 Chron. 21.1–22.1, ends with the purchase of the site of the Temple and the building of the altar and leads directly to the preparations for the building of the Temple in 1 Chron. 22.2-5.

7. Botterweck, 'Zur Eigenart der chronistischen Davidsgeschichte', p. 412.

reference to Saul is made in the same narrative through Saul's daughter's disapproval of David's cultic dance in 1 Chron. 15.29. Even in the absence of such explicit occurrences of the name of Saul, the contrast of the Chronistic David to the Saul paradigm would be obvious, for David is everything that Saul was not: David is the king concerned with the cultus whose campaigns make Israel secure in the land and who is blessed with the dynasty.

However, according to the paradigm, one should expect that these elements in the David story be not isolated, but interrelated; Israel's security and David's dynasty should flow from his attention to the cultus, as a manifestation of the blessings expected according to the general pattern of ancient Near Eastern ideology. This is, in fact, what the story line of the Davidic narrative implies: David first demonstrates his concern for the Ark (1 Chron. 13.2-5), and is then given victories against the very enemies that had defeated Saul[1] as well as being promised the dynasty (1 Chron. 17.10-14).

The Chronicler's strong interest in the dynastic promise is indicated by his references to Nathan's oracle within the Davidic material.[2] The strength of his dynastic concern understandably gives rise to the interpretation of many commentators that the Chronicler was expressing a hope for a Davidic restoration; however, if the Chronicler has not expressed such a hope, then his concern with the dynastic promise must be linked to a larger concern, and concentration on his treatment of the dynastic promise in isolation from the larger concern could be misleading.

The memory of the dynastic promise continued to live in the postmonarchic reality of Israel through the cultic hymns. Psalms 89 and 132 are of special interest, for they enunciate most explicitly the Davidic covenant in which dynasty and Temple are combined; they have been referred to as a 're-reading of Nathan's oracle'.[3] The origin of both psalms is now generally located in the pre-exilic cultus,[4]

---

1. 1 Chron. 14.8-17; the taking of towns from the Philistines in 1 Chron. 18.1 counterbalances the loss of Israelite cities to them consequent to the defeat of Saul in 1 Chron. 10.7.

2. 1 Chron. 17.1-27; 22.8-10; 28.3-7; cf. Newsome, 'Toward a New Understanding of the Chronicler and his Purposes', pp. 209-10.

3. Coppens, *Le messianisme royale*, p. 47.

4. The lament found in Ps. 89.39-53 has posed particular problems concerning the unity and dating of this psalm, and it has sometimes been seen as a lamentation

although the earlier tendency to place their composition in post-exilic times[1] itself indicates how well the terms of these psalms could be interpreted against the post-exilic background. By its very nature, the continuing invocation of the dynastic promise in the cultus created a tension which had to be resolved in one of two ways: either the promise could be taken along the broad lines of its pre-exilic significance and a political Davidic restoration be seen as guaranteed, or else the promise would have to be re-examined in order that its true significance in the postmonarchical reality be found.[2]

Both the Chronicler's Saul paradigm and the story line of his Davidic narrative indicate the essential connection that the author has made between David's cultic concern and the granting of a dynasty, a connection already implied in Psalm 132. It is possible, therefore, that the cultus provides the larger concern to which the Chronicler's interest in the dynastic promise is subordinate and against which that

over the collapse of the dynasty. H.-J. Kraus, *Psalmen*, II, pp. 616-17, identifies the singer of the psalm as the king himself and dates the entire composition to the period of the monarchy. A.R. Johnson, *Sacral Kingship in Ancient Israel*, pp. 110-13, sees in these verses a reference to the ritual humiliation of the king during the Autumn Festival. J.M. Ward, 'The Literary Form and Liturgical Background of Psalm LXXXIX', pp. 334-39, situates the lament in a historical military disaster which seemed to frustrate the promises to David. Even A.A. Anderson, *Psalms*, II, p. 631, who tends to view the psalm as a post-exilic composition in hope of the restoration of the Davidic kingdom, also suggests that the psalmist used older material for Ps. 89.1-37 (38). The explicit mention of the Ark and prayer for the king in Ps. 132.8-10 makes the pre-exilic origin of the psalm nearly undeniable; cf. Weiser, *The Psalms*, pp. 779-80.

1. See for instance, H. van den Busshe, 'Le Texte de la prophétie de Nathan sur la Dynastie Davidique (II Sam.,VII–I Chron., XVII)', pp. 388-91, who argues that these psalms represent an intermediate stage of thought in the transmission of Nathan's oracle between the Chronicler (whom van den Busshe judges to be more faithful to the tradition) and the Deuteronomistic Historian.

2. Christian messianism itself should be seen as belonging more to the second of these paths than to the first. Even though Christian belief concentrates on the rule of the Davidide, this rule differs fundamentally from the political reality implied in Nathan's oracle. The Gospels stress that the kingship of Jesus is eschatological and thus cannot simply conform to the expectations associated with kingship in the present world-order; cf. Mt. 25.31-46; Mk 8.29-38; 10.35-45; 12.35-37; 13.24-27; Lk. 4.1-13; 22.24-30; Jn 6.15; 18.33-37. The Gospels also show the need to re-examine the Scriptures so that they may yield their true meaning; see especially Lk. 24.25-27, 44-47.

promise's true significance is given its Chronistic interpretation. Such a possibility must be examined firstly in the Chronicler's Davidic narrative, but can only be fully investigated by tracing the theme further into the Chronicler's History.

The dynastic promise first appears in Chronicles in the account of Nathan's oracle in 1 Chron. 17.1-15, largely taken from the *Vorlage*.[1] The major differences between the Chronistic and Deuteronomistic texts may be identified as follows: 1 Chron. 17.1 lacks the reference to Yahweh's granting David rest from his enemies; whereas 2 Sam. 7.5 uses an ironic question to deny David the privilege of constructing the Temple, 1 Chron. 17.4 makes an indicative statement to the same effect; 2 Sam. 7.6 states that Yahweh was going about באהל ובמשכן while 1 Chron. 17.5 says that Yahweh was there מאהל אל־אהל וממשכן; the reference to rest in 2 Sam. 7.11 (והניחתי) is again lacking in 1 Chron. 17.10 with no effective change in meaning; the phrase יהיה מבניך in 1 Chron. 17.11 replaces the more general יצא ממעיך of the *Vorlage*;[2] the reference to possible punishment in 2 Sam. 7.14b is not to be found in 1 Chron. 17.13; a reference to מאשר היה לפניך in 1 Chron. 17.13 corresponds to the more explicit mention of Saul in 2 Sam. 7.15; differences in pronominal suffixes identify the house and kingdom as God's and the throne as belonging to the promised successor in 1 Chron. 17.14, whereas 2 Sam. 7.16 identifies all three as David's.

The overall effect of the differences to be found in 1 Chronicles 17 when compared to its *Vorlage*, especially taken in the larger context of the Chronicler's later references to the oracle,[3] shows that the Chronicler has applied the promise first and foremost to Solomon.[4]

---

1. 2 Sam. 7.1-17. The hypothesis of van den Busshe, 'Le Texte de la prophétie de Nathan sur la Dynastie Davidique (II Sam., VII–I Chron., XVII)', pp. 388-91, to the effect that Chronicles represents the more original text of the oracle, has not gained wide acceptance; although it is, of course, possible that individual phrases in the MT of 2 Samuel 7 not found in 1 Chronicles 17 may be expansions. Such a possibility is explored by McKenzie, *The Chronicler's Use of the Deuteronomistic History*, p. 63.

2. The LXX of 1 Chron. 17.11 reads ἐκ τῆς κοιλίας, however.

3. 1 Chron. 22.9; 28.6.

4. Rudolph, *Chronikbücher*, p. 133; Botterweck, 'Zur Eigenart der chronistischen Davidsgeschichte', p. 422; Michaeli, *Les livres des Chroniques, d'Esdras et de Néhémie*, p. 101; Williamson, 'Eschatology in Chronicles', pp. 134-35; Willi, *Die*

This, in fact, is in line with the general pattern of dynastic thought in the ancient Near East according to which the guarantee of dynasty extended to a single generation.[1] The identification of the house and the kingdom as belonging to Yahweh in 1 Chron. 17.14, generally admitted to be one of the more characteristically Chronistic touches in the oracle,[2] adds to the impression that the emphasis has been somewhat removed from David and placed more on Solomon and Yahweh.[3]

It would seem that the Chronicler has, in fact, made full use of the link between Temple and dynasty in his presentation of Nathan's oracle, a link which was already central to his *Vorlage*. By emphasizing Solomon, the Chronicler is also underlining the fact that Solomon has been chosen primarily for the purpose of temple-building. By eliminating the references to David's rest, the Chronicler maintains consistency with his portrayal of David as one who must establish the conditions for the rest as part of his preparations for the construction of the Temple, rather than as one who enjoys that rest himself. Most telling of all is the change of suffix for בית in 1 Chron. 17.14; whereas the reading of 2 Sam. 7.16, ביתך, must be taken to refer to David's dynasty, the Chronistic בביתי can only refer to the establishment of Solomon in regard to the Temple.[4] The Chronicler,

---

Chronik als Auslegung, p 186; De Vries, 'The Schema of Dynastic Endangerment in Chronicles', pp. 62-63. Of the exegetes mentioned, Botterweck and Williamson also find a messianic emphasis in the Chronicler's re-presentation of Nathan's oracle. Others find a strong messianism here rather than a reference to Solomon, especially in 1 Chron. 17.11; cf. Harvey-Jellie, *Chronicles*, pp. 125-26; von Rad, *Das Geschichtsbild des chronistischen Werkes*, p. 123; A. Noordtzij, 'Les intentions du Chroniste', p. 163; Galling, *Die Bücher der Chronik, Esra, Nehemia*, p. 54.

1.   B. Halpern, *The Constitution of the Monarchy in Israel*, p. 41 (cf. also pp. 1-11).

2.   Curtis and Madsen, *A Critical and Exegetical Commentary on the Books of Chronicles*, p. 228; Noth, *The Chronicler's History*, p. 101; Brunet, 'Le Chroniste et ses sources', p. 505; Welten, 'Lade–Tempel–Jerusalem: Zur Theologie der Chronikbücher', p. 178. McKenzie, *The Chronicler's Use of the Deuteronomistic History*, p. 64, offers an alternative explanation based on scribal confusion of *yod* and *waw*; the coincidence of the MT reading for 1 Chron. 17.14 with the Chronicler's outlook weighs heavily against such an argument.

3.   Braun, *1 Chronicles*, p. 199; De Vries, *1 and 2 Chronicles*, pp. 154-58.

4.   Although the opinion is given by Curtis and Madsen, *A Critical and Exegetical Commentary on the Books of Chronicles*, p. 228, that בביתי must refer to

in the final analysis, shows that the gift of the dynasty is not simply occasioned by David's desire to build the Temple, but is given primarily for the purposes of temple-building. This can also be seen in the Chronicler's recalling of Nathan's oracle in 1 Chron. 22.8-10 and in 1 Chron. 28.3-7, as well as in the fact that 'the sole task laid upon Solomon, and that repeatedly, is the construction of the temple'.[1]

This picture of the dynasty and the Temple contained in the Chronistic presentation of Nathan's oracle, both in 1 Chronicles 17 and in the later references in 1 Chronicles 22 and 28, is consistent with the liturgical remembrance of David reflected in the cultic poetry. In Ps. 78.67-72 the choice of David is placed within the context of the choice of Zion and the building of the sanctuary.[2] Psalm 89 implicitly links the choice of David with the Jerusalem Temple through the praise of Yahweh's throne in v. 15.[3] The prime example of this twofold choice of David and Zion occurs in Ps. 132.11-18; the beginning of the psalm (Ps. 132.1-6), like the Chronistic narrative, celebrates David's concern for the Ark and provides a context for the statement of the dynastic promise in Ps. 132.11-12.

The importance of Psalm 132 for the Chronicler is indicated by his use of it in the conclusion to Solomon's prayer of dedication.[4] If the Chronicler intended to import the royal ideology of this psalm into his

---

the whole people of Israel, the common Hebrew idiom for Temple suggests otherwise, and 1 Chron. 17.14 is read accordingly by a number of exegetes. See Randellini, *Il libro delle Cronache*, p. 203; Ackroyd, *I & II Chronicles, Ezra, Nehemiah*, pp. 67-68; Saebø, 'Messianism in Chronicles? Some Remarks to the Old Testament Background of the New Testament Christology', pp. 99-100; McCarthy, 'Covenant and Law in Chronicles–Nehemiah', p. 26; Mangan, *1–2 Chronicles, Ezra, Nehemiah*, p. 47; Becker, *1 Chronik*, p. 78.

1. Braun, 'Solomon, the Chosen Temple Builder: The Significance of 1 Chronicles 22, 28, and 29 for the Theology of Chronicles', p. 587.

2. It should be noted, however, that this passage emphasizes the political role of David in affirming Yahweh's choice of him, although this does not substantially affect the underlying unity of the twofold choice.

3. C. Stuhlmueller, *Psalms 2*, p. 64.

4. 2 Chron. 6.41-42. A connection between Psalm 132 and 1 Chronicles 28, based on the מנוחה of Yahweh, has also been observed; cf. von Rad, 'The Levitical Sermon in I & II Chronicles', p. 276, and McConville, 'I Chronicles 28:9: Yahweh "Seeks Out" Solomon', pp. 106-107. Braun, *1 Chronicles*, pp. 273-74, also notes a connection between Psalm 132 and 1 Chronicles 28 through occurrence of the rare term לעד.

work, then he brought an explicit element of conditionality into
his total picture of the dynastic promise:

> If your sons keep my covenant
> > and my solemn charges which I shall teach them,
> Then their sons, too, in perpetuity
> > shall sit upon your throne (Ps. 132.12).

The conditionality of the royal covenant has been much discussed in
its origin, its demands and its effect.[1] For the post-exilic author of
Chronicles, there was no discussion: the cultic poetry presented him
with a promise to David that explicated faithfulness to the covenant as
a condition for the granting of rule to his descendants, and the picture
given by the cultic poetry seems to express the pre-exilic reality of the
conditioned nature of the royal covenant.[2] The pre-exilic royal
covenant, in keeping with ancient Near Eastern temple theology,
seems to have placed special emphasis on the responsibilities of the
king toward the Temple;[3] that such is the Chronicler's understanding
is indicated by the close connection between the dynastic promise and
the task of temple-building evident in his Davidic narrative.

Perhaps Psalm 132 provides the best context in which to consider one
of the most striking differences between 1 Chronicles 17 and its

---

1.   Thus some, such as J. Bright, *Covenant and Promise: The Prophetic
Understanding of the Future in Pre-Exilic Israel*, pp. 58-60 and 64, and
Brueggemann, *David's Truth in Israel's Imagination*, p. 94, would hold that the
royal covenant was unconditioned, at least in the official presentation of the later
monarchy. Others suggest that the royal covenant was conditioned and that this
conditionality was expressed through the investiture of the king with the עֵדוּת (as in 2
Kgs 11.12); see G. von Rad, 'The Royal Ritual in Judah', pp. 224-26, and
Johnson, *Sacral Kingship in Ancient Israel*, pp. 23-25.

2.   In support of the conditionality of Israelite kingship, Halpern, *The
Constitution of the Monarchy in Israel*, p. 17, notes that Saul's fall is due to dis-
obedience to Yahweh. M. Tsevat, 'The House of David in Nathan's Prophecy',
pp. 353-56, analyses 2 Samuel 7 in the light of David's prayer (2 Sam. 7.18-29)
and suggests that the apparent unconditionality of a perpetual dynasty contained in 2
Sam. 7.13-16 is alien to the thought of the original story and is possibly an addition
which goes back to the time of Solomon. The conditionality of the biblical royal
covenant is also indicated by the Deuteronomistic History's portrayal of a prospect of
dynasty offered to Jeroboam (1 Kgs 11.37-38) and its negation because of
Jeroboam's behaviour (1 Kgs 14.7-16).

3.   Cf. D.J. McCarthy, *Old Testament Covenant: A Survey of Current Opinions*,
p. 51.

Vorlage, the omission of 2 Sam. 7.14b: אשר בהעותו והכחתיו בשבט אנשים ובנגעי בני אדם. The absence of this clause has been variously explained: the Chronicler presents the more original reading which the Deuteronomistic Historian has expanded;[1] the lack is to be explained by the Chronistic idealization of David and Solomon;[2] or the Chronicler omits the phrase to accommodate his messianic hope.[3]

While suggesting a messianic explanation for the omission, Botterweck notes that the lack of this phrase has reduced the unconditionality of Yahweh's favour towards the House of David,[4] a suggestion reinforced by Japhet with reference to ancient Near Eastern parallels.[5] This observation assumes added strength if one postulates that the hope for Davidic restoration was missing in the Chronicler's outlook. The absence of the phrase, together with the new emphasis on Solomon in the oracle, allows for the possibility that lack of faithfulness may lead to an end to the dynastic promise, at least in its political expression,[6] just as the Chronistic expressions of the oracle allow the possibility of an everlasting dynasty if the kings remain faithful (cf. 1 Chron. 28.7). The omission of 2 Sam. 7.14b displays greater consistency with Ps. 132.12 as read in the non-monarchical post-exilic context, for it removes the safety valve (unknown to Ps. 132) which could be seen as guaranteeing the rule of individual members of the dynasty even in the face of overwhelming unfaithfulness to Yahweh. That such an unconditional guarantee does not form part of the Chronicler's picture is demonstrated by the warning to Solomon in 1 Chron. 28.9. The omission of 2 Sam. 7.14b, and of the unconditional promise that

1. Van den Busshe, 'Le Texte de la prophétie de Nathan sur la Dynastie Davidique (II Sam., VII–I Chron., XVII)', pp. 388-89.

2. For example Wellhausen, *Prolegomena to the History of Ancient Israel*, p. 177; Brunet, 'Le Chroniste et ses sources', p. 505; Rudolph, *Chronikbücher*, p. 135; Williamson, *1 and 2 Chronicles*, pp. 135-36; Runnalls, 'The King as Temple Builder: A Messianic Typology', p. 24; McKenzie, *The Chronicler's Use of the Deuteronomistic History*, p. 63; Braun, *1 Chronicles*, p. 199.

3. For example Harvey-Jellie, *Chronicles*, pp. 125-26; Noordtzij, 'Les intentions du Chroniste', p. 163; Galling, *Die Bücher der Chronik, Esra, Nehemia*, p. 54; Michaeli, *Les livres des Chroniques, d'Esdras et de Néhémie*, p. 101; Virgulin, *Libri delle Cronache*, pp. 175-76.

4. 'Zur Eigenart der chronistischen Davidsgeschichte', pp. 422-23.

5. Japhet, *The Ideology of the Book of Chronicles and its Place in Biblical Thought*, p. 464.

6. Cf. Coggins, *The First and Second Books of the Chronicles*, pp. 94-95.

it can be made to imply, eventually allows the Chronicler to bring the story of the dynasty to the historical end known to him, and to do so in line with both his Saul paradigm and his vision of divine retribution.

The conditionality of Nathan's oracle, especially in relation to the Solomonic focus of its Chronistic form in 1 Chronicles 17, receives its most lucid expression in the assurance, or warning, of David to Solomon in 1 Chron. 28.9b: אם־תדרשנו ימצא לך ואם־תעזבנו יזניחך לעד. Even though he is the son upon whom the promise of 1 Chronicles 17 centres, Solomon must be warned that his actions could make Yahweh forsake him forever.[1] The presence of the verb דרש in the first condition of this admonition, as well as the adverse possibility contained in the second condition, invoke the Saul paradigm for the very first successor in the Davidic line.[2] In Solomon, the Chronicler's David seems to be addressing the entire Davidic dynasty to come, placing the conditionality of the dynastic promise in plain terms before the narrative of the subsequent members of the dynasty begins.

In this context of a conditioned covenant, the significance of the Chronicler's alterations in 1 Chron. 17.14 becomes more obvious: the oracle is brought to a final crescendo with the promise והעמדתיהו בביתי ובמלכותי עד־העולם וכסאו יהיה נכון עד־עולם. The oracle culminates in the promise that Solomon will be a vassal to Yahweh, stationed for duty in the Temple,[3] and that Solomon's throne (not David's) will be established in perpetuity. The Chronicler affirms that the kingship and the kingdom belong to Yahweh, not to the House of David[4]—an

---

1. 'Therefore in one sense the Chronicler has balanced his statement of Solomon's eternal election with at least the possibility of an eternal rejection!' (Braun, *1 Chronicles*, pp. 273-74); cf. also J.G. McConville, *Chronicles*, pp. 99-100. Becker, *1 Chronik*, p. 110, suggests that this warning refers to the infidelity of Solomon which is unexpressed but presupposed in Chronicles; such an argument from silence is hard to maintain given the Chronicler's control over his material (although the Chronicler's presentation of Solomon contains problems in this regard, as shall be seen). It seems far more appropriate to interpret the Chronicler as applying the warning to later members of the dynasty.

2. Williamson, *1 and 2 Chronicles*, p. 181.

3. The meaning 'station, set... for duty' is suggested for the *hiphil* of עמד by BDB, p. 764; although 'establish' is the meaning suggested specifically for this passage by BDB, 'station for duty' seems to make better sense of the locative ב.

4. Cf. De Vries, 'The Schema of Dynastic Endangerment in Chronicles', pp. 62-64.

affirmation which is repeated in the great doxology at the end of the Davidic narrative (1 Chron. 29.11-12).

The Chronicler's interest in the Davidic dynasty can therefore be seen as more concerned with the role of the dynasty in relation to the Temple than with the dynasty's unending rule over Israel, and this interest manifests itself as early as the Chronistic presentation of Nathan's oracle. The narrative stage is set not so much for an eternal dynasty as for David's dynastic successor whose primary function is to finish what David has begun in bringing the Ark to Jerusalem[1] and to carry out the תבנית given to David.[2] For the Chronicler, the centre of the covenant with David is not formed by the dynastic promise, but by the task of temple-building, and the fulfilment of the covenant is to be sought in the completed Temple rather than in an unending Davidic rule.[3]

Yet even within the Davidic material, the Chronicler may have indicated the *terminus ad quem* for the dynastic promise in the eventuality that the dynasty prove unsatisfactory. This indication of a possible *terminus* is contained in the final Davidic admonition to Solomon in Chronicles:

> And David said to Solomon his son, 'Be strong, be brave and act! Do not fear and do not be terrified, for Yahweh God, my God, is with you; he will not forsake you and he will not abandon you before all the work of the service of the House of Yahweh is finished' (1 Chron. 28.20).

Commentators sometimes propose that this passage depends upon Josh. 1.5-7 in which there is not only a great correspondence of vocabulary, but also of occasion.[4] However, there is nothing in Josh. 1.5-7 which corresponds to the temporal clause עד־לכלות כל־מלאכת עבודת בית־יהוה in 1 Chron. 28.20. This clause certainly 'serves to point to the *goal*

---

1.   Although David has brought the Ark to Jerusalem, he has left the Tent at Gibeon according to 1 Chron. 16.39. From a narrative consideration the presence of the Tent outside Jerusalem points to the incompletion of the Jerusalem cultus in David's day and sets the story firmly on the road towards its eventual completion under Solomon.

2.   Clements, *God and Temple*, p. 129; De Vries, 'Moses and David as Cult Founders in Chronicles', p. 633.

3.   McCarthy, 'Covenant and Law in Chronicles–Nehemiah', pp. 26-27.

4.   For example, cf. Curtis and Madsen, *A Critical and Exegetical Commentary on the Books of Chronicles*, p. 300; Rudolph, *Chronikbücher*, p. 189; Braun, *1 Chronicles*, p. 273.

of the divine presence, the construction of the temple';[1] it may also
indicate the goal of the election of the dynasty, and the point to which
the rule of that dynasty is guaranteed.[2]

True to the paradigm established in his Saul narrative, the
Chronicler presents his audience with a view of the dynastic promise
through a cultic lens. David's cultic concern has ensured that he did
not become another failed king like his predecessor; instead, his reign
is presented as an idealized *Urzeit* for both the dynasty and the cultus.
David, the second founder of the cultus, becomes the founder of the
dynasty to which fell the task of putting the Davidic תבנית for the
Temple and its services into effect; the task and the promise will be
especially important in the Chronistic narrative concerning Solomon
which complements the Davidic story. The Chronicler's insights into
king and cultus, contained initially in the Davidic *Urzeit*, etched their
own pattern on his record of how David's legacy was to fare in the
hands of his descendants, as shall be seen.

Solomon, Temple-Builder

When approaching the Chronicler's picture of Solomon and
attempting to delineate the opening parameter of the narrative, the
unity of the Solomonic material with the Davidic is particularly
striking; the Chronicler is careful to show that Solomon's royal inauguration takes place while David is still reigning over Israel (1 Chron.
23.1) and pictures Solomon ascending the throne while David is yet
alive.[3] Three references to Solomon in the narratives of the post-
Solomonic monarchs also link Solomon and David as a unit: 2 Chron.
11.17 says of the Israelites who came down to Judah after the schism
הלכו בדרך דויד ושלמה; according to 2 Chron. 33.7 the divine promise
to dwell in the Temple was spoken אל־דויד ואל־שלמה בנו; in 2 Chron.
35.4, Josiah instructs the Levites to prepare themselves for the
Passover according to their courses בכתב דויד מלך ישראל ובמכתב שלמה
בנו. These joint references to David and Solomon in the

___

1. Braun, *1 Chronicles*, p. 273.
2. Caquot, 'Peut-on parler de messianisme dans l'oeuvre du Chroniste?',
p. 118.
3. 1 Chron. 29.22-23. While this can also be said of the picture presented in 1
Kgs 1.32-40, the portrayal of David as incapacitated by old age is decidedly lacking
in Chronicles.

post-Solomonic narrative serve to verify the impression of an underlying unity in the Chronistic treatment of these two kings; they also indicate that the Solomonic material shares, at least to some extent, in the *Urzeit* nature which has been already identified for the Davidic narrative.[1]

While the underlying unity of the Davidic and Solomonic material cannot be denied, parameters for a narrative that has Solomon for its primary focus are easily established. The summary statement of David's reign in 1 Chron. 29.16-30 forms the conclusion to the Davidic narrative, and the similar summary of Solomon's reign in 2 Chron. 9.29-31 allows the block of material in 2 Chron. 1.1–9.31 to be identified as the specifically Solomonic narrative. This unit of material constitutes the main concern for the present section of this chapter, while appropriate attention must also be given to the larger Chronistic unit of the Davidic and Solomonic narrative to which the specifically Solomonic narrative belongs.

Solomon's Temple-Building Destiny

The Chronicler relates more about Solomon than just his temple-building activities; however, the construction and dedication of the Jerusalem Temple constitutes a major part of the Solomonic narrative. The Chronicler's concern with Solomon as temple-builder can be discerned firstly by the very proportion of the Solomonic material that the author assigns to the Temple narration,[2] and also by the central place that he has given to the dedication of the Temple in the

---

1.   'The combined reigns of David and Solomon are regarded as the inauguration of a temple age which persisted to the Chronicler's day' (Allen, 'Kerygmatic Units in 1 & 2 Chronicles', p. 24). On the *Urzeit* nature of David's reign, see especially De Vries, 'Moses and David as Cult Founders in Chronicles', p. 639.

2.   If the later division of the material into chapters may be taken as an approximation, the distribution may be summarized in this way: 2 Chron. 3.1–7.11 specifically deals with the building of the Temple and its inauguration liturgies; 2 Chron. 2.1-18, which deals with preparations for the Temple and the palace, and 2 Chron. 7.12-22, which relates the revelation of Yahweh to Solomon in response to his dedicatory prayer, should also be seen as parts of this block, resulting in a total of six out of nine chapters given to this concern. The corresponding material in the Deuteronomistic History (1 Kgs 5.15–6.38; 7.15–9.9) represents a lesser proportion of the Solomonic narrative of that work—less than five chapters out of a total of approximately ten chapters of narrative (1 Kgs 2.12–11.43).

framing of the story of Solomon's reign.[1]

The Chronicler's concern with the Temple is evident even in material related to Solomon's accession to the throne, an event which both the Deuteronomistic Historian and the Chronicler place during the reign of, and according to the designs of, David himself.[2] While Solomon only reaches the throne in the Deuteronomistic narrative through a tortuous path lined with the unsavoury realities of adultery, incest, murder and two separate attempts by Solomon's siblings to seize the kingship,[3] the Chronistic portrayal of Solomon shows no such negativity in telling the story of how he achieved the royal inauguration; the absence of this aspect of the *Vorlage* must itself be judged as dependent upon the Chronicler's purpose.[4] Instead of giving the inside story of Solomon's rise to power, the Chronicler reveals only Solomon's destiny for kingship, which is also his destiny for temple-building;[5] these two concepts are linked from the very first narrative mention of a successor to David in 1 Chron. 17.11-12.

The Chronicler has inherited a narrative connection between the issues of succession to David and temple building in Nathan's oracle from his *Vorlage* (2 Sam. 7.12-13); however, in 1 Chron. 22.7-10 the Chronicler has enhanced this connection and has made of it a direct pointer to Solomon as the only possible successor among David's sons. The author accomplishes this effect through his use of the theme of rest, together with the technique of paronomasia,[6] to indicate Solomon

1. R.B. Dillard, 'The Literary Structure of the Chronicler's Solomon Narrative', pp. 87-88, proposes that, in the Solomonic narrative, the Chronicler has formed a chiasm centring on the Temple dedication and the divine response (2 Chron. 5.2-7.22). According to Dillard, this chiastic centre is framed by narrative blocks concerned with Solomon's building projects, his recognition by the Gentiles, and reference to Solomon's wealth and wisdom.

2. 1 Kgs 1.32-40; 1 Chron. 22.6-23.1; 29.20-24.

3. It is sometimes suggested that the Succession Narrative often identified in 2 Samuel 9–1 Kings 2 is written to show how it was Solomon and not another Davidide who ascended the throne, justifying his claim to kingship. See Hertzberg, *I & II Samuel*, pp. 375-79; R.N. Whybray, *The Succession Narrative: A Study of II Sam. 9–20 and I Kings 1 and 2*, pp. 50-55.

4. Brunet, 'Le Chroniste et ses sources', pp. 252, 261-62.

5. Rudolph, *Chronikbücher*, p. 225.

6. Although this is especially evident in the use of שלום in 1 Chron. 22.9, less explicit paronomasia may also be involved in the occurrences of the root שלם in the Solomonic material, especially when these occur in close proximity to Solomon's

as the divinely designated heir to David's throne who is destined to be the builder of the Temple:

> And David said to Solomon his son: 'It was in my heart to build a House for the name of Yahweh my God. But the Word of Yahweh came to me saying, "Much blood have you shed and great wars have you waged. You shall not build a House for my name for much blood have you shed on the earth before me. There will be a son born to you; he will be a man of rest: I will give him rest from all his enemies round about, for Solomon will be his name, and I will give peace and quiet to Israel in his days. He will build a House for my name, and he will become a son to me[1] and I a father to him; and I will establish the throne of his reign over Israel forever"' (1 Chron. 22.7-10).

This passage establishes a contrast between David, who because of bloodshed and wars is ineligible to build the Temple,[2] and his successor whose quality of being איש מנוחה enables him to carry out the project, thus providing an explanation for the irrefutable historical fact that Solomon and not David had undertaken the actual construction.[3] The significance for the Chronicler of the stated reason for Yahweh's disqualification of David from this central activity is ambiguous and so has given rise to various interpretations: Harvey-Jellie,[4] Curtis and Madsen[5] and Slotki[6] interpret the reference to David as a man of blood as a reflection of 1 Kgs 5.17 which sees David's wars as consuming the time and resources needed if a temple were to be built; Rudolph,[7] followed by Randellini[8] and Michaeli,[9] finds here a recognition that warfare and bloodshed are incompatible with work dedicated to the glory of God; Mangan suggests that a strong psychological

---

name. Cf. 1 Chron. 18.9; 29.19; 2 Chron. 5.1; 8.16.

1. Such a translation of the idiom היה with ל by 'become' is noted in BDB, p. 226, with specific reference to its presence in the Chronicler's account of Nathan's oracle (1 Chron. 17.3). The same translation is suggested by G. Cooke, 'The Israelite King as Son of God', p. 207, who argues however that it should be understood metaphorically.

2. Cf. also 1 Chron. 28.3.

3. Willi, *Die Chronik als Auslegung*, p. 208.

4. *Chronicles*, p. 144.

5. *A Critical and Exegetical Commentary on the Books of Chronicles*, p. 257.

6. *Chronicles*, p. 122.

7. *Chronikbücher*, p. 151.

8. *Il libro delle Cronache*, p. 237.

9. *Les livres des Chroniques, d'Esdras et de Néhémie*, pp. 117-18.

reaction against bloodshed may lie behind the text;[1] Coggins associates
the rejection of the warrior-king as temple-builder with Israel's situation in the Chronicler's day in such a way that post-exilic Israel's lack
of warfare has been reflected in the Chronistic portrayal of the era of
Solomon.[2]

The contrast established by the Chronicler in 1 Chron. 22.8-9
indicates that the disqualification of David should be interpreted in
light of the acceptability of Solomon. Reference has already been
made to the association in the ancient Near East of temple with rest, a
connection reflected elsewhere in the Hebrew Bible; the importance of
this asso-ciation between temple and rest in the Chronicler's thought
can be seen by the presence of the fourfold paronomasia upon the
name שלמה in 1 Chron. 22.9.[3] In this way, the specific qualification
that the Chronistic Solomon possesses as a royal temple-builder—that
of being איש מנוחה—speaks within the context of an association of
concepts common to the ancient Near Eastern world.[4] In utilizing this
association, the Chronicler has departed somewhat from the more
pragmatic consideration proposed in the *Vorlage* to explain why it
was Solomon and not David who actually built the Temple,[5] and has
proposed a reason within the ideological network surrounding the
cultus itself: the Temple must be associated with rest. That the concern
with rest is directly involved with the building of the Temple is
also indicated by the Chronistic reference to Solomon's warfare,
without manifest disapproval, after the Temple is constructed;[6] since
the purpose of Solomon's lack of warfare has been completed, he

---

1. *1–2 Chronicles, Ezra, Nehemiah*, p. 56.

2. Coggins, *The First and Second Books of the Chronicles*, pp. 114-15.

3. Such paronomasia should be seen in the use of מנוחה, *hiphil A* of נוח, שפט
and שלם in this verse. A further dimension of the paronomasia may lie in an association of שלום with the concept of 'fulfilment' by the Chronicler; see J.I. Durham,
'שלום and the Presence of God', pp. 276-77, 283.

4. The Chronicler has, of course, used this association according to its
specifically Israelite expression which includes not only the concept of rest for the
Deity (as in 2 Chron. 6.41), but also rest for the nation (as in 1 Chron. 22.9). Cf.
Braun, 'Solomon, the Chosen Temple Builder: The Significance of 1 Chronicles 22,
28, and 29 for the Theology of Chronicles', pp. 582-84.

5. I.e., David's preoccupation with establishing Israel's security; cf. 1 Kgs
5.17-18.

6. 2 Chron. 8.3. This campaign is not mentioned in 1 Kings.

is now free to engage in military action.

Viewing David's disqualification in the cultic terms of Solomon's contrasting eligibility, one is led to agree with those exegetes who have found in the Chronicler's reference to David's warfare and bloodshed a statement of David's ritual impurity for the sacred action of temple-building.[1] This ineligibility of David to perform the actual construction of the Temple does not detract from David's role of cult founder, nor does it imply immorality; it does, however, show that both David and Israel are in need of Solomon if what David has begun and what Yahweh has promised to him is to reach its full implementation.

The disqualification of David from building the Temple expressed in Chronicles, and his consequent need of Solomon to bring to completion the groundwork which he had laid, remind the audience of the exclusion of Moses from entering the Promised Land and his consequent need of Joshua to lead Israel into its possession.[2] This correspondence has been highlighted by the Chronicler through the use of parallel verbal material between the commissioning of Solomon in 1 Chronicles 22 and 28 and the earlier narratives relating to the commissioning of Joshua, as has been noted by several exegetes.[3] Porter,[4] Braun[5] and Williamson[6] point beyond the similarity of phraseology in the Joshua and Chronistic Solomon texts to an underlying pattern consisting of encouragement, the description of the task and the assurance of the divine presence and aid. Viewed together with the Chronistic portrayal of David as a second Moses seen above, the

1. Ackroyd, *I & II Chronicles, Ezra, Nehemiah*, p. 79; Myers, *I Chronicles*, p. 154; Virgulin, *Libri delle Cronache*, p. 200; J.G. McConville, *Chronicles*, p. 77; Williamson, *1 and 2 Chronicles*, p. 154. Virgulin, Williamson and Cazelles, *Les livres des Chroniques*, p. 104, all note the affinity of this disqualification of David with the Priestly laws on ritual impurity.

2. R.B. Dillard, *2 Chronicles*, pp. 3-4; cf. Deut. 31.2-8 in this context.

3. For example Curtis and Madsen, *A Critical and Exegetical Commentary on the Books of Chronicles*, pp. 257, 300; Rudolph, *Chronikbücher*, p. 189; Virgulin, *Libri delle Cronache*, pp. 201, 236; Coggins, *The First and Second Books of Chronicles*, p. 115. The correspondence of 1 Chron. 28.20 with Josh. 1.5-7 has already been noted.

4. J.R. Porter, 'The Accession of Joshua', pp. 104-105, 118.

5. 'Solomon, the Chosen Temple Builder: The Significance of 1 Chronicles 22, 28, and 29 for the Theology of Chronicles', pp. 586-88.

6. Williamson, *1 and 2 Chronicles*, pp. 155-56.

literary parallels to the commissioning of Joshua suggest that the
Chronicler has presented Solomon in the role of a second Joshua who
is there, not to innovate, but to bring to completion; in this context it
is significant that, just as the giving of the written Mosaic תורה had
been closely associated with the commissioning of Joshua in
Deuteronomy,[1] so the Davidic תבנית is associated with the commissioning of Solomon in a narrative already linked by the Chronicler
to the Joshua episode by verbal correspondence.[2]

The Chronistic use of the theme of rest in the narratives relating to
David and Solomon may well be dependent in part upon the place of
this idea in the Deuteronomistic treatment of Joshua. The excision of
references to rest for David from the Chronicler's account of
Nathan's oracle is noteworthy in this context, for rest thus becomes
something that Israel enjoys only at the end of David's reign (which
overlaps with the beginning of Solomon's), and is an indication that
the time for building the Temple has come.[3] Similarly, in the
Deuteronomistic outlook, rest is not something enjoyed under Moses,
but belongs to a time after Moses; the Deuteronomist further specifies
that the granting of Israel's rest will signify that the central sanctuary
must be used exclusively.[4] This rest is actually granted to Israel under
Joshua.[5] Although the parallels between Solomon and Joshua are not
drawn with mathematical precision, the Chronicler's use of this key
element of rest to indicate Solomon's destiny seems to hark back to
terms which are to be found in material related to the Mosaic *Urzeit*[6]
and to the completion of this period under Joshua,[7] an *Urzeit* which,

---

1.   Deut. 31.7-13, 23-27.
2.   1 Chron. 28.8-21. Note especially the use of the verbs חזק and אמץ in both
the Deuteronomistic and the Chronistic passages, as well as the formalized promise
of Yahweh's presence with both Joshua and Solomon in 1 Chron. 28.20 and Deut.
31.8, 23.
3.   1 Chron. 22.18-19. This passage gives some substantiation to the suggestion
of Kapelrud, 'Temple Building, a Task for Gods and Kings', p. 60, that the peace
of Solomon's day signified to him 'that the omens for temple-building were
favourable'.
4.   Deut. 12.8-11. This passage employs both the *hiphil A* form of נוח and the
noun מְנוּחָה.
5.   Josh. 21.44; 22.4; 23.1. These texts all employ the *hiphil A* form of נוח.
6.   Cf. Deut. 3.20; 12.9-11; 25.19.
7.   Cf. Josh. 1.13,15; 21.44; 22.4; 23.1.

for the Chronicler, was complemented by the similar nature of the Davidic period.

Solomon as Faithful Accomplisher of the Davidic Task

The parallels that the Chronicler has constructed between Solomon and Joshua help to clarify the precise role of Solomon in the Chronistic schema: the Chronicler has shown Solomon to have been commissioned to put into effect the promise and the command which Yahweh had given through David,[1] just as it was Joshua's role to bring the commandment and promise given through Moses into full reality.[2] For Solomon, the Chronistic narrative clearly identifies the task as centring on the construction of the Jerusalem Temple.[3]

In order to assess the role of Solomon as temple-builder, the pattern and elements identified by Kapelrud for temple-building in the ancient Near East, already noted in relation to the Chronistic treatment of David, can serve as a guide.[4] With the exception of perceiving the need for the Temple and receiving its plan through divine revelation (Kapelrud's first and third elements), all of the elements identified by Kapelrud in the temple-building pattern applied to David by the Chronicler[5] are, in fact, also performed in some way by Solomon. However, the initiative that the Chronicler attributes to David in the performance of many of these elements transforms the function of Solomon: he is less the initiator of the Temple than he is the one who completes what David has begun. This contingent function of Solomon

1. Cf. 1 Chron. 28.7-20. In this passage, Solomon is entrusted with the תבנית given through David for the Temple. In 1 Chron. 22.11-16, wherein Solomon is also commissioned to build the Temple, the commission includes keeping the commandments given to Moses.

2. Deut 31.7; Josh. 1.6-9.

3. 1 Chron. 22.14-16; 28.9-10.

4. 'Temple Building, a Task for Gods and Kings', p. 62. The constitutive elements of Kapelrud's pattern of royal temple building are cited in the section *The Cultic Role of David*, above.

5. These elements applied to the Chronistic David are the announcing of the intention, the provision of raw materials, the fixing of norms and the promise of everlasting domination. Since Kapelrud's schema is partially based on a consideration of Solomon's temple-building activity in 1 Kings, it is far more significant that the Chronicler assigns elements of this function to David than that these same elements are shared by Solomon in the Chronistic account which reflects its *Vorlage* and the received historical traditions of Israel.

is particularly evident in the bestowal of the detailed תבנית which the Chronistic David gives to his son when he commissions Solomon to construct the Temple (1 Chron. 28.10-19). In addition to those references that assign to David the preparations for the construction of the Temple yet to be built,[1] 1 Chron. 22.1 and 2 Chron. 3.1 make David's setting up of an altar on the threshing-floor of Ornan into the first real act of cultic construction on the site of the Jerusalem Temple.[2] The overall effect is that David has done everything possible for the building of the Temple apart from the actual construction; it only remains for Solomon to carry on where David left off and to complete the task in hand. This continuity between David's incipient cultic action and Solomon's completion is marked in the narrative by an *inclusio* bounded by fire from heaven coming upon the Jerusalem altar, firstly for David after the Temple site is purchased and then for Solomon after the dedication prayer has been made at the completed Temple construction.[3]

---

1.   1 Chron. 22.2-4, 14-16; 29.2-5.
2.   Ackroyd, *I & II Chronicles, Ezra, Nehemiah*, p. 77; C.L. Meyers, 'David as Temple Builder', p. 370. The construction of the altar was distinct from the act of temple-building proper, but the Chronicler implies that this altar is not a temporary construction but the definitive structure, according to Cazelles, *Les livres des Chroniques*, p. 102; cf. also A. Parrot, *Le temple de Jérusalem*, pp. 8-10. Becker, *2 Chronik*, pp. 5-6, takes a contrasting, but similar, position, for Becker also finds that the Chronicler is concerned with a legitimate succession; however Becker sees it as referring ultimately to the Mosaic altar at Gibeon rather than the Davidic altar in Jerusalem. The subsequent building of the bronze altar mentioned in 2 Chron. 4.1, perhaps unmentioned in the MT of the *Vorlage* because of textual corruption (cf. Rudolph, *Chronikbücher*, p. 207 and Dillard, *2 Chronicles*, p. 34), need not contradict the interpretation of Cazelles, for it was the continuity of the site of the act of construction rather than the continuity of materials used that was important to the Chronicler and his audience, as is evidenced by the legitimacy of the construction of the Second Temple itself. One might note the similar attitude implicit in the dismantling and reconstruction of the altar referred to in 1 Macc. 4.44-47. The importance of the construction of the altar in establishing the sacred site is also shown by the fact that, according to the book of Ezra, the first reconstruction on the Temple site after the exile was the rebuilding of the altar which served for the cultic focus of restored pilgrimage festivals even before the foundations of the Temple were laid; cf. Ezra 3.1-6.
3.   1 Chron. 21.27; 2 Chron. 7.1; cf. 1 Chron. 22.1; 2 Chron. 3.1.

In terms of the elements of ancient Near Eastern royal temple-building identified by Kapelrud, the Chronistic Solomon performs the following functions: he visits the high place at Gibeon overnight (2 Chron. 1.3-13); he announces his intention to build the Temple (2 Chron. 2.3-6); he procures the master builder, workers and materials for the task (2 Chron. 2.7-17); he finishes the Temple according to plan (2 Chron. 3.1–5.1); he presides at the dedication and offerings (2 Chron. 6.1-42; 7.4-10); he assembles the people (2 Chron. 5.2-14); and, as a result of Solomon's work and in response to his prayer, Yahweh manifests his presence in the Temple (2 Chron. 5.13-14; 7.1-3); Solomon is blessed and promised an everlasting reign.[1]

All of these elements in the Solomonic temple-building reflect the activities of Solomon in the Deuteronomistic *Vorlage*.[2] The Chronistic passage relating to each element also makes reference to the Davidic story in either implicit or explicit terms, and some of these Davidic echoes are proper to the Chronicler's account of Solomon's temple-building activity. Thus, during his night vision at Gibeon, Solomon recalls Yahweh's חסד to David and asks that the divine word to David be fulfilled;[3] Solomon's announcement of his intention to build continues the trade relationship with Tyre which was begun by David;[4] Solomon's request for workers is intended to supplement the skilled workers already provided by David;[5] the Chronistic account of the actual construction begins by identifying the site with the place that David had prepared, and ends with those things that David had

---

1. 2 Chron. 7.12, 16-22. It should be noted that the promise of an everlasting reign is conditioned.

2. Thus 2 Chron. 1.3-13 has a parallel in 1 Kgs 3.4-15, 2 Chron. 2.3 in 1 Kgs 5.19, 2 Chron. 2.7-17 in 1 Kgs 5.20-32, 2 Chron. 3.1–5.1 in 1 Kgs 6.1–7.51, 2 Chron. 6.1-42 in 1 Kgs 8.12-32 and 2 Chron. 7.4-10 in 1 Kgs 8.62-66, 2 Chron. 5.2-14 in 1 Kgs 8.1-11, and 2 Chron. 7.12, 16-22 in 1 Kgs 9.2-6.

3. 2 Chron. 1.8-9. The request concerning the divine word to David does not find a parallel in 1 Kings 3. The connection of this episode with temple-building is strengthened for the Chronicler since he shows that Solomon's wisdom is exemplified by his construction of the House of God (as in 2 Chron. 2.11); cf. Brunet, 'Le Chroniste et ses sources', p. 354.

4. 2 Chron. 2.3 ‖ 1 Kgs 5.19.

5. 2 Chron. 2.6-7. This allusion is not found in 1 Kings 5.

dedicated being brought into the finished construction;[1] the dedication of the Temple contains many references to the promise made to David and the deeds done by him, both in the words of Solomon[2] and in the account of the liturgical action;[3] the account of the assembly of the people and the bringing of the Ark into the Temple echoes explicitly the Ark liturgy of the Chronistic David,[4] just as the manifestation of Yahweh's presence in Solomon's Temple is reminiscent of the manifestation in the story of David at Ornan's threshing-floor;[5] Yahweh's blessing of Solomon and promise to him makes a double reference to David's deeds and covenant.[6]

Seen against the background of the common elements of royal temple-building, the Chronistic account of Solomon's activity has strengthened and supplemented the Davidic references already contained in the Deuteronomistic History; all of the key Solomonic temple-building actions are now presented with conscious allusions to David, ensuring that Solomon's action is perceived as the faithful completion of David's initiative.

The final provision made by Solomon for the Temple in the Chronistic narrative, the organization of the priests and Levites (2 Chron. 8.14-15), falls outside the pattern identified above; yet it seems that, especially in the final form of the Chronistic History,[7] the

1   2 Chron. 3.1; 5.1. 2 Chron. 5.1 is parallel to 1 Kgs 7.51, but the Davidic reference in 2 Chron. 3.1 stands in place of the Deuteronomistic dating of the temple-building in relation to the exodus (1 Kgs 6.1).

2.   2 Chron. 6.4-10 (|| 1 Kgs 8.15-20); 2 Chron. 6.15-17 (|| 1 Kgs 8.24-26); 2 Chron. 6.42. The reference to David in 2 Chron. 6.42 depends upon Psalm 132 and Isa. 55.3, but has no parallel in the Deuteronomistic *Vorlage*.

3.   2 Chron. 7.6, 10. The reference in 2 Chron. 7.6 harkens back to David's cultic arrangements and is proper to the Chronicler, whereas 2 Chron. 7.10 finds a parallel in 1 Kgs 8.66.

4.   2 Chron. 5.11b-13. This passage has no parallel in 1 Kings 8.

5.   2 Chron. 7.1-3. The fire from heaven in 2 Chron. 7.1 has no parallel in 1 Kings 8, but finds its parallel in 1 Chron. 21.26; David's liturgy is also echoed in 2 Chron. 7.3.

6.   2 Chron. 7.17-18 || 1 Kgs 9.4-5.

7.   Concern for the organization of the cultic personnel is particularly evident in the section 1 Chron. 23.2–27.34, which probably belongs to one or more later redactions of Chronicles. See the discussion in H.G.M. Williamson, 'The Origins of the Twenty-Four Priestly Courses: A Study of 1 Chronicles XXIII–XXVII', pp. 251-68. This concern is, of course, present elsewhere in the Chronicler's Davidic narra-

organization of the cultic personnel is an essential if separate part of the foundational story of the Temple and its service.[1] In this specifically Chronistic emphasis in the story of the Temple one also finds the explicit mention of David who is given as the authority for the assignation of duties for the cultic personnel (2 Chron. 8.14) just as Moses is named as the authority for the statutory sacrifices (2 Chron. 8.13).

This analysis of David's place in Solomon's temple-building in Chronicles confirms the observation of De Vries that the Chronistic Solomon's major function is to carry out the rules and plan of David,[2] and the observation made by Flanagan that, in Chronicles, David remains the figure who legitimizes Solomon's temple-building action.[3] The very unity to be found in the Chronistic accounts of David and Solomon can be attributed to the Chronicler's concern for the Temple; the Davidic period has become for him primarily one of royal temple-planning (and temple-foundation) while the Solomonic period has become primarily one of royal temple-building.[4]

Solomon, Temple and the Davidic Promise
Yahweh's covenant with David, which the Chronicler's *Vorlage* had already presented as combining the Temple theme with the dynastic promise,[5] takes on particular prominence in the Chronistic account of

tive, and can be found in 1 Chron. 15.16-24 and 1 Chron. 16.4-6, 37-42, although questions are also raised at times concerning the stage at which these passages became part of the Chronistic work, as can be seen in the commentaries of Galling, *Die Bücher der Chronik, Esra, Nehemia*, pp. 11, 49, 51, and Randellini, *Il libro delle Cronache*, pp. 179-81, 185.

1.   Although the completed construction of the Temple proper is marked in 2 Chron. 8.1, it is only after this action that the Chronicler asserts in 2 Chron. 8.16 ותעד־כלתו שלם בית יהוה. Strictly speaking, this element forms part of a larger concern, which is the establishment of the regular services of the Temple, including the mandatory sacrifices; cf. 2 Chron. 8.12-16. For evidence of the importance of ordering the cultic personnel in the king's establishment of the cult elsewhere in the ancient Near East, cf. the texts cited by Wright, 'The Legacy of David in Chronicles: The Narrative Function of 1 Chronicles 23–27', pp. 238-40.

2.   'Moses and David as Cult Founders in Chronicles', pp. 631-33.

3.   *David's Social Drama: A Hologram of Israel's Early Iron Age*, pp. 212-13.

4.   Throntveit, *When Kings Speak: Royal Speech and Royal Prayer in Chronicles*, p. 115.

5.   This is evident in 2 Sam. 7.12-13 and 1 Kgs 9.3-5.

Solomon's temple-building. This prominence is particularly evident in the more explicit references to the Davidic covenant in the Solomonic narrative, most of which have parallels in the Deuteronomistic History. These explicit references are characterized by mention of the divine promise to David or by mention of the חסד operative between Yahweh and David[1] or by a combined reference to both חסד and divine promise; such references to the Davidic covenant are to be identified as 2 Chron. 1.7-10,[2] 6.4-11,[3] 6.14-17,[4] 6.41-42,[5] and 7.17-22.[6] The author of Chronicles also alludes to the Davidic promise less explicitly in other parts of his Solomonic narrative.[7]

Consideration of the Davidic material has already shown that the Chronicler has made the dynastic promise to David apply first and foremost to Solomon, both in the Chronistic narration of Nathan's oracle and in later reference to it. However, the Chronicler does not hold that the mere accession of Solomon to the throne of Israel fulfils the promise, for after his succession Solomon can pray:

---

1. חסד has often been linked in a fundamental relationship to covenant by commentators. Thus N.H. Snaith, *The Distinctive Ideas of the Old Testament*, pp. 94-95, differentiates between חסד and אהבה by stating that חסד 'in all its varied shades of meaning, is conditional upon there being a covenant'. More recently, M. Weinfeld, 'Covenant, Davidic', p. 189, goes so far as to state that חסד 'is synonymous with ברית'. The assumption that חסד automatically operates as a covenant term is not always supported by the evidence, and it is neither necessary nor convincing to postulate the covenant overtone in all instances (for example Gen. 20.13; 24.49; Ruth 3.10). However, some passages (such as Deut. 7.9, 12; 1 Kgs 8.23 [ǁ 2 Chron. 6.14]; Ps. 89.29, 34; 106.45; Neh. 9.32) do show that for the biblical authors the notions conveyed by the nouns חסד and ברית can be closely related in both Davidic and non-Davidic contexts. The covenant connotations of חסד for the Chronicler are indicated by the fact that the three occurrences of the term unique to the Chronicler (2 Chron. 24.22; 32.32; 35.26) all occur in contexts in which a covenant has been made (cf. 2 Chron. 23.16; 29.10; 34.29-32).

2. ǁ 1 Kgs 3.5-10.

3. ǁ 1 Kgs 8.15-21.

4. ǁ 1 Kgs 8.23-26.

5. There is no parallel in the Deuteronomistic History; cf. Ps. 132.8-10.

6. ǁ 1 Kgs 9.4-9.

7. For example 2 Chron. 2.11; 7.10.

You yourself have done great kindness[1] with David my father and have made me king after him. Now, Yahweh God, may your word with David my father be established, for you have made me king over a numerous people like the dust of the earth. Now give me wisdom and knowledge so that I may go out and come in before this people, for who could govern this great people of yours? (2 Chron. 1.8-10).

The request to establish the word to David, not to be found in the *Vorlage*, links the request for wisdom with the establishment of the divine promise. The narrative juxtaposition of this request and the promise of its granting with the initiation of Solomon's Temple project[2] shows that the real proof for the Chronicler of Solomon's wisdom lies in his successful construction of the Temple, as has been noted by several exegetes;[3] the request for the establishment of the word to David also points the audience in this direction, serving as a reminder that, along with the accession of Solomon, the construction of the Temple forms an essential part of the divine promise.[4] Solomon's address at the dedication of the finished construction in 2 Chron. 6.4-11 reiterates the dual nature of the promise (as delineated in 1 Chronicles 22 and 28) which has now received its initial fulfilment in the kingship of Solomon and his building of the Temple.[5]

However, the promise to David has still not been exhausted, even by the dual phenomena of Solomon's reign and the construction of the Temple. This is indicated by the prayer of Solomon at the dedication which acknowledges that initial fulfilment has taken place, and yet which seeks that a further dimension of the promise be kept:

1. The idiom עשׂה חסד could also be rendered 'kept great loyalty'; cf. W.L. Holladay, *A Concise Hebrew and Aramaic Lexicon of the Old Testament*, p. 111.

2. The intervening material in 2 Chron. 1.14-17 illustrates the fulfilment of Yahweh's promise of the riches and honour given in 1.12, leaving the demonstration of Solomon's wisdom for the building of the Temple. Cf. Williamson, *1 and 2 Chronicles*, pp. 196; Becker, *2 Chronik*, pp. 7-8.

3. For example, Brunet, 'Le Chroniste et ses sources', p. 354; Virgulin, *Libri delle Cronache*, pp. 250-51; Williamson, *1 and 2 Chronicles*, p. 195; Dillard, *2 Chronicles*, p. 10.

4. 1 Chron. 17.11-12; 22.9-10; 28.5-6.

5. Williamson, *Israel in the Books of Chronicles*, p. 65; McCarthy, 'Covenant and Law in Chronicles–Nehemiah', pp. 26-27.

> [You] have kept for your servant David, my father, what you had said to
> him: you have spoken with your mouth and you have fulfilled with your
> hand as this day. And now, Yahweh God of Israel, keep for your servant
> David, my father, that which you have spoken to him, saying: There shall
> not be cut off for you a man from before me sitting on the throne of Israel,
> if only your sons keep their way to walk in my law as you have walked
> before me. And now, Yahweh God of Israel, let your word which you
> have spoken to your servant David be established (2 Chron. 6.15-17).

This request, which is to be found in almost identical form in the
Vorlage,[1] contains an undeniably conditional element reminiscent of
that found in Ps. 132.12.[2] As in the case of Psalm 132, it is not
immediately clear whether the non-fulfilment of the condition will
result in the replacement of the offending monarch alone or in the fall
of the dynasty, although the universal quality of the apodosis
contained in 2 Chron. 6.16 indicates that the latter is more probable;[3]
in any event, the conditionality of the promise should exclude the
assignation of a facile messianism to this passage.[4]

The dependence of 2 Chron. 6.16 upon 2 Kgs 8.25 should not distract the interpreter from recognizing the importance of this verse for
the Chronicler. Willi points to 2 Chron. 6.16 as one of the key verses
in Chronicles, providing a common denominator for much of
Chronistic thought.[5] Certainly 2 Chron. 6.16 encapsulates the
Chronicler's doctrine of retribution and applies it to the members of
the Davidic dynasty, and perhaps applies this doctrine to the dynasty
as a whole.

The conditioned Psalm 132, as well as the Davidic theme and the
theme of rest, is echoed once more in the concluding verses of the

---

1. 1 Kgs 8.24-26. The only significant difference lies in the Chronicler's ללכת
בתורתי in place of the Deuteronomistic Historian's ללכת לפני, which arguably
strengthens—or, at the least, explicates in terms of the post-exilic emphasis on
תורה—the conditional quality of the promise; cf. Harvey-Jellie, *Chronicles*, p. 203;
Cazelles, *Les livres des Chroniques*, p. 142; Ackroyd, *I & II Chronicles, Ezra,
Nehemiah*, p. 112; M. Fishbane, *Biblical Interpretation in Ancient Israel*, p. 386.
2. Curtis and Madsen, *A Critical and Exegetical Commentary on the Books of
Chronicles*, p. 342. The conditionality is also a feature of the *Vorlage* reflected elsewhere in Kings with particular reference to Solomon (1 Kgs 3.14; 6.12; 9.4-5).
3. לא־יכרת לך איש מלפני יושב על־כסא ישראל. Cf. Becker, *2 Chronik*, p. 26.
4. As, for instance, has been readily offered by Galling, *Die Bücher der
Chronik, Esra, Nehemia*, p. 93.
5. *Die Chronik als Auslegung*, pp. 125-26.

prayer, supplying a type of Davidic framework to the entire prayer of dedication which it does not have in the *Vorlage*:

> Now, my God, do let your eyes be opened and your ears attentive to the prayer of this place. And now, rise up, Yahweh God, to your resting, yourself and the Ark of your strength. May your priests, Yahweh God, be clothed with salvation and your faithful ones rejoice in the good. Yahweh God, do not turn back the face of your Anointed; remember the loyalties of your servant David (לחסדי דויד עבדך) (2 Chron. 6.40-42).

The Chronicler begins to depart from the conclusion of his *Vorlage* with the omission of references to the captors of Israel from 1 Kgs 8.50 and to the exodus from 1 Kgs 8.51. Although the transition verse (2 Chron. 6.40) is reminiscent of 1 Kgs 8.52, it shares exact correspondence with only two words of the verse in Kings.[1] Entirely unique to the Chronicler, however, is the expression לתפלת המקום הזה which occurs in the Hebrew Bible only here and in 2 Chron. 7.15, a verse which signifies that the petition of 6.40 has been heard and accepted. Thus it would appear that the transition verse is a Chronistic composition and not, as Virgulin implies,[2] a mere abridgement of the Deuteronomistic *Vorlage*. The transition verse has the effect of erasing the exodus reference of 1 Kgs 8.51 and allowing the dedicatory prayer to end on the crescendo of the psalmic citation.

Within this context, it is possible to see that the Chronicler may be making 'the prayer of this place' explicit in his use of Psalm 132. The phrase refers not only to prayers offered in the Temple as occasion demands, but to the persistent requests which the very existence of the Temple implies and which the cultic poetry enunciates: that Yahweh dwell with his people in this place so that their worship be a joyful celebration of the salvation and benefits which his presence brings. It is also noteworthy that these concluding verses contain many terms with cultic overtones,[3] giving substance to the impression that they represent the prayer that arises from the newly constructed Temple.

The ending phrase of Solomon's prayer, זכרה לחסדי דויד עבדך, wherein the Chronicler diverges markedly from the text of Psalm

---

1. עיניך פתחות. The full phrase יהיו־נא עיניך פתחות ואזניך קשבות is closer to a phrase found in Neh. 1.6, תהי נא אזנך־קשבת ועיניך פתחות, although even here the parallel is far from exact.

2. *Libe delle Cronache*, p. 277.

3. Among these should be included חסד; שמח; כהן; ארון; נוח (as in the refrain given in 1 Chron. 16.34, 41 and in 2 Chron. 5.14 and 7.3).

132, contains both an allusion to David's faithful actions and an invocation of the promises made to David;[1] by means of this dual reference, the phrase manages to evoke much of the content of Psalm 132.[2] The ending phrase in 2 Chron. 6.42 is beloved of commentators who see the hope for a Davidic restoration in the Chronicler's work;[3] however, if the phrase is taken from Isa. 55.3, as many commentators suggest, then it comes from a source that has already transferred the Davidic promises from the dynasty to the nation.[4] The Chronicler may be importing the phrase from Isa. 55.3 in order to import the same radical interpretation of the Davidic promises as that made by Deutero-Isaiah.[5]

The democratization of the Davidic covenant is possible for the Chronicler at this point in the narrative because the dynastic promise has received its initial fulfilment in Solomon and in his completion of the Temple, a fact to which the Chronicler has already referred in 2 Chron. 6.10. Although Yahweh's promise stands fulfilled, the divine pronouncement in 2 Chron. 7.17-18 shows that the Davidic covenant

1. The term חסד has already been used in the Solomonic material with obvious reference to the promises to David (cf. 2 Chron. 1.8 and 6.14-15). However, the use of the plural here (and even more in the summary statements of 2 Chron. 32.32 and 35.26) inclines the audience to the sense of 'faithful deeds, kindnesses'. Since all three of the kings to whom the word is applied were explicitly involved in covenant, it would seem that both the gracious promise of Yahweh's covenant and the faithful deeds of the king are intended in all three occurrences of the plural. On the use of the term in 2 Chron. 6.42, see K.D. Sakenfield, *The Meaning of HESED in the Hebrew Bible: A New Inquiry*, pp. 156-58; Welten, 'Lade–Tempel–Jerusalem: Zur Theologie der Chronickbücher', p. 181; Japhet, *The Ideology of the Book of Chronicles and its Place in Biblical Thought*, pp. 457-59.

2. M. Adinolfi, 'Le "opere di pietà liturgica" di David in 2 Cron. 6,42', p. 35; Welten, 'Lade–Tempel–Jerusalem: Zur Theologie der Chronickbücher', p. 181. Welten also notes the relationship between this phrase and Ps. 89.50 as well as Isa. 55.3.

3. For example Brunet, 'La théologie du chroniste: théocratie et messianisme', pp. 390-91; J.M. Myers, *II Chronicles*, p. 38; Williamson, *1 and 2 Chronicles*, pp. 220-21. Williamson postulates in his commentary that the Chronicler has given the phrase a royalist interpretation of the promises to David quite unlike the use of the phrase in Isa. 55.3; cf. H.G.M. Williamson, '"The Sure Mercies of David": Subjective or Objective Genitive?', pp. 31-49.

4. C. Westermann, *Isaiah 40–66*, pp. 283-84; J. Becker, *Messiaserwartung im Alten Testament*, pp. 63-64; R.N. Whybray, *The Second Isaiah*, p. 51.

5. Goldingay, 'The Chronicler as a Theologian', pp. 114-15.

still has potential for great blessings for the nation and the dynasty, but now according to the same type of condition as that expressed in Psalm 132.

The conditionality of the Davidic promise is also evident in another passage which demonstrates strong dependence upon the *Vorlage*,[1] that of the vision which answers Solomon's prayer of dedication:

> As for you, if you walk before me, as David your father walked, and do according to all that I have commanded you and keep my statutes and my judgments—then I will establish the throne of your kingdom just as I covenanted with David your father, saying: There shall not be cut off for you a man governing in Israel. And if you[2] turn away and forsake my statutes and my commandments which I have placed before you, and you walk [after] and serve other gods and worship before them—then I will root them[3] out from off my land which I gave to them,[4] and this House which I have made holy for my name I will cast away from my face, and I let it become a taunt and a mockery among all the peoples. As for this House, which was exalted, everyone who travels to it shall be appalled and say: 'Why has Yahweh acted like this towards this land and this House?' And they shall say [to him]: 'Because they had forsaken Yahweh the God of their fathers who brought them out of the land of Egypt and they took hold of other gods and worshipped before them and served them; that is why he has brought all this evil upon them' (2 Chron. 7.17-22).

It is noteworthy that this vision, and the prayer to which it is a response, cover a span of events which seems to embrace all the history of monarchical Israel, including the exile.[5] The entire episode of

---

1. ‖ 1 Kgs 9.4-9. Although there is obvious dependence upon the *Vorlage*, the Chronistic passage here exhibits a marked difference from the MT of Kings; this divergence is most noticeable in the omission of two entire phrases which are found in 1 Kgs 9.4-5 (בתם־לבב ובישר in 1 Kgs 9.4 and על־ישראל לעלם in 1 Kgs 9.5). McKenzie, *The Chronicler's Use of the Deuteronomistic History*, p. 97, shows that the omitted phrases have parallels elsewhere in Chronicles and suggests that both are later expansions to the text of Kings.

2. There is a change of subject here, marked in the Hebrew by a change from the second person singular to the second person plural.

3. The Septuagint and Vulgate here have the second person plural pronoun: 'then I will root you out'.

4. The Septuagint and Vulgate here have the second person plural pronoun: 'which I gave to you'.

5. 2 Chron. 6.36-39; 7.20.

the vision which responds to Solomon's prayer, and in particular the Chronicler's addition of 2 Chron. 7.13-15, can be seen as a programmatic statement which embodies many of the key concepts of the Chronistic retribution theology and some of its characteristic vocabulary.[1] In the context of the conditionality attached to the promise and the negative possibility for the future described in vv. 19-22, and in the wider context of a passage imbued with Chronistic retribution theology, the Chronicler's use of the covenant verb כרת is significant. The specific use of a covenant term with reference to the promise to David in such a highly conditioned passage makes nearly inescapable the conclusion that the Davidic covenant was conditioned in the Chronistic outlook consistent with the expression of such a condition in Ps. 132.12.

On the other hand, several commentators point to 2 Chron. 7.17-18 as containing the Chronistic expression of an inviolable Davidic covenant, sometimes of messianic proportions, and alert their readers to the presence of the specifically Chronistic phrase מושל בישראל,[2] seen as an echo of Mic. 5.1, which for them provides certain grounds for this interpretation.[3] This purported connection of 2 Chron. 7.18 with Mic. 5.1 has several weaknesses. First, the verbal correspondence is so weak as to be negligible, leading one exegete to refer to the supposed linking of the two passages as far-fetched.[4] Secondly, the Septuagint of 3 Kgdms 9.5 reads ἡγούμενος ἐν Ισραηλ with the Chronicler and against the MT of Kings, as noted by Curtis and Madsen,[5] which indicates that the Chronicler may simply have been following his *Vorlage* rather than introducing an alteration charged with meaningful nuance. Thirdly, the very passage from Micah in its

---

1. Dillard, 'Reward and Punishment in Chronicles: The Theology of Immediate Retribution', p. 166; Williamson, *1 and 2 Chronicles*, pp. 225-26. Characteristic vocabulary to be found here includes the verbs כנע and בקש, both of which have cultic overtones; Williamson indicates other terms which he judges to be used in a specifically Chronistic manner.

2. Compare 1 Kgs 9.5: מעל כסא ישראל.

3. For example von Rad, *Das Geschichtsbild des chronistischen Werkes*, p. 124; Myers, *II Chronicles*, p. 44; Randellini, *Il libro delle Cronache*, p. 334; Ackroyd, *I & II Chronicles, Ezra, Nehemiah*, p. 116; Virgulin, *Libri delle Cronache*, pp. 281-82; Dillard, *2 Chronicles*, pp. 58-59.

4. Becker, *2 Chronik*, p. 32.

5. *A Critical and Exegetical Commentary on the Books of Chronicles*, p. 351.

original context seems to point outside of the direct line of David in its hope for the future ruler of Israel.[1] Taken together, these observations seriously undermine an interpretation of an inviolable dynastic promise which is akin to messianism in these verses.

The messianic or quasi-messianic interpretation of 2 Chron. 7.17-18 also runs contrary to the conditioned character of the larger passage into which these verses are situated. The conditionality expressed in 2 Chron. 7.17-18, together with the dire consequences for the failure to meet Yahweh's demands which are outlined in 2 Chron. 7.19-22,[2] echoes the same condition expressed in the Davidic exhortation to Solomon: אם־תדרשנו ימצא לך ואם־תעזבנו יזניחך לעד (1 Chron. 28.9). The repetition of a condition for the establishment of Solomon's reign in this final explicit reference to the Davidic promise in the Solomonic narrative indicates that the conditions for the promise have at this point been neither violated nor permanently fulfilled, not even by the building of the Temple. The passage points to a condition which can never be finally fulfilled but which must be continually fulfilled; therefore the conditionality, expressed here in 2 Chron. 7.17-18 and earlier in 2 Chron. 6.16, is necessarily a constant and continuing part of the dynastic promise to David in the Chronicler's theology.[3]

---

1. J.L. Mays, *Micah: A Commentary*, p. 113.

2. The change to the second person plural here creates certain difficulties for identifying the intended referent; these difficulties are not alleviated by the variant pronominal readings in the versions referred to above. Some commentators, and most notably those who find an inviolable dynastic promise in 2 Chron. 7.17-18, solve the difficulty by proposing two referents—Solomon for the first part and Israel for the second; cf. Randellini, *Il libro delle Cronache*, p. 334, Ackroyd, *I & II Chronicles, Ezra, Nehemiah*, pp. 116-17, and Dillard, *2 Chronicles*, p. 59. While this is a possibility, especially if the variant readings of the versions are accepted as the more authentic, the Chronicler may also have intended to apply these consequences to the entire dynasty which is therefore addressed in the plural, as in the *Vorlage* at 1 Kgs 9.6; the omission of ובניכם from 1 Kgs 9.6 does not weaken a dynastic application, as Williamson suggests (*1 and 2 Chronicles*, pp. 226-27), but rather strengthens it, since the plural pronominal ending indicates that Solomon alone is not being addressed in the *Vorlage*.

3. This conclusion is contrary to those interpreters who see that the dynasty is eternally established in the Chronistic outlook by Solomon's completion of the Temple, a point of view which is espoused by Williamson, 'Eschatology in Chronicles', p. 142. A similar interpretation is proposed by Halpern, 'Sacred History and Ideology: Chronicles' Thematic Structure—Indications of an Earlier

Thus, even in the success of the House of David portrayed in the accomplished construction of the Temple by Solomon, the Chronicler has shown that future success and continued endorsement of the Davidic dynasty can only be guaranteed by the Davidides' continual adherence to Yahweh's demands. Since the Chronicler was writing at a time when the Davidic dynasty was no longer reigning, these references to the conditionality of the promise become especially significant. The Davidic heritage is shown more and more to reside in the cultic life of Israel, and the allusion to Isa. 55.3 in 2 Chron. 6.42 may well be a conscious attempt to remind the audience that the real promise to David now rests with the nation gathered at the Temple of the Davidic covenant rather than with a dynasty.[1] Even at the height of Solomonic achievement, the shadow of the Saul paradigm is implicit in the admonitions and conditions which are present throughout the narrative related to Solomon's temple-building.[2]

Nevertheless, the Chronicler's Solomonic narrative marks true progress in the story of the Jerusalem cultus, not only in fulfilling the Davidic תבנית but also in uniting the Tent with the Davidic site to provide the single legitimate cultic place for Israel (2 Chron. 5.5). In many ways, the Chronistic Solomon, cleansed of the sins and failures narrated in the Deuteronomistic History (1 Kgs 11.1-8), provides a picture of the ideal Davidide. However, the Temple in Chronicles does not gain in prestige because it has been built by someone so sinless; rather, Solomon becomes sinless in the Chronistic History because he has fulfilled the task laid upon him and built the Temple.[3] For this, Solomon is rewarded in the narrative: he receives cities and secures the land (2 Chron. 8.1-6; an action reminiscent of the effects of temple-building in ancient Near Eastern mythology);[4] foreign

Source', pp. 44-45, and McConville, *Chronicles*, pp. 138-39; Halpern and McConville acknowledge that conditionality pertains to the dynasty during Solomon's reign, but suggest that after Solomon has completed the task laid upon him, the conditionality no longer applies to the dynastic promise.

1. Caquot, 'Peut-on parler de messianisme dans l'oeuvre du Chroniste?', pp. 118-19; Dumbrell, 'The Purpose of the Books of Chronicles', p. 263.

2. Cf. 1 Chron. 28.7, 9; 2 Chron. 6.16; 7.17-22.

3. Harvey-Jellie, *Chronicles*, p. 176; Caquot, 'Peut-on parler de messianisme dans l'oeuvre du Chroniste?', pp. 115-16.

4. Baal, in one of several places in the Ugaritic material which make a connection between the divine dwelling-place and the lordship of the land, seizes towns

monarchs help to increase his wealth and prestige, recognizing his accomplishments.[1] Solomon continues to implement faithfully the cultus of the Jerusalem Temple and, by implication, is shown to fulfil constantly the condition embedded in the Davidic promise.[2] Solomon's completed construction, however, signals neither the final stage of the Jerusalem Temple nor the perfection of the Jerusalem cultus; to tell that story, the Chronicler must continue his history through the Davidic dynasty of Judah.

The Post-Solomonic Kings to Josiah: The Cultus Completed

Having established and described his cultic *Urzeit* by re-presenting the story of the United Monarchy, the Chronicler turns his attention to the remaining kings belonging to the Davidic dynasty. As in the case of the Davidic and Solomonic narratives, the author of Chronicles imbues these stories with his special concerns; this is evident both from the major differences between the Chronistic text and its Deuteronomistic *Vorlage*, and from the general patterns that can be discerned in the final form of this part of his work. In this section, the Chronicler's re-presentation of the Jerusalem monarchy in the period from Rehoboam to Josiah will be considered; the post-Josian kings are treated in a highly stylized manner by the Chronicler and will be discussed separately in the next section of this chapter.

If the Chronicler's interest in these post-Solomonic monarchs as a group corresponds approximately to the amount of narration he affords them, then the Chronicler has left the realm of his fascination—the Davidic and Solomonic *Urzeit*—to bring his audience to a consideration of characters and events in the history of Judah which are of a lesser interest to him. However, the audience can quickly discern that telling this part of Judah's story is also necessary for the Chronicler's purpose, for from it the author draws many lessons and continues the story of the Jerusalem cultus which he had begun

---

after the completion of his temple as a sign of his kingly might; cf. G.R. Driver, *Canaanite Myths and Legends*, p. 101. Cf. also Ginsberg, 'Poems about Baal and Anath', p. 138; R.J. Clifford, *The Cosmic Mountain in Canaan and the Old Testament*, pp. 69-72; Clements, *God and Temple*, p. 6.

1.   2 Chron. 8.17–9.12, 14, 23-24.
2.   2 Chron. 8.12-16; cf. also 2 Chron. 8.11; 9.11.

negatively with the Saul paradigm and presented positively with the *Urzeit* of the United Monarchy.

This section will deal with 2 Chron. 10.1–35.27, the division of the narrative that treats of the monarchs from Rehoboam to Josiah, by considerations of the relationship of the king to the cultus, of the presentation of the Davidic promise and of the progress of the Jerusalem cultus. In keeping with the character of this chapter as a final form study and with the nature of the Chronicler's work as narrative, each of these three concerns in turn will be surveyed according to the denouement of the Chronicler's presentation of this period in Israel's history.

Post-Solomonic Retribution in Relation to the Cultus

Because this section of the Chronicler's work compresses its narration into shorter units encompassing whole reigns, the Chronistic theme of retribution is more apparent here than in the narratives of David and Solomon. Several other themes are evident in this section of the Chronicler's history, all of which can be related at least in part to the retribution theme; mention should be made in particular of the all-Israel theme,[1] of the recurring theme of foreign alliances[2] and of the inattention to the word of God, whether contained in תורה or oracle.[3] Without denying the importance of these and other themes in Chronicles, exegetes often advert to a close, although not exclusive, relationship between the cultic concern of the Chronicler and the retribution theme in both its positive and negative workings.[4]

---

1. Cf. Rudolph, *Chronikbücher*, p. ix; Braun, 'The Message of Chronicles: Rally 'Round the Temple', p. 510; Williamson, *Israel in the Books of Chronicles*, pp. 110-18.

2. Cf. Dillard, 'Reward and Punishment in Chronicles: The Theology of Immediate Retribution', p. 167.

3. Cf. Wellhausen, *Prolegomena to the History of Ancient Israel*, pp. 203-11; Welch, *The Work of the Chronicler: Its Purpose and Date*, pp. 46-48; Willi, *Die Chronik als Auslegung*, pp. 216-29; Mosis, *Untersuchungen zur Theologie des chronistischen Geschichtswerkes*, pp. 35-39; Newsome, 'Toward a New Understanding of the Chronicler and his Purposes', p. 203.

4. Noordtzij, 'Les intentions du Chroniste', p. 161; Brunet, 'Le Chroniste et ses sources', pp. 376, 385; Caquot, 'Peut-on parler de messianisme dans l'oeuvre du Chroniste?', p. 119; Virgulin, *Libri delle Cronache*, p. 50; Runnalls, 'The King as Temple Builder: A Messianic Typology', p. 26; Dillard, 'Reward and Punishment in Chronicles: The Theology of Immediate Retribution', p. 167-68; Duke, *The*

Von Rad has observed that the Chronicler has portrayed retribution as applicable, first and foremost, to the Davidide.[1] Mosis, while concurring with this observation, treats it as a corollary of the fact that the Davidic kings constitute the principal characters of the work.[2] However attractive the suggestion of Mosis may be in its simplicity, it seems to ignore the cultic element which is often a factor in royal retribution; the recurring connections that the Chronicler makes in this section between monarchy, retribution and cultus suggest that the ramifications of this combination should be traced much deeper and further into the ancient Near Eastern temple ideology.

As has been seen, the Chronicler has retained the ancient Near Eastern picture of the king as temple-builder in his portrayal of David and Solomon. Similarly, the ancient Near Eastern temple ideology also placed the continuing responsibility of temple maintenance upon the king. The Chronicler has reflected this outlook in his own narrative of the post-Solomonic kings and in his application of the retribution theme, allowing the Temple to bestow legitimacy upon its royal custodians in proportion to their faithfulness.[3] However, this aspect of the Chronicler's narrative is not confined simply to the Temple itself, but extends to the entire life of worship in Israel, from the eradication of illicit cults to the assembly of the nation for authentic liturgical celebration. It has been correctly observed that the cultus is not simply a question of rite for the Chronicler, but a way of speaking of the whole field of religion,[4] a proof of the attachment of individuals and of the nation to Yahweh[5] and the expression of the continuity of the bond between Israel and Yahweh.[6] The Chronistic use of themes such as harkening to the word of Yahweh and dependence upon him rather than upon foreign allies shows that what is at stake for the Chronicler

---

Persuasive Appeal of the Chronicler: A Rhetorical Analysis, p. 93.

1. *Das Geschichtsbild des chronistischen Werkes*, p. 120.

2. *Untersuchungen zur Theologie des chronistischen Geschichtswerkes*, p. 169.

3. Flanagan, *David's Social Drama: A Hologram of Israel's Early Iron Age*, p. 244.

4. Barnes, 'The Religious Standpoint of the Chronicler', p. 17.

5. G. von Rad, *Old Testament Theology 1: The Theology of Israel's Historical Traditions*, p. 353.

6. Japhet, *The Ideology of the Book of Chronicles and its Place in Biblical Thought*, p. 222.

is absolute allegiance to Yahweh and not a purely formal cultic loyalty.[1] Within this context, the king assumes a role that is more demanding than the simple task of temple maintenance: he becomes the figure responsible for guiding the nation in the seeking of Yahweh and in fulfilling the conditions of the covenant.[2] While the workings of retribution depend upon more than simply cultic factors, a brief survey will indicate that the correspondence between retribution and cultus has been presented with a consistency which is remarkable for a narrative work.

The first Judaean king of the Divided Monarchy, Rehoboam, suffers two great misfortunes in the Chronistic narrative, both of which are to be found in the Deuteronomistic History and neither of which is linked explicitly to cultic offences.[3] However, two positive links between Rehoboam's reign and the cultus may be noted, neither of which have corresponding references in the Deuteronomistic History: the Northern priests and Levites who immigrated into Judah are said to have strengthened Rehoboam's kingship (2 Chron. 11.13-17) and the humbling of Rehoboam and the princes of Judah averted worse disasters that could have taken place in the invasion of Shishak.[4] The Chronicler seems to pass a mixed verdict on Rehoboam, noting that during his reign וגם ביהודה היה דברים טובים,[5] but still declaring in the last analysis that ויעש הרע כי לא הכין לבו לדרוש את־יהוה.[6] Some slight positive judgment may be seen in the Chronicler's note that Rehoboam was buried in the city of David.[7]

1. Schumacher, 'The Chronicler's Theology of History', p. 16.
2. Brunet, 'Le Chroniste et ses sources', pp. 376.
3. Thus Rehoboam suffers the schism in 2 Chron. 10.16-19 (‖ 1 Kgs 12.16-19), which will be discussed below, and the invasion by Shishak which was occasioned through the abandoning of the Law by Rehoboam and Israel (2 Chron. 12.1-9; cf. 1 Kgs 14.22-26). The reference to Judah's unfaithful behaviour in 1 Kgs 14.22-24 suggests that the phrase עזב את־תורת יהוה in 2 Chron. 12.1 may have signified cultic offences for the Chronicler; cf. Harvey-Jellie, *Chronicles*, p. 230; Virgulin, *Libri delle Cronache*, p. 304.
4. 2 Chron. 12.5-8, for which there is no corresponding passage in Kings. The cultic significance of כנע has already been noted.
5. 2 Chron. 12.12. There is no parallel passage for this verse in the *Vorlage*.
6. 2 Chron. 12.14; 1 Kgs 14.22 reads simply ויעש הרע בעיני יהוה.
7. 2 Chron. 12.16 (‖ 1 Kgs 14.31). Von Rad, *Old Testament Theology 1: The Theology of Israel's Historical Traditions*, p. 350, notes that the Chronicler often uses the burial of a king as the last indicator of divine retribution. While the

Whereas the Deuteronomistic Historian portrays Abijah as walking in the sinful ways of Rehoboam,[1] Abijah is portrayed as a model king by the Chronicler. His sermon is, in part, a contrasting of the cultic rebellion of the North with the cultic faithfulness of Abijah and his kingdom,[2] the reward of which is victory over the North in battle,[3] as well as the acquisition of cities from the vanquished schismatic kingdom.[4] This cultically faithful king is also buried in the city of David.[5]

The reign of Asa is more complicated in its cultic aspect, reflecting a certain ambiguity concerning Asa in the Deuteronomistic History (cf. 1 Kgs 15.9-16); the Chronicler solves this ambiguity by dividing the reign of Asa into two periods. The beginning of Asa's reign is characterized by the eradication of illicit cults and the seeking of Yahweh (2 Chron. 14.1-4); as a reward for this faithfulness, Yahweh gives rest to the kingdom, allowing Asa to strengthen the kingdom with fortified cities and a well-equipped army and to meet the attempted Cushite invasion victoriously.[6] The oracle of Azariah,

Chronicler does not display unequivocal consistency in this regard, there are instances where the record of burial obviously stands as a final statement of the Chronicler's judgment upon a monarch; cf. 2 Chron. 24.25; 35.24-25. The inconsistency may be partially explained if the records of burial are taken to indicate a gradual degeneration with exceptions for the better monarchs.

1. 1 Kgs 15.3. Apart from the opening and concluding formulae of 1 Kgs 15.1-2 and 1 Kgs 15.7-8 and the notice of war with Jeroboam in 1 Kgs 15.7, the Chronicler does not seem to be much indebted to his *Vorlage* for his account of Abijah's reign.

2. 2 Chron. 13.8-12. D.G. Deboys, 'History and Theology in the Chronicler's Portrayal of Abijah', p. 51, demonstrates that the Chronicler has taken care to portray solidarity between Abijah and his people in their faithfulness and thus in their victory.

3. 2 Chron. 13.18. The battle is even won through cultic actions according to 2 Chron. 13.14-16, for the priests blowing on their trumpets, the cry and the shout are all evocative of cultic actions and are the only actions that the Judaean army performs in order to win the battle.

4. 2 Chron. 13.19. The taking of cities has resonances with ancient Near Eastern temple thought, although it is more likely here to be simply an indication of divine reward.

5. 2 Chron. 13.23 (∥ 1 Kgs 15.8).

6. 2 Chron. 14.4-12; there is no correspondent to this incident in the *Vorlage*. The seeking of Yahweh is given as a grounds for confidence in undertaking new projects in 2 Chron. 14.6. This is reminiscent of the response of the assembly to Gilgamesh's request for advice on a proposed war with Kish wherein the assembly,

which is unique to the Chronicler and which neatly summarizes the
principles of retribution (2 Chron. 15.1-7), is followed by further
cultic reform which stretches into what had been the territory of the
Northern Kingdom and includes an assembly gathered from a number
of tribes for sacrifice and covenant-making;[1] the reward, once more,
is rest for the nation.[2] However, the Chronicler also portrays a negative side to Asa's relationship to the cultus in the latter period of his
reign: his reliance upon Ben-hadad for help, itself a grave error in the
Chronistic evaluation, is compounded by the taking of gold and silver
from the Temple to substantiate the request.[3] This reliance results in
the removal of rest, as announced through the oracle of Hanani.[4] In
the disease of the feet with which Asa is afflicted in the last two years
of his reign, Asa fails to seek Yahweh, but makes a vain seeking of
physicians;[5] implicit in this is a cultic failure which brings Asa
directly into the shadow of Saul.[6] Asa's burial could represent a partial rehabilitation of Asa by the Chronicler in recognition of his former cultic contribution,[7] although the burial בקברתיו אשר כרה־לו בעיר

---

in responding positively, draws courage from Gilgamesh's care for the temple; cf.
Kramer, 'Gilgamesh and Agga', pp. 45-46.

    1.   2 Chron. 15.8-15; cf. also 15.16-19.

    2.   2 Chron. 15.15, 19; this contrasts with the note in 1 Kgs 15.16 that there
was constant war between Asa and Baasha of Israel.

    3.   2 Chron. 16.2 (|| 1 Kgs 15.18).

    4.   2 Chron. 16.7-10; there is no corresponding passage in the *Vorlage*. This
oracle shows that Asa's lack of reliance on Yahweh, more than the removal of wealth
from the Temple treasury, constitutes the offence. Just as the period of Asa's faithfulness involves the building up of the treasury (2 Chron. 15.18), so the period of
his unfaithfulness is marked by the impoverishment of the Temple in the execution of
his act of infidelity.

    5.   לא־דרש את־יהוה כי ברפאים; 2 Chron. 16.12. Asa's disease of the feet is
referred to in 1 Kgs 15.23, but the phrase cited is only to be found in Chronicles.
'His resorting to PHYSICIANS may... be understood as a reference to undesirable
practices, since the word, literally "healers", may also be understood as having connections with the spirits of the dead. Necromantic or magical practices may be in the
Chronicler's mind' (Ackroyd, *I & II Chronicles, Ezra, Nehemiah*, p. 141).

    6.   Mosis, *Untersuchungen zur Theologie des chronistischen Geschichtswerkes*,
p. 175.

    7.   2 Chron. 16.14 (|| 1 Kgs 15.24). See Michaeli, *Les livres des Chroniques,
d'Esdras et de Néhémie*, p. 185.

דויד[1] may indicate a certain distancing from the burial with the fathers/kings so beloved of the Chronicler for more worthy kings.[2]

The reign of Jehoshaphat begins with a statement of cultic faithfulness, noting that the king הלך בדרכי דויד אביו הראשנים ולא דרש לבעלים, the seeking of the Baals being identified with the deeds of the Northern Kingdom in 2 Chron. 17.3-4. The Chronicler seems to be expanding upon the sparse note of approval that the Deuteronomistic Historian awards Jehoshaphat in 1 Kgs 22.43.[3] The Chronicler's more detailed statements note Jehoshaphat's eradication of the high places and Asherim (2 Chron. 17.6), and the sending out of princes, priests and Levites to teach תורה to the people.[4] The reward of his faithfulness can be seen in his wealth, rest from warfare and military strength.[5] The joint military venture that Jehoshaphat undertakes with the Northern Kingdom represents a mark against him and a grave danger, but his cultic faithfulness preserves him from total disaster;[6] the Chronicler even prefaces Jehoshaphat's salvation in battle with the cultic term זעק.[7] The power of cultic faithfulness is drawn with great explicitness when Jehoshaphat overcomes the threat of foreign invasion through liturgical supplication and action, and once more enjoys

1.   This phrase is not to be found in 1 Kgs 15.24.
2.   For example 2 Chron. 21.1; 24.16; 25.28. Negative examples also illustrate the Chronicler's use of this image in 2 Chron. 21.20 and 24.25.
3.   Apart from the episode of the attack against Ramoth-Gilead and possibly the venture of sending ships to Tarshish (in which Jehoshaphat refuses to allow the North to participate according to 1 Kgs 22.49, whereas he joins a disastrous joint venture with the North according to 2 Chron. 20.36), the Chronicler does not depend on the Deuteronomistic History for his narratives concerning Jehoshaphat.
4.   2 Chron. 17.7-9. Jehoshaphat later establishes the priests and Levites as judges to apply תורה in 2 Chron. 19.8-11. Albright, 'The Judicial Reform of Jehoshaphat', pp. 78-79, refers to a temple inscription at Karnak which indicates that Egyptian priests fulfilled a judicial function by royal appointment in the 14th century BCE.
5.   2 Chron. 17.2, 5, 10-19.
6.   2 Chron. 18.2-34 (|| 1 Kgs 22.2-35); cf. 2 Chron. 19.2-3.
7.   2 Chron. 18.31. While the term זעק itself is drawn from the *Vorlage*, the Chronicler's addition of an explicitly divine response gives the word a more cultic flavour. This brings this passage into conformity with the other occurrences of the verb in Chronicles which all refer explicitly to an appeal for divine help; cf. 1 Chron. 5.20; 2 Chron. 13.14; 20.9; 32.20.

the gift of rest.[1] The Chronistic judgment does not give total approval to Jehoshaphat, for high places are left to stand and Jehoshaphat himself persists in joint ventures with the Northern Kingdom;[2] however, he is granted burial with his fathers.[3]

The cooperation with the Northern Kingdom initiated by Jehoshaphat bears its first bitter fruit in Jehoram, whose wife is Athaliah, the daughter of Ahab.[4] His cultic offences include the generic crime of walking in the way of the kings of Israel,[5] and the establishment of high places.[6] The narrative notes several punishments for these crimes: the loss of Moab and Edom,[7] attack and pillage from foreign forces,[8] debilitating disease,[9] and Jehoram's burial outside of the royal tombs.[10]

1.   2 Chron. 20.1-30. The ritual that brings the victory is firmly centred on the Jerusalem Temple, as is evident from the framing of the battle with Temple worship in vv. 4-19 and 28. The actual triumph is brought about by the singing of the liturgical refrain associated elsewhere in the Chronicler's work with the official cultus. The Temple emphasis is made most explicit in the prayer of Jehoshaphat in v. 9 which grounds the appeal to Yahweh in Solomon's dedication prayer. The promise of victory through the cultic prophet in one sense locates the victory in the Temple itself; this assurance of victory is so certain that the proper response is no longer supplication, but worship and praise even before the victory itself, as can be seen in vv. 18-19.

2.   2 Chron. 20.33, 35-37. Willi, *Die Chronik als Auslegung*, pp. 61-62, notes the oxymoron between 2 Chron. 20.33 and 2 Chron. 17.6 and suggests that it arises from the Chronicler's use of his *Vorlage*; the author, therefore, might intend to note and explain the presence of high places, as in 1 Kgs 22.43, by attributing it to the failure of the people to set their hearts on Yahweh. A similar understanding of 2 Chron. 20.33 is proposed by G.N. Knoppers, 'Reform and Regression: The Chronicler's Presentation of Jehoshaphat', p. 519.

3.   2 Chron. 21.1 (∥ 1 Kgs 22.51).

4.   2 Chron. 21.6 (∥ 2 Kgs 8.18). More probably, Athaliah was the daughter of Omri; cf. Rudolph, *Chronikbücher*, p. 264.

5.   2 Chron. 21.6 (∥ 2 Kgs 8.18). That this involves the illicit worship of the North is shown by 2 Chron. 17.3-4 (which is without a parallel passage in the *Vorlage*).

6.   2 Chron. 21.11; there is no corresponding passage in the *Vorlage*.

7.   2 Chron. 21.8-10 (∥ 2 Kgs 8.20-22).

8.   2 Chron. 21.16-17; there is no corresponding passage in the *Vorlage*.

9.   2 Chron. 21.18-19; there is no corresponding passage in the *Vorlage*.

10. 2 Chron. 21.20. This contrasts with 2 Kgs 8.24, according to which Jehoram was buried with his fathers.

Ahaziah similarly follows the ways of the North in cultic error, aided by the counsel of Athaliah and the House of Ahab;[1] this results in a joint campaign with the North against Aram.[2] As a result of wounds received during this campaign, Ahaziah is to be found with the House of Ahab when Jehu brings the judgment upon them and the same fate is inflicted upon Ahaziah as upon the dynasty with which he has sided.[3] Although buried (for the sake of his ancestor Jehoshaphat), there is no place of burial identified, implying a burial in Samaria where he was slain, rather than in Jerusalem as stated in the Deuteronomistic History.[4]

The two reigns of Jehoram and Ahaziah combine to bring the House of David to a situation not unlike that portrayed for Saul in 1 Chronicles 10: cultic unfaithfulness has resulted in the loss of territory and the lack of a suitable successor to the throne.[5] Athaliah, the queen mother, quickly fills the power vacuum;[6] the Chronicler need not recount her cultic crimes since he has already implied that she stood behind the offences of Jehoram and Ahaziah.[7]

Joash, whose very survival and accession to the throne depended in the Chronicler's eyes upon the cultic personnel and cultic action,[8] falls

---

1. 2 Chron. 22.3-5; the Chronicler has strengthened the reference to the relationship between Ahaziah and the House of Ahab already to be found in 2 Kgs 8.27 by mentioning the role of the latter as Ahaziah's counsellors.

2. 2 Chron. 22.5 (|| 2 Kgs 8.28).

3. 2 Chron. 22.6-9; this passage represents a Chronistic version of the death of Ahaziah which is told in 2 Kgs 9.21-28. According to the Deuteronomistic Historian, Ahaziah was pursued and wounded in his chariot, after which he died at Megiddo, whereas in the Chronicler's History, Azariah was slain in the presence of Jehu.

4. 2 Chron. 22.9; 2 Kgs 9.28. Some exegetes interpret the Chronistic burial notice as the final condemnation of Ahaziah, linking him more closely to the House of Ahab than to the House of David; cf. Coggins, *The First and Second Books of the Chronicles*, p. 232; Becker, *2 Chronik*, p. 73.

5. Mosis, *Untersuchungen zur Theologie des chronistischen Geschichtswerkes*, pp. 178-79.

6. 2 Chron. 22.9-10 (|| 2 Kgs 11.1-2).

7. 2 Chron. 21.6; 22.3; cf. also 24.7. Although 2 Chron. 21.6 corresponds to 2 Kgs 8.18, the Chronicler has added a specific reference to Athaliah's evil influence in 2 Chron. 22.3 which is lacking in 2 Kgs 8.27. 2 Chron. 24.7 is unique to Chronicles.

8. 2 Chron. 22.10–23.21 (|| 2 Kgs 11.1-20). Through a series of minor additions, omissions and modifications, rather than through lengthy additions or exten-

heir to the task of reform initiated by the priest Jehoiada as part of Joash's enthronement.[1] Joash continues the good work and furthers it, collecting money from the nation for the upkeep of the Temple[2] and effecting the needed repairs (2 Chron. 24.12-13) However, the Chronistic narrative breaks suddenly in a way unknown to the Deuteronomistic Historian with the death of Jehoiada (who is buried in the tombs of the kings),[3] and thereafter Joash becomes a king who forsakes the Temple to serve idols (2 Chron. 24.18). The punishment of Joash can be seen in the successful invasion by Aram,[4] the assassination of the king and the final narrative condemnation of a burial outside the royal tombs.[5]

Amaziah is commended for doing what is right before Yahweh, but no specific cultic allusion is made in this note of approval.[6] He commits a fatal cultic crime by bringing the gods of Seir to Jerusalem and worshipping them,[7] the result of which was defeat at the hands of Israel, the looting of Jerusalem and Amaziah's eventual assassination in Lachish.[8] However, he is given burial with his

---

sive alterations to his *Vorlage*, the Chronicler has emphasized the liturgical nature of this episode of Davidic restoration; he achieves this liturgical emphasis especially through the heightened role given to the cultic personnel. Thus Jehoshabeath is portrayed as the wife of the priest Jehoiada in 2 Chron. 22.11, the Levites are gathered to Jerusalem in preparation for the revolt in 2 Chron. 23.2 and the task of guarding the Temple and the king is transferred to the priests and the Levites in 2 Chron. 23.4-7. The cultic aspect of the whole people is also to be inferred from their designation as קהל in 2 Chron. 23.3; cf. Cazelles, *Les livres des Chroniques*, p. 189 and Virgulin, *Libi delle Cronache*, p. 364.

1. 2 Chron. 23.17-19; cf. 2 Kgs 11.18.

2. 2 Chron. 24.4-11; the passage 2 Chron. 24.4-14 is a reshaping of the episode contained in 2 Kgs 12.5-17.

3. 2 Chron. 24.16; there is no corresponding passage in the *Vorlage*. The reason given for affording Jehoiada this privilege כי־עשה טובה בישראל ועם האלהים וביתו, implies that Jehoiada has exercised a kingly function in his action on behalf of the Temple.

4. 2 Chron. 24.23-24; cf. 2 Kgs 12.18.

5. 2 Chron. 24.25-26 (‖ 2 Kgs 12.21-22); according to the account in Kings, Joash is buried with his fathers.

6. 2 Chron. 25.2 (‖ 2 Kgs 14.3). The only specification of Amaziah's righteousness is that he followed the precept of Deut. 24.16 in dealing with his father's assassins in 2 Chron. 25.4 (‖ 2 Kgs 14.6).

7. 2 Chron. 25.14-16; there is no corresponding passage in the *Vorlage*.

8. 2 Chron. 25.20-27; cf. 2 Kgs 14.11-19. The Chronicler has made the

fathers, presumably for his earlier faithfulness.[1]

Uzziah is also credited with doing what is right,[2] explained through use of the cultic term דרש,[3] which results in his prosperity and in his military and building achievements.[4] However, his cultic offence of attempting to burn incense in the Temple leads to the immediate punishment of leprosy and his banishment from the Temple.[5] His burial takes place in a field because of his leprosy, but is still classified as a royal burial with his fathers, again presumably because of his earlier zeal for Yahweh.[6]

Jotham is presented as possessing all the positive qualities of Uzziah, but the Chronicler notes that Jotham did not enter the Temple.[7] He is rewarded with success in building and in battle,[8] as well as royal burial.[9]

The cultic crimes of Ahaz are presented as multitudinous: he makes images, offers illicit sacrifices, even ויבער את־בניו באש.[10] The

divinely punitive nature of these events more explicit than had his *Vorlage*; cf. 2 Chron. 25.20, 27.

1. 2 Chron. 25.28 (|| 2 Kgs 14.20).
2. 2 Chron. 26.4 (|| 2 Kgs 15.3).
3. 2 Chron. 26.5; there is no corresponding passage in the *Vorlage*.
4. 2 Chron. 26.5-15; there is no corresponding passage in the *Vorlage*.
5. 2 Chron. 26.16-21; while this episode is unique to Chronicles, the Deuteronomistic History notes Uzziah's leprosy in 2 Kgs 15.5.
6. 2 Chron. 26.23; this contrasts with 2 Kgs 15.7, according to which Uzziah was buried in the City of David.
7. 2 Chron. 27.2; cf. 2 Kgs 15.34-35. Although no specific cultic act is cited by the Chronicler (it is probably presumed in the allusion to Uzziah), a positive cultic note may be contained in the identification of the queen mother as the daughter of Zadok (cf. 2 Kgs 15.33) whom the Chronicler may have associated with the priest Zadok listed in 1 Chron. 6.12; see Ackroyd, *I & II Chronicles, Ezra, Nehemiah*, p. 172.
8. 2 Chron. 27.3-6; this passage is largely lacking in the *Vorlage*, except for mention of the building of the Upper Gate of the Temple in 2 Kgs 15.35.
9. 2 Chron. 27.9 (|| 2 Kgs 15.38).
10. 2 Chron. 28.2-4. Compare the phrase quoted from 2 Chron. 28.3 with the *Vorlage* in 2 Kgs 16.3 where it reads וגם את־בנו העביר באש. Although the phrase in Kings may refer to a rite of passage rather than immolation, the Chronicler has eliminated this possible reading and has multiplied the occurrences of this abomination. Cf. Rudolph, *Chronikbücher*, p. 288; Randellini, *Il libro delle Cronache*, p. 432-33; Coggins, *The First and Second Books of the Chronicles*, p. 258; M.E.W. Thompson, *Situation and Theology: Old Testament Interpretations of the*

punishment is defeat by Aram with a deportation to Damascus[1] and defeat by the Northern Kingdom with pillage and deportation,[2] as well as loss of captives to Edom and territory to the Philistines.[3] Ahaz himself despoils the Temple to substantiate a request for help to Tiglath-pileser,[4] and his continuing distress leads to the further cultic offences of sacrificing to the gods of Damascus, the further despoiling of the Temple (as well as the shutting of its doors) and the construction of high places.[5] Ahaz is buried in Jerusalem, but not in the tombs of the kings.[6]

The majority of the Chronistic narrative concerning Hezekiah deals with that king's cultic action, with his restoration of the Temple and Passover celebration,[7] with the eradication of both Northern and Judaean illicit cultic sites,[8] with provisions for such matters as the courses of priests and Levites, the regular sacrifices and the support of the cultic personnel.[9] Hezekiah is rewarded for his cultic faithfulness

---

Syro–Ephraimite War, p. 96; C. Conroy, *1–2 Samuel, 1–2 Kings*, p. 220.

1.   2 Chron. 28.5; this contrasts with 2 Kgs 16.5 which presents the Aramean attack against Ahaz as unsuccessful.

2.   2 Chron. 28.5-8; there is no corresponding passage in the *Vorlage*.

3.   2 Chron. 28.17-18; there is no corresponding passage in the *Vorlage*.

4.   2 Chron. 28.21; cf. 2 Kgs 16.8.

5.   2 Chron. 28.22-26; the cultic offence in 2 Kgs 16.10-18 consists of alterations to the Temple to conform with the altar which Ahaz had seen during his visit with Tiglath-pileser rather than worship of the Syrian deities and the shutting of the Temple doors.

6.   2 Chron. 28.27; this contrasts with the notice in 2 Kgs 16.20 that Ahaz was buried with his fathers.

7.   2 Chron. 29.3–30.27; there is no corresponding passage for this extensive account of Hezekiah's cultic action in the *Vorlage* apart from the brief notice of righteousness and reform in 2 Kgs 18.3-4. 2 Chron. 29.3–31.1 comprises two distinct liturgical scenes—the reforming liturgies in 2 Chron. 29.3-36 and the Passover celebration in 2 Chron. 30.1–31.1. Although these two scenes are delineated by their own distinct introductions and conclusions, they are drawn into unity by shared thematic and narrative features, in particular by the progression of reform described within them involving firstly the purification of the Temple from its former uncleanness, then the removal of illegitimate altars from the city and finally the destruction of altars, high places and sacred groves in the territories of Judah, Benjamin, Ephraim and Manasseh.

8.   2 Chron. 31.1; cf. 2 Kgs 18.4. This can be considered as the concluding action of the reform liturgies (Rudolph, *Chronikbücher*, p. 305).

9.   2 Chron. 31.2-21; there is no corresponding passage in the *Vorlage*.

by the divine protection afforded him against the daunting threats of Sennacherib[1] (who is ironically killed by his own sons in the temple of his god),[2] as well as riches and other achievements.[3] However, negative indications have also been included in the Chronistic portrayal of Hezekiah—an ominous note about his pride, for which Hezekiah had to humble himself to avoid the wrath of Yahweh in his day,[4] and the necessity for Yahweh to test him by means of the incident of the Babylonian ambassadors.[5] He is afforded a fitting burial במעלה קברי בני־דויד.[6]

As Hezekiah is one of the cultic high points in the Chronicler's narrative, so Manasseh is one of the deep valleys. His evil deeds, compared to the nations which had been cast out of Palestine to make way for Israel,[7] include the erection of high places, pagan altars and idols,[8] as well as sorcery and divination.[9] His punishment culminated in his personal exile to Babylon, where he humbled himself, and so was brought back to rule in Jerusalem, an exile and change of heart which

1.   2 Chron. 32.1-22; this is a shorter version of the account of this episode which is to be found in 2 Kgs 18.13–19.37. One detail which the Chronicler omits is Hezekiah's depletion of the Temple treasuries and removal of gold from the Temple in order to provide a gift for the king of Assyria (cf. 2 Kgs 18.15-16).

2.   2 Chron. 32.21; cf. 2 Kgs 19.37 which names the assassins but does not specify the relationship between the assassins and their victim. Given the Chronistic concerns with such questions as Temple and dynasty, this end for Sennacherib must be seen as the height of divine judgment visited upon the Assyrian king. The Chronicler may be aware of a Babylonian tradition that Sennacherib died at the hand of one of his sons; cf. J. Gray, *I & II Kings*, p. 696.

3.   2 Chron. 32.23, 27-30; there are no corresponding passages in the *Vorlage*, but cf. 2 Kgs 20.13.

4.   2 Chron. 32.24-26; 2 Kgs 20.1a parallels 2 Chron. 32.24a, but the remainder of this passage is Chronistic.

5.   2 Chron. 32.31; cf. 2 Kgs 20.12-19. The results of the test, though unstated, must be taken to be positive, since Hezekiah has been blessed.

6.   2 Chron. 32.33; the phrase במעלה קברי בני־דויד is lacking in 2 Kgs 20.21. ' "In the ascent"; this literalistic rendering makes no sense. In view of the Chronicler's frequent use of this root to express the superlative (and its use later with the meaning "excellence"), it may be better rendered "in a privileged place amongst"'; Williamson, *1 and 2 Chronicles*, p. 388. Cf. also Rudolph, *Chronikbücher*, p. 314.

7.   2 Chron. 33.2 (|| 2 Kgs 21.2).

8.   2 Chron. 33.3-5, 7 (|| 2 Kgs 21.3-5, 7).

9.   2 Chron. 33.6 (|| 2 Kgs 21.6).

is not narrated in the Deuteronomistic History.[1] Upon his reinstatement, Manasseh engages in a programme of cultic reform and restores the proper sacrifices in the Temple.[2] His burial is apart from the royal tombs, perhaps an indication that Manasseh is more to be remembered for the effects of his apostasy than for his repentance.[3]

Amon continues the cultic infidelities of his father Manasseh, though without the repentance, sacrificing to the idols Manasseh had established.[4] The Chronicler records nothing further about this king than his assassination in his own house; even his burial passes without mention.[5]

The Chronicler's portrayal of Josiah, as in the case of Hezekiah, concentrates on his cultic reform. This is introduced by the statement that Josiah walked in the ways of David[6] and even in his youth began לדרוש לאלהי דויד אביו.[7] The evidence for this dedication to the seeking of Yahweh is to be found in Josiah's eradication of high places and idols, firstly in Jerusalem and Judah and then in the territories of the Northern tribes.[8] This is followed by the task of repairing the Temple,[9] during which the Book of the Law is found.[10] The reform

---

1. 2 Chron. 33.11-13. The cultic verb כנע is used to describe Manasseh's repentance in v. 12.

2. 2 Chron. 33.15-16.

3. 2 Chron. 33.20 (|| 2 Kgs 21.18). Such an interpretation is in keeping with the tone of the summary statement in v. 19. Cf. Virgulin, *Libri delle Cronache*, p. 431.

4. 2 Chron. 33.22-23 (|| 2 Kgs 21.20-22).

5. 2 Chron. 33.24; cf. 2 Kgs 21.23. The burial of Amon in the royal garden is noted in 2 Kgs 21.26.

6. 2 Chron. 34.2 (|| 2 Kgs 22.2).

7. 2 Chron. 34.3; there is no corresponding passage in the *Vorlage*.

8. 2 Chron. 34.3-7; whereas Josiah's cultic reform receives much attention in 2 Kgs 23.4-20, this is placed after the discovery of the Book of the Law in the Deuteronomistic History.

9. 2 Chron. 34.8-13; this passage represents a Chronistic reworking of the material to be found in 2 Kgs 22.3-7, including a heightened place for the cultic personnel, especially in v. 12.

10. 2 Chron. 34.14; there is no corresponding passage in the *Vorlage*, although the fact that the Book of the Law is discovered is stated in 2 Kgs 22.8 (|| 2 Chron. 34.15). Although it is generally conceded that the Book of the Law mentioned in 2 Kings 23 corresponds to the core of Deuteronomy, no such consensus emerges for the work mentioned in the Chronistic parallel. While some maintain that the

continues in the narrative with a covenant-making ceremony which embraces the words written in the Book of the Law,[1] and culminates with a Passover celebration.[2] Although Josiah is killed in battle as a result of his disregard for the Word of God (in the mouth of Neco),[3] his burial is the most splendid of all the royal burials of the sons of David: as he is placed in the royal tombs, all Judah and Jerusalem are in mourning, and the lamentations stem from no less a source than the prophet Jeremiah.[4]

This synopsis of the Chronistic material demonstrates that retribution often invokes the cultic action of a king, be it in terms of faithfulness or unfaithfulness. In order to achieve this, the Chronicler has relied at times upon material already contained in his *Vorlage*, at other times has expanded upon brief notices contained there, and at still other times has given an account which is at variance with the Deuteronomistic History. Although other factors are undeniably present in the workings of retribution for the Chronicler, those monarchs who serve as the outstanding Chronistic examples of reward or

Chronicler has kept the reference to the discovery of some version of Deuteronomy (for example Barnes, *The Books of Chronicles*, p. 282, Slotki, *Chronicles*, p. 329, and Ackroyd, *I & II Chronicles, Ezra, Nehemiah*, p. 202), other commentators suggest that the Chronicler has made a reference to the discovery of the entire Pentateuch. This latter interpretation derives in part from the phrase ויקרא־בו in 2 Chron. 34.18 which is taken to imply that the scroll was too long to be completed at one reading. Cf. Cazelles, *Les livres des Chroniques*, p. 233; Randellini, *Il libro delle Cronache*, p. 485; Michaeli, *Les livres des Chroniques, d'Esdras et de Néhémie*, p. 245. However the Chronistic reference to the Book of the Law is interpreted in terms of existing canonical material, the question of its significance for the Chronicler is a different matter. Chronicles' two previous references to written תורה (2 Chron. 17.9; 25.4) lead the reader to the conclusion that the Chronicler thought of the discovery under Josiah as supplementing the Mosaic traditions which were already available in some type of written form, a conclusion borne out by the various reactions to the discovery which treat of at least some of the material in the recently discovered book as new both to Josiah and to others.

1. 2 Chron. 34.29-32; cf. 2 Kgs 23.1-4.
2. 2 Chron. 35.1-19; this passage is an expansion of the brief notice of the Passover celebration given in 2 Kgs 23.21-23.
3. 2 Chron. 35.22. There is no reference to Neco as bearer of the divine utterance in the brief account of Josiah's death in 2 Kgs 23.29.
4. 2 Chron. 35.24-25; in 2 Kgs 23.30, Josiah's burial in Jerusalem lacks the splendour of the Chronistic version.

punishment, such as Jehoshaphat, Joash, Ahaz, Hezekiah, Manasseh and Josiah, are always portrayed carefully and explicitly in relation to the cultus with the appropriate dues of their cultic action afforded them.

*Chronistic Treatment of the Dynastic Promise
in the Post-Solomonic Narrative*

Flanagan observes that the unity of the Davidic and Solomonic narratives in Chronicles has the effect of postponing the question of the dynasty's endurance until after the Northern schism.[1] This observation finds particular substantiation in those passages where the dynastic promise to David is made to apply first and foremost to his immediate successor[2] (as can be the case in ancient Near Eastern dynastic thought),[3] giving rise to the possibility that its further application to later members of the dynasty is secondary and non-essential. Such passages, which are often linked with indications of the conditionality of the promise,[4] provide a background for observing the dynastic concern in the Chronistic stories of the post-Solomonic kings.

The investigation of the dynastic promise in this section of the Chronistic History cannot be limited to explicit statements concerning that promise. Since the Chronicler has produced his work as a narrative, his thought is often to be sought in the movements of the narrative as a whole, as well as in the movements and statements to be found within the smaller units; North even draws the attention of the interpreter to the importance of the Chronicler's eloquent silences for this dynastic issue as for others.[5]

The first dynastic note in the post-Solomonic period is a dangerous one, as the Chronicler begins the period with the crisis in the Davidic dynasty's rule over Israel, constituted by Israel's rebellion under Jeroboam against the Davidide Rehoboam.[6] Whereas the

---

1. *David's Social Drama: A Hologram of Israel's Early Iron Age*, p. 225.

2. 1 Chron. 17.11-15; 22.7-11; 28.5-7, 10; 29.1; 2 Chron. 6.8-10; 7.17-18.

3. Cf. the evidence given in Halpern, *The Constitution of the Monarchy in Israel*, pp. 45-47.

4. 1 Chron. 22.12-13; 28.7, 9; 2 Chron. 7.17, 19-22.

5. 'Theology of the Chronicler', pp. 376-77.

6. 2 Chron. 10.1-18. Although many commentators presume that the reference to Israel in this episode refers to the Northern tribes, it would seem that, for the Chronicler, this only becomes the case after Rehoboam's failure to conciliate the

Deuteronomistic Historian has prepared his audience for this event by including such relevant material as the civil war David fought against Ishbaal,[1] the sins of Solomon (1 Kgs 11.1-13), and the proleptic revolt of Jeroboam (together with Ahijah's oracle concerning the future kingship of Jeroboam, 1 Kgs 11.26-40), the Chronicler has presented a schism without prior warning. Some commentators find here a direct allusion to the Deuteronomistic account, concluding that the Chronicler presumes a knowledge of the causes given there.[2] However, there are problems with this approach. The Chronicler's reference to the visions of Iddo (2 Chron. 9.30) cannot be a direct reference to the oracle of kingship for Jeroboam since the prophet concerned is named as Ahijah in Kings and, although Ahijah is cited in 2 Chron. 9.30, the name Iddo does not appear in the Deuteronomistic History. This problem is relatively minor, especially since direct reference is made to the oracle of Ahijah in 2 Chron. 10.15.[3] A more fundamental problem remains: while the Deuteronomistic viewpoint attributes the schism to Solomon's sins, the Chronicler has been resolute in portraying a sinless Solomon in contrast to his *Vorlage*;[4] acceptance of the Deuteronomistic line of causality for the Northern schism would undermine the Chronistic picture of Solomon and his reign which has been so carefully presented. A further fundamental consideration arises from the amount of material that the Chronicler has

grievances; cf. Williamson, *1 and 2 Chronicles*, p. 238. Williamson's point receives validation from the use of Israel in 2 Chron. 10.17 (ובני ישראל הישבים בערי יהודה) and serves as a warning against interpreting even those Chronistic passages which rely most heavily upon the *Vorlage* as if they were still being presented as part of the Deuteronomistic History.

1.   2 Sam. 2.8–4.12. Ishbaal is, of course, referred to as איש בשׁת in the MT of Samuel.

2.   For example Curtis and Madsen, *A Critical and Exegetical Commentary on the Books of Chronicles*, p. 363; Rudolph, *Chronikbücher*, p. 227; Randellini, *Il libro delle Cronache*, p. 353; Michaeli, *Les livres des Chroniques, d'Esdras et de Néhémie*, p. 173.

3.   However, there is no indication there to place Ahijah's oracle in Solomon's reign nor that its contents imply that the schism is a result of the failures of Solomon, as in the case of 1 Kgs 11.31-39, especially in the Septuagint and Vulgate. There is nothing in Chronicles to prevent the oracle having been delivered even as late as the time of Rehoboam.

4.   As in the contrast, for instance, between 2 Chron. 8.11 and 1 Kgs 11.1-8. Cf. Braun, 'The Message of Chronicles: Rally 'Round the Temple', p. 508.

repeated from his *Vorlage*: the presumption must be that the
Chronicler reproduces all the material that is important for his interpretation of history. Although the material from the Deuteronomistic
Vorlage that he has not included is often significant for a close reading
of Chronicles, it is significant precisely as omission; the meaning of an
episode in the Chronistic History cannot be imported from the very
material that the author has excluded from his historical re-
presentation.

If the evidence from the Deuteronomistic History concerning the
reasons for the schism is judged inadmissible in discerning the
Chronistic interpretation of this tragic event, then Solomon and his
sins can no longer be seen as the cause of division in the Chronicler's
eyes.[1] The Chronicler's clearest statement of causality simply ascribes
the event to Yahweh's action;[2] however, the Chronistic doctrine of
retribution encourages the interpreter to seek a further cause for the
divine action in human failure. While Jeroboam himself is undoubtedly portrayed as more culpable by the Chronicler,[3] divine acquies-
cence in the event signifies that those who are the victims of the rebellion, Rehoboam or Judah, have deserved the rebellion in the
Chronicler's eyes. The underlying blame for the schism in Chronicles
devolves, without moralizing emphasis, on Rehoboam for his folly
and his failure to be concerned for the whole people of Israel.[4]

Although the Chronicler has not completely set aside his doctrine of
immediate retribution in his treatment of the schism, the lack of clear
and emphatic definition of the human factor in this chain of retribution throws the emphasis upon the schism as act of Yahweh rather
than upon the human act which precipitated it; this emphasis can be

1. Mosis, *Untersuchungen zur Theologie des chronistischen Geschichtswerkes*,
p. 169; Coggins, *The First and Second Books of the Chronicles*, p. 183.
2. 2 Chron. 11.4; cf. 1 Kgs 12.24.
3. Cf. 2 Chron. 13.6-7, for which no parallel exists in the *Vorlage*. See
Ackroyd, *I & II Chronicles, Ezra, Nehemiah*, p. 125; Becker, *2 Chronik*, pp. 40-
41. It should be noted that in the account of the events leading to the schism,
Jeroboam is noticeably active, but no blame attaches to him (unless one reads the
verb פשע in 2 Chron. 10.19, which is applied to Israel and not just to Jeroboam, as a
condemnation); the evidence of his guilt is given later at 2 Chron. 11.14-15 which
speaks of Jeroboam's illicit cult.
4. Cf. Williamson, *1 and 2 Chronicles*, pp. 238-40; McConville, *Chronicles*,
pp. 152-53.

seen in the Chronicler's two references, taken from his *Vorlage*, to Yahweh's action in bringing about the schism.[1] Those who see the Chronicler as evoking the familiarity of his audience with the Deuteronomistic History tend to find no real significance in these references.[2] However, it must be noted that, while the Chronicler has kept the Deuteronomistic Historian's note of divine causality, he has discarded the emphatic portrayal of his *Vorlage* of the human factors which led to this turn of events.[3] By de-emphasizing the retribution theme of his own outlook as well as by avoiding the causal explanation to be found in the Deuteronomistic *Vorlage*, the Chronicler has shown that Yahweh remains profoundly free in bestowing kingship, both upon Davidides and elsewhere. It is thus significant that, as a divine act affecting kingship, the schism in Chronicles is reminiscent of the turning of the kingdom from Saul to David;[4] it is also noteworthy that the Chronicler does not consider the Davidic promise to have been violated during the reign of Rehoboam by the removal of the majority of the nation from the rule of the Davidide.[5] The opening episode of the Chronicler's post-Solomonic history, therefore, can be seen to portray Yahweh as limiting the dynastic promise by his own free act without the expected emphasis on a human failure which provokes such a startling turn of events.

A more positive and explicit reference to the dynastic promise is made at the beginning of the speech of Abijah, for which the Chronicler owes no debt to the Deuteronomistic History:

1.   2 Chron. 10.15; 11.4 (|| 1 Kgs 12.15, 24).

2.   Curtis and Madsen, *A Critical and Exegetical Commentary on the Books of Chronicles*, p. 363; Harvey-Jellie, *Chronicles*, p. 227; Michaeli, *Les livres des Chroniques, d'Esdras et de Néhémie*, pp. 172-73.

3.   1 Kgs 11.9-13, 30-35.

4.   McConville, *Chronicles*, p. 152, sees such a correspondence between the Saul narrative and the schism in the theme of the loss of land. P.R. Ackroyd, 'The Chronicler as Exegete', p. 9, sees a connection between these two episodes implicit in the Chronicler's use of the verb סבב.

5.   Japhet, *The Ideology of the Book of Chronicles and its Place in Biblical Thought*, pp. 293-94, observes that, through emigrations from the Northern Kingdom, the Chronicler retains a limited rule of the Davidide over people from all Israel: 'The people remain one even after the monarchy is split in two, and all its elements and tribes continue to be represented in the kingdom of Judah'.

> Abijah stood upon the mountain of Zemaraim which is in the mountains of
> Ephraim and said: 'Listen to me, Jeroboam and all Israel. Is it not yours to
> know that Yahweh, the God of Israel, gave the kingdom to David over
> Israel forever, to him and to his sons—a covenant of salt'
> (2 Chron. 13.4-5).

A further reference to the Davidic rule proper to the Chronicler is
made later in the speech:

> And now you intend to be strong before the Kingdom of Yahweh in the
> hand of the sons of David; and you are a great crowd, and with you are
> the calves of gold which Jeroboam made as gods for you (2 Chron. 13.8).

For von Rad, to cite but one example, this speech is a proof of the
Chronicler's unequivocal messianic hope;[1] however, von Rad has
expressed elsewhere his opinion that the Chronicler is an author of
limited ability,[2] and such a low opinion may have prevented him from
perceiving that the Chronicler has stated his outlook with some subtlety. When more than a superficial reading of the Davidic references
in Abijah's speech is allowed, it becomes clear that the Chronicler has
not abandoned his view that the kingdom still belongs to Yahweh and
is held by the Davidides only on trust.[3]

The phrase ברית מלח, 'covenant of salt', deserves special consideration. It is usually taken to indicate a perpetual covenant, and the
justification for this interpretation is often given by referring the
reader to similar usages in either Lev. 2.13 or Num. 18.19;[4] this
interpretation has also been proposed on the basis of the common
bond created by a common meal as among the Arab tribes, although
this evidence is not as clear cut as it might at first appear.[5] The

---

1.   *Das Geschichtsbild des chronistischen Werkes*, p. 124.

2.   '. . . we must therefore go on to ask whether it is likely that the Chronicler
himself invented this mode of instruction, expressly for the purpose of putting over
his own point of view. But he really is quite the last person whom we should credit
with the creation of anything, let alone a new literary form!' (von Rad, 'The Levitical
Sermon in I & II Chronicles', p. 277).

3.   Compare 2 Chron. 13.8 with 1 Chron. 17.14 or 1 Chron. 29.11. See De
Vries, 'The Schema of Dynastic Endangerment in Chronicles', p. 64.

4.   For example Cazelles, *Les livres des Chroniques*, p. 162; Ackroyd, *I & II
Chronicles, Ezra, Nehemiah*, p. 132; Mangan, *1–2 Chronicles, Ezra, Nehemiah*,
p. 98.

5.   So Curtis and Madsen, *A Critical and Exegetical Commentary on the Books
of Chronicles*, p. 375; however, the common meal bond among the Arabs as

covenant of salt in Num. 18.19 seems to signify a permanent covenant, as is indicated by the word עולם which follows the phrase; it is another question whether the addition of עולם is a pleonasm or the addition of a further concept into the understanding of ברית מלח. A similar question can be raised about the Chronicler's use of לעולם in the phrase immediately preceding his mention of ברית מלח.[1] The repetition of the mixing of מלח ברית with sacrifices in Lev. 2.13 might be taken as an indication that a covenant of salt needs constant renewal in order to be perpetuated.[2]

It is possible to construe the significance of the phrase ברית מלח in Num. 18.19 somewhat differently, taking the primary significance to be rooted in the bond that arises from a common meal and not in a notion of permanency. As a result of their service, the priests receive a portion of the sacrifices as specified in Num. 18.8-19; the constant consumption of these by the priests and their families is the perpetuation of a bond with Yahweh in whose portion they share. The bond ultimately depends on the liturgical role which the priests have been called upon to exercise in Israel, and the perpetuity of the bond is linked to the perpetuity of their function.

The Chronicler may have a similar significance in mind for his use of ברית מלח in 2 Chron. 13.5, even though there is no explicit reference to a common meal.[3] Yahweh has truly given the kingship to

expounded by W.R. Smith, *Lectures on the Religion of the Semites*, pp. 269-71 (the authority referred to by Curtis and Madsen for this approach), need not imply a permanent bond at all. Thus it often refers to a bond that lasts as long as the salt is in the stomach and so needs to be renewed at periods varying from 24 hours to three and a third days. M. Noth, *Leviticus*, p. 29, also refers to the Arab practice in interpreting Lev. 2.13, but makes no mention of a permanent relationship in that context.

1. For the difficulties posed by the word עולם itself, see J. Barr, *Biblical Words for Time*, pp. 122-26, 191.

2. Cf. Smith, *Lectures on the Religion of the Semites*, p. 270.

3. One cannot exclude the possibility that the Chronicler did, in fact, mean to imply the type of bond that resulted from a common meal. If references such as 2 Chron. 30.24 and 35.7 indicate that the Chronicler is aware of Ezekiel's injunction on the prince to supply Temple offerings (Ezek. 45.17; cf. Coggins, *The First and Second Books of the Chronicles*, p. 300), then the Chronicler would also be aware of Ezekiel's provision for the prince to eat bread before Yahweh in Ezek. 44.3. Assuming that Ezekiel's provisions are not innovations but a scaling down of the traditional place of the king in the cultus, it is not necessary to assert that the

David and his house; their functioning in this role brings about the
perpetuation of a bond which can be described as ברית מלח; as in the
case of the Aaronide priests in Num. 18.19, the bond arises from a
function with a cultic dimension,[1] and the Chronicler may be using the
expression to emphasize this aspect of the bond. A notion of eternity
which would imply a Davidic restoration is thus not necessarily contained in the phrase, not even when considered with the preceding
לעולם, and would indeed be excluded if the Chronicler saw that the
cultic function of the Davidic kings had fulfilled its role and come to
its conclusion.

This cultic interpretation of ברית מלח receives some substantiation
from the text of Abijah's speech itself, for it is apparent that the
Chronicler's main indictment of Jeroboam and Israel is that by abandoning the Davidic rule they have abandoned the proper cult; as a
result, the Northern Kingdom lacked the legitimate cultic personnel,
the legitimate sacrifices and the legitimate cultic equipment. Their
defeat would come through the very cultic personnel and instruments
which they lacked (2 Chron. 13.12, 14). Abijah's confidence does not
stem from his position as the descendant of David so much as from the
loyalty that his kingdom has shown towards the legitimate cultus.[2]

When these two elements of the Abijah speech are taken together,
they can be viewed as part of the larger ancient Near Eastern awareness that the king who is faithful to his cultic responsibilities has his
rule divinely established, while the rule of the faithless monarch is
liable to divine subversion.[3] Abijah, whose own words portray him as
a king faithful to the Jerusalem cultus, can rely upon his Davidic lineage and make reference to the dynastic promise. Whether these
words would be as valid for the Chronicler in the mouth of a less

Chronicler has Ezekiel's cultic provisions in mind in associating the king with a
sacred meal of fellowship.

1.   Note also the cultic context in which מלח ברית occurs in Lev. 2.13.
2.   Harvey-Jellie, *Chronicles*, p. 234.
3.   For example, cf. A.L. Oppenheim, 'Nabonidus and his God', p. 562; *idem*,
'Cyrus (557–529)', p. 315; W.L. Moran, 'Divine Revelations', p. 625. In the
prophetic text edited and translated by Moran, the god Adad promises the Mari king
'throne upon throne, house upon house, territory upon territory, city upon city; even
the land from east to west will I give him' in return for a hereditary property which
should be seen as land given either for cultic use or for the support of the cultus; cf.
A. Malamat, 'A Forerunner of Biblical Prophecy: The Mari Documents', p. 36.

faithful monarch is a very different question; the defeat of Ahaz and his forces at the hands of the Northern Kingdom shows that the dynastic promise alone cannot guarantee success when an unfaithful Davidic king faces a similar challenge.[1]

While no overt reference to the dynastic promise is made in the Chronistic narration of Asa's reign, the beginning of Azariah's oracle is of interest in this regard:

> And he went out before Asa and said to him, 'Listen to me, Asa and all Judah and Benjamin. Yahweh is with you while you are with him, and if you seek him, he will be found for you. But if you abandon him, he will abandon you' (2 Chron. 15.2).

The language used in the admonition to Solomon in 1 Chron. 28.9 in the context of Solomon's divine election[2] has been echoed and re-addressed to the Davidic king, together with his subjects. While it is true that the oracle lacks specific and essential connection to the narratives which surround it[3] (and may therefore be intended by the Chronicler as a generic exhortation addressed to the audience of his own time),[4] Azariah's oracle has been situated in a narrative flow which reveals the Chronicler's understanding of the oracle's message:[5] being with Yahweh and seeking Yahweh entails the cultic actions of reform and engagement in the Jerusalem cultus, as demonstrated by the immediate response of Azariah's audience (2 Chron. 15.8-15). This oracle, through its initial echo of the admonition to Solomon, indicates that the Chronicler's outlook has broadened the Davidic cultic task beyond the Davidide alone; the cultic task is addressed to the entire people, albeit with the Davidide at their head, a process which the Chronicler had already begun in his narrative of David.[6]

---

1.   2 Chron. 28.5-8; this episode has no parallel in the *Vorlage*.

2.   אם־תדרשנו ימצא לך ואם־תעזבנו יזניחך לעד. Both 1 Chron. 28.9 and 2 Chron. 15.2 are without parallel in the *Vorlage*.

3.   Curtis and Madsen, *A Critical and Exegetical Commentary on the Books of Chronicles*, p. 384; von Rad, 'The Levitical Sermon in I & II Chronicles', p. 271.

4.   Harvey-Jellie, *Chronicles*, pp. 241-42; Rudolph, *Chronikbücher*, p. 245; Michaeli, *Les livres des Chroniques, d'Esdras et de Néhémie*, p. 184; Virgulin, *Libri delle Cronache*, p. 321. Von Rad, 'The Levitical Sermon in I & II Chronicles', pp. 270-71, considers Azariah's oracle a key example of the Levitical sermon form.

5.   Dillard, *2 Chronicles*, p. 120.

6.   Cf. 1 Chron. 28.21. It might also be noted that in the Davidic narratives, the dynastic promise is linked to the cultic task demanded of the House of David; cf. 1

Although the reign of Jehoshaphat contains a note of high praise for the king with specific reference to David (but without specific mention of the dynastic promise,[1] the beginning of the narrative concerned with his son Jehoram pertains more explicitly to the matter of the dynastic promise:

> And Jehoram rose over the kingdom of his father; he was strong and he killed all his brothers with the sword and even some of the princes of Israel. Jehoram was thirty-two years old when he began to rule, and he was king for eight years in Jerusalem. He walked in the way of the kings of Israel, doing just as the House of Ahab did, for the daughter of Ahab was his wife; and he did evil in the eyes of Yahweh. But Yahweh was not willing to destroy the House of David because of the covenant which he made with David, and according to what he had said—that he would give a lamp for him and for his sons all days (2 Chron. 21.4-7).

In 2 Chron. 21.4, the Chronicler introduces the element of Jehoram's mass fratricide which has no correspondent in the Deuteronomistic *Vorlage*; through this episode, a new dimension is given to the possible endangerment of the continuation of the Davidic dynasty,[2] a theme that is also addressed by 21.7.[3] This new dimension is tantamount to a reintroduction of the possibility of endangerment which was raised obliquely by the division of the Davidic kingdom under Rehoboam.[4]

In 2 Chron. 21.7, the Chronicler has expressed the importance for him of the continuation of the dynastic line; this verse is often taken as a statement of the Chronicler's belief that the Davidic line will be maintained.[5] However, another possibility must be considered in approaching this verse—that the Chronicler is indeed stating that it

Chron. 17.11-12; 22.9-10; 28.2-7.

1. 2 Chron. 17.3.

2. Williamson, *1 and 2 Chronicles*, p. 304.

3. 2 Chron. 21.7 echoes 2 Kgs 8.19 with notable differences. Thus, whereas the *Vorlage* indicates that Yahweh is unwilling to destroy Judah, the Chronicler specifies that Yahweh is unwilling to destroy the House of David; whereas the *Vorlage* states that this is because of דוד עבדו, the Chronicler says that it is because of the covenant made with David; the conjunction in the Chronicler's ולבניו may be purely stylistic or may represent an error in the transmission of the MT of Kings (cf. *BHS*, p. 633).

4. Cf. 2 Chron. 10.1-18; 11.4.

5. Curtis and Madsen, *A Critical and Exegetical Commentary on the Books of Chronicles*, p. 414; Myers, *II Chronicles*, p. 121; Virgulin, *Libri delle Cronache*, p. 356.

is important for the Davidic dynasty to continue beyond Jehoram, but not necessarily that the dynasty continue in power indefinitely. The interpretative crux lies in the referent of the word נֵיר, which is sometimes seen as referring either to the Davidic dynasty itself[1] or to its rule over Judah.[2] A different suggestion has been made for this term, however;[3] it may be an allusion to the light which symbolizes the presence of Yahweh in his Temple[4] and to that relationship between Yahweh and the dynasty of which the Temple is evidence.[5] An interpretation which sees a reference to the permanent establishment of the Temple in the Chronistic use of this image has one definite advantage over the suggestion that the Chronicler has understood נֵיר to refer to the dynasty itself, since the lamp is stated as having been given for the sake of David's sons who themselves constitute the dynasty. Such an interpretation also conforms to the Chronicler's presentation of the Davidic covenant as the instrument through which the Temple is granted to David and to Israel. Accordingly, Yahweh is shown to be unwilling to destroy the House of David because the covenant which ensures that the Temple will endure as a lamp for David and his sons has not yet been fulfilled.

A further aspect of this passage merits attention. The Chronicler has already narrated the action of Jehoram which endangers the dynasty; the statement in 2 Chron. 21.7 (ולא־אבה יהוה להשחית את־בית דויד)[6] can thus be seen as implying that Yahweh himself has been involved in this action, even though he stops short of the actual destruction of the dynasty. In this way, Yahweh's specific concern with and control over matters of kingship is once more asserted in the text.[7]

---

1. De Vries, 'The Schema of Dynastic Endangerment in Chronicles', pp. 64-65; *idem, 1 and 2 Chronicles*, p. 333.

2. This interpretation follows from its use in 1 Kgs 11.36. Cf. Dillard, *2 Chronicles*, p. 166. It should be noted that the Deuteronomistic Historian places some emphasis on the lamp for David being established in Jerusalem in this verse.

3. Cf. Coppens, *Le messianisme royal*, p. 51; Gray, *I & II Kings*, p. 297.

4. Cf. Exod. 27.20, 1 Sam. 3.3 in which the perpetual lamp of the sanctuary is referred to by the cognate word נֵר; the plural נֵרֹת is the usual term used to designate the lamps of the Menorah (cf. Exod. 25.37 and 30.7-8).

5. The cognate word נֵר is used in Ps. 132.17 where the context points to the Temple as the intended referent of the image. See Anderson, *Psalms*, p. 885.

6. Cf. 2 Kgs 8.19 which reads ולא־אבה יהוה להשחית את־יהודה.

7. Cf. also 1 Chron. 10.14; 2 Chron. 10.15; 11.4.

The fortunes of the dynasty continue to deteriorate in the Chronicler's account of Jehoram when, at the end of his reign and in accordance with the warning given in Elijah's letter,[1] all his sons were taken or slain in battle except Ahaziah (or Jehoahaz), the youngest.[2]

The death of Ahaziah after a reign of only one year brings the Davidic dynasty to a lower point still. The Chronicler remarks that Ahaziah's downfall[3] was מאלהים, and notes that he fell in the slaughter of the House of Ahab by Jehu אשר משחו יהוה להכרית את־בית אחאב.[4] The verse (and its subsequent narrative) identifies Ahaziah's dynastic heritage as much with Ahab, whose seed God eradicates, as with David.[5] In the face of this identification, Ahaziah cannot survive. The Chronicler feels it necessary to state that Ahaziah's downfall is not simply an accident of being caught in the crossfire; his death is מאלהים.

The lowest point on the spiral is reached when Athaliah slays the royal seed and puts an effective, if temporary, end to the rule of the Davidic dynasty, reminiscent of the fate of the House of Saul.[6] After a Davidic lacuna of more than six years, however, the Davidic line is restored, as the Chronicler narrates in a passage teeming with dynastic possibilities (2 Chron. 22.10–23.21): even when the Israelite princess and Judaean queen mother appears to have succeeded in eliminating the Davidic line and usurping the throne, one surviving Davidide is brought to the throne to fulfil the ancient promise.

1.   2 Chron. 21.12-15; there is no parallel for Elijah's letter in the *Vorlage*.

2.   2 Chron. 21.17; 22.1. See Randellini, *Il libro delle Cronache*, pp. 401-402, on the possibility of different sources for the apparent differences between these verses. There is no corresponding account of such an incident in the *Vorlage*.

3.   'Downfall' presumes that the *hapax legomenon* תבוסה (construct case) in MT is correct. Several authors suggest emendations based on the root סבב and bring this verse into conformity with the language of divine action in relation to the kingship used in 1 Chron. 10.14 and 2 Chron. 10.15. See Rudolph, *Chronikbücher*, p. 268; Ackroyd, *I & II Chronicles, Ezra, Nehemiah*, p. 156; Williamson, *1 and 2 Chronicles*, p. 312.

4.   2 Chron. 22.7. There is no parallel of this verse in the *Vorlage*.

5.   This identification flows not only through Ahaziah's physical descent and his relation to the House of Ahab (or, better, the House of Omri) through his mother Athaliah, but especially through his use of the House of Ahab as advisers. Cf. 2 Chron. 22.3-4; Michaeli, *Les livres des Chroniques, d'Esdras et de Néhémie*, p. 201.

6.   2 Chron. 22.10 (ǁ 2 Kgs 11.1). See Mosis, *Untersuchungen zur Theologie des chronistischen Geschichtswerkes*, p. 180.

It is well to note that the Deuteronomistic Historian (upon whom the Chronicler has depended greatly for the narration of this episode)[1] has already treated this story as a fulfilment of the Davidic promise illustrating one of the foundations of his theology.[2] It is also significant that the Deuteronomistic account of the coronation of Joash undeniably describes an action with liturgical elements, especially in 2 Kgs 11.12 which notes that the new king is crowned, presented with the testimony, anointed and proclaimed in the Temple.[3] This liturgical aspect is hardly surprising, since both biblical texts[4] and texts from other ancient Near Eastern settings[5] indicate that the inauguration of the king was a liturgy, sometimes linked with the king's divine sonship.[6] However, the Chronicler has built further on the considerable base that his *Vorlage* has provided. The greater involvement of priests and Levites,[7] the heightened portrayal of Jehoiada,[8] the designation of

1. The Chronicler has made many changes, but most of them are minor. Only 2 Chron. 23.19 consists of material entirely unique to the Chronicler, and not a single complete verse of the *Vorlage* has been omitted.

2. C. Levin, *Der Sturz der Königin Atalja*, pp. 11-12; Conroy, *1–2 Samuel, 1–2 Kings*, p. 213.

3. The royal inauguration cannot be simply limited to these elements in the text of Kings; Halpern, *The Constitution of the Monarchy in Israel*, pp. 140-41, and Levin, *Der Sturz der Königin Atalja*, pp. 93-94, rightly include the elements of covenant-making in 2 Kgs 11.17 and enthronement in 2 Kgs 11.19 as part of the ritual of king-making. However, the portrayal of the crowning and anointing of Aaron as part of his being installed as a high priest in Exod. 29.6-7 and Lev. 8.9-12 indicates that these two parts of the ritual can be seen as the central acts of kingly inauguration, so central that they are later applied to the high priest.

4. For example 1 Kgs 1.32-40; Psalms 2 and 110. Although the inauguration of Solomon is not a Temple liturgy (since the Temple has yet to be built), it is portrayed as a cultic activity involving the priest Zadok who anoints the new king (1 Kgs 1.39).

5. Cf. Frankfort, *Kingship and the Gods*, pp. 245-48 and the texts there cited.

6. For example Wilson, 'The Divine Nomination of Thut-Mose III', pp. 446-47. Note also Ps. 2.6-7.

7. For example the statement that Jehoshabeath was the wife of Jehoiada in 2 Chron. 22.11 or the heightened role of the priests and Levites in 2 Chron. 23.4-7.

8. Among many small additions to Jehoiada's role, two slight textual changes introduced by the Chronicler might be noted as examples of the more exalted picture of the priest. Firstly, the Chronicler names Jehoiada and his sons as those who anoint the king in 2 Chron. 23.11 (the verb is without an explicit subject in 2 Kgs 11.12). The second is the alteration of 2 Kgs 11.17 in 2 Chron. 23.16 to the effect

the assembly as קהל (2 Chron. 23.3), as well as the use of musical instruments (2 Chron. 23.13) and rejoicing (2 Chron. 23.18, 21) and praise (2 Chron. 23.13), all show that the episode is the story of a liturgy, not of a political coup. Although the Davidic element is not lacking, it has been made subordinate to the concern with the Temple liturgy in much the same way that Joash has been made subordinate to the priest Jehoiada. The Temple, through its cultus and especially through its personnel, is shown to be the means through which the Davidic dynasty is rescued from impending extinction. The careful nuancing that the Chronicler gives to his narration indicates both the essential relationship that exists between king and cultus in his theology and the relative importance that he assigns to the reigning monarch and the Temple.

Although the effect of the Chronistic treatment of this episode is to underscore the necessity of the Davidic reign (at least for the period under consideration),[1] a striking connection between the Temple and the Davidic dynasty has been made. Just as the Temple emerged from the Davidic dynasty, now in the incident of Joash's enthronement the Temple cultus saves the dynasty from permanent eradication and restores the dynasty to the Jerusalem throne. However, the supremacy of the Temple cultus in the Chronicler's concerns may be discerned in the contrast between the noble end of the priest Jehoiada, buried among the kings (2 Chron. 24.16), and the ignominious end of Joash who is assassinated and buried outside the royal tombs (2 Chron. 24.25), a contrast which is not to be found in the *Vorlage*. Moreover, before Joash's death the people were issued with a prophetic condemnation couched in language associated with the conditionality of the

that Jehoiada becomes the covenant partner of the king.

1. 2 Chron. 23.3. Some commentators point to this phrase as an indication that the Chronicler wrote in earnest hope of a Davidic restoration; see for example von Rad, *Das Geschichtsbild des chronistischen Werkes*, p. 124; Williamson, 'Eschatology in Chronicles', pp. 147-48, and Dillard, *2 Chronicles*, p. 181. However, this interpretation is only necessary when the passage is removed from its narrative context. The problem for the Chronicler's Jehoiada is not created by an empty throne, but by a non-Davidic usurper; this might account for the emphasis on בן־המלך which the Chronicler has indicated by the word order of the sentence (cf. GKC p. 455). The Chronicler obviously accepts that as long as there is a king of Israel/Judah, it should be a Davidide; this does not necessitate that Davidic kingship itself was essentially a permanent institution in the Chronicler's theology.

dynastic promise: כי־עזבתם את־יהוה ויעזב אתכם.[1] This prophetic condemnation (and Joash's callous reaction to it) suggests why the
Davidide who had been placed on the throne by Yahweh's promise can
end as a man assassinated by his own household and by the judgment
of Yahweh.[2]

After the Chronistic treatment of Joash, concern with the dynastic
promise seems to wane in this section of the Chronicler's narrative.
The promise is not referred to explicitly again, and even though
Yahweh is still seen to bring about the downfall of an individual king
such as Amaziah,[3] the danger to the dynasty is not emphasized as it
was in the reigns of Jehoram and Ahaziah.[4] The Chronicler's concern
with the dynastic theme is evident in the prominence and careful construction that he affords the statements and narratives which reflect
the dynastic promise; however, while the statements are positive in
tone, the narrative is largely negative, showing the dynasty surviving
by the thin and ultimately unworthy thread of Joash. The sudden disappearance of this dynastic theme from prominence in the Chronistic
history in the middle of the post-Solomonic period indicates that the
dynastic promise was subordinate, both in the Chronicler's theology
and in his perception of history, to an even greater concern.

The Story of the Temple and its Cultus from Rehoboam to Josiah
Chronistic texts dealing with the accession of Solomon demonstrate
that an essential element in his election is the construction of the
Temple edifice,[5] just as the Temple itself is an important part of the

1.   2 Chron. 24.20. Cf. 1 Chron. 28.9; 2 Chron. 15.2. None of these three texts
find corresponding texts in the *Vorlage*.
2.   This is implied in the dying imprecation of Zechariah given in 2 Chron. 24.22
(ירא יהוה וידרש), and perhaps also by the Gentile parentage (possibly reflecting the
book of Ezra) identified for the assassins in 2 Chron. 24.26, since Gentiles are often
used by the Chronicler in the divine chastisement of erring monarchs. Cf.
M.P. Graham, 'A Connection Proposed between II Chr 24,26 and Ezra 9–10',
pp. 256-58; Coggins, *The First and Second Books of the Chronicles*, p. 242.
3.   2 Chron. 25.16, 27-28.
4.   De Vries, 'The Schema of Dynastic Endangerment in Chronicles', pp. 71-
72, suggests that the assassination of Amaziah is the concluding note of an epilogue
to the theme of dynastic endangerment which culminated in the massacre by Athaliah.
5.   For example 1 Chron. 22.10-11; 28.5-6, 10; 2 Chron. 2.11; 6.4-10, 15.
Braun, 'Solomon, the Chosen Temple Builder: The Significance of 1 Chronicles 22,
28, and 29 for the Theology of Chronicles', pp. 581-90.

promise given to David in the oracle of Nathan (1 Chron. 17.12). However, the mere construction of the edifice does not itself exhaust the ancient Near Eastern notion of founding a temple;[1] the ancient Near Eastern texts further indicate that the responsibility for the temple, its sacrifices and its maintenance continues well past the act of construction.[2] It is therefore to be expected that the Chronicler, who has already established in his narrative an essential link between monarch and Temple akin to the general patterns of the ancient Near East and a concern with temple foundation which goes far beyond the erection of the edifice,[3] should continue the story of the fortunes of the Jerusalem Temple under the monarchs as part of his monarchical history.[4] Outlining the nature and narrative of the continuing relationship of king to Temple in the Chronistic work gives the focus to this part of the study.

The opportunities that modern discoveries have given exegetes to understand the biblical traditions against the wider background of the ancient Near East have sometimes undermined former scholarly observations; among these must be listed the suggestion of Wellhausen that the Chronicler has punished a king such as Joash for interfering with the Mosaic arrangements for the cultus.[5] However, in this suggestion, Wellhausen has made the useful observation that the post-Solomonic kings in Chronicles do change the cultic arrangements.[6] These monarchs act as the authoritative regulators of the Temple

1. This is clear from the pattern proposed by Kapelrud, 'Temple Building, a Task for Gods and Kings', p. 62. One might note in particular Kapelrud's seventh element which includes the fixing of norms and the eighth and ninth elements which deal with the temple dedication.

2. For example, cf. J.A. Wilson, 'The Divine Nomination of an Ethiopian King', pp. 447-48; Sachs, 'Temple Program for the New Year's Festivals at Babylon', p. 334; Oppenheim, 'Cyrus (557–529)', p. 315; *idem*, 'Antiochus Soter (280–262/1)', p. 317.

3. This is especially evident in the listing of the contents of the Davidic תבנית in 1 Chron. 28.11-19.

4. The Deuteronomistic History was also concerned with the kings in relationship to the Temple, and so it is only natural that many of the references that the Chronicler makes to the Temple and its cultus have been drawn from his *Vorlage*.

5. *Prolegomena to the History of Ancient Israel*, p. 200.

6. Wellhausen himself denies this elsewhere with relation to Josiah, and interprets Josiah's reforms as the simple reintroduction of Mosaic arrangements; *Prolegomena to the History of Ancient Israel*, p. 203.

cultus who derive their authority from their royal position; they are not simple guardians of the Temple, but heirs to its founders.

Since the Chronicler has shown the תבנית of David to have been implemented by Solomon, the post-Solomonic monarchs no longer face the *Urzeit* task of temple construction, even though they do bear the continuing burden of temple maintenance common to ancient Near Eastern kings. However, one major task in forming the Temple cultus has not yet been addressed in the narrative, and that is the full establishment of the festivals and their celebration in the Temple. The Chronicler displays a concern to place the festal celebrations known to his own community back into the liturgical life of the pre-exilic community[1] as he uses some of the faithful post-Solomonic kings in bringing his own liturgical experience into the pre-exilic era.

The relationship between the post-Solomonic kings and the Temple cultus has a negative aspect as well as a positive one: just as he shows the progress of the Temple and its cultus in his work, the Chronicler also sketches a contrasting movement towards the exile through the unfaithfulness of Judah and its rulers.[2] Some of the material relating to the Chronicler's theme of retribution which is cast in terms of the Temple provides the reader with a continuing saga of threats to the Holy Place and assaults upon its sanctity; these threats and assaults arise because of the actions of the kings who should have been its royal guardians. These two aspects, positive and negative, of the royal relationship to the Temple and its cultus are woven together in the narrative through the Chronicler's concern with the sacred vessels, the cultic personnel, the sacrifices, festivals and the Temple building itself.

In the reign of Rehoboam, the first post-Solomonic king, the Chronicler notes that the Temple is looted by Shishak of Egypt who removes various Temple treasures, including the gold shields of

---

1. H. Cancik, 'Das judische Fest: Ein Versuch zu Form und Religion des chronistischen Geschichtswerkes', p. 333; Weinberg, 'Das Eigengut in den Chronikbüchern', p. 174.

2. Mosis, *Untersuchungen zur Theologie des chronistischen Geschichtswerkes*, pp. 30-39; Ackroyd, 'The Chronicler as Exegete', p. 3. Torrey, *The Chronicler's History of Israel*, pp. xxv-xxviii, goes so far as to suggest that the whole purpose of the Chronicler was to invent an exile which had never taken place, in order to justify an existing social stratification of his own day.

Solomon.[1] The Chronicler gives his own interpretation to this episode
by linking it to the unfaithfulness of Rehoboam and the people and to
the consequent abandonment of them by Yahweh.[2]

The Chronistic account of the reign of Asa divides the reign into a
time of faithfulness and blessing and a time of faithlessness and mis-
fortune, using a pattern characteristic of the Chronicler's outlook and
style.[3] The positive narrative of Asa notes that ויבא את־קדשי אביו
וקדשיו בית האלהים כסף וזהב וכלים.[4] However, if the Temple benefits
from the good period of Asa's reign, it also suffers from his
unfaithfulness, for Asa takes treasures from the Temple to persuade
Ben-hadad to break his treaty with Baasa.[5] Whereas in the
Deuteronomistic History, Asa's reliance upon Ben-hadad, which
included his impoverishment of the Temple, is part of a successful
operation (1 Kgs 15.18-22), the Chronicler makes it the cause of a
divine condemnation revealed through prophetic oracle (2 Chron.
16.7-10).

The Chronistic narrative of Asa's predecessor Abijah demonstrates
much cultic interest without making explicit reference to any
significant development in the story of the Temple and its cultus. A
similar situation arises with the Chronicler's narrative concerning
Asa's successors Jehoshaphat and Jehoram.[6]

---

1.   2 Chron. 12.9-11. This incident depends upon the *Vorlage* at 1 Kgs 14.26-
28.
2.   2 Chron. 12.1-8. This material is proper to the Chronicler, but cf. 1 Kgs
14.22-24.
3.   Dillard, 'The Reign of Asa (2 Chronicles 14–16): An Example of the
Chronicler's Theological Method', pp. 211-13; *idem*, 'The Chronicler's
Jehoshaphat', pp. 17-18.
4.   2 Chron. 15.18 (‖ 1 Kgs 15.15).
5.   2 Chron. 16.2-3 (‖ 1 Kgs 15.18-19).
6.   This is not to say that the Chronicler has lost interest in the Temple and its
cultus in these narratives. Thus the cultic personnel are prominent in Jehoshaphat's
promulgation of תורה and act as judges at his behest, perhaps in keeping with the role
of cultic personnel elsewhere in the ancient Near East (cf. 2 Chron. 17.7-9; 19.8-11;
Albright, 'The Judicial Reform of Jehoshaphat', pp. 78-79); the mention of אמריהו
כהן הראש in 2 Chron. 19.11 does not seem of particular cultic significance given that
his function is complemented by the layman Zebadiah. The Temple provides the
grounds for Jehoshaphat's ability to repel the invasion which threatens Judah in his
day, as is evident from 2 Chron. 20.8-9. As has already been seen, the ניר for David
and his sons referred to in 2 Chron. 21.7, best interpreted as referring to the Temple,

The periods of Ahaziah and Athaliah are treated as one reign by the Chronicler,[1] and there is no note of the Temple's fortunes within the narratives dealing with them. However, an important retrospective reference within the Joash narrative gives notice of the horrors inflicted upon the Jerusalem Temple during their rule:

> For Athaliah—that wickedness!—her sons broke down the House of God and even all the holy things of the House of Yahweh they made into[2] Baalim (2 Chron. 24.7).

Although the Temple can still function as the place of concealment for the infant Joash and as the locus of his inauguration, it—like the Davidic dynasty itself—has been brought to a low ebb by the activities of Athaliah and Ahaziah. This picture is reinforced by reference to the rival temple of Baal in Jerusalem, implicitly an edifice constructed by Athaliah and her family.[3]

The liturgical nature of the Chronistic account of the accession of Joash acts as an overture to a reign which has great consequences for the Temple. Although the cultic reforms begin within the king's inauguration, it is the priest Jehoiada who reappoints the Temple officials, albeit according to the provisions established by David.[4] In doing so, Jehoiada is shown to be at least participating in a royal function, and this is in harmony with the royal burial that he is afforded later in the Chronistic account.[5]

---

shows that the Chronicler has not lost sight of the Jerusalem cultus in the Jehoram narrative.

1.   Cf. 2 Chron. 22.2-5. The Chronicler does not afford Athaliah the usual literary courtesies of a proper reign, such as beginning and concluding notices, demonstrating that she is a mere usurper in his history. Cf. Michaeli, *Les livres des Chroniques, d'Esdras et de Néhémie*, pp. 203-204; Myers, *II Chronicles*, p. 130.

2.   This translation follows the suggestion of Slotki, *Chronicles*, p. 270. Rudolph, *Chronikbücher*, p. 274, and Williamson, *1 and 2 Chronicles*, p. 321, suggest that בָּנֶיהָ might be repointed בְּנָיהָ and thus interpret the entire verse as seeing the Temple plundered for the raw materials of the temple of Baal and its cultus. This verse has no parallel in the *Vorlage*.

3.   2 Chron. 23.17; cf. 2 Chron. 21.6, 11; 22.2-4.

4.   2 Chron. 23.18; this verse represents a considerable expansion of 2 Kgs 11.18b and thus brings the action of Jehoiada into the cultic rather than the military realm.

5.   2 Chron. 24.16. This verse notes that the reason for this high honour is that Jehoiada עשה טובה בישראל ועם האלהים וביתו, linking the royal status given to the

Joash himself is not inactive as regards the Temple. He works towards its restoration after the tragedies imposed upon it by Athaliah and her family (2 Chron. 24.4-7). Following his *Vorlage* (2 Kgs 12.4-16), the Chronicler narrates how Joash's concern for the Temple results in the collection of monies and the repair of the Temple (2 Chron. 24.8-14). However, the Chronicler's account differs in several respects: the money is identified with the tax for the Tent (both revealing a post-exilic practice and reinforcing the Chronicler's identification of Temple and Tent);[1] the rebuke in the Deuteronomistic History for the failure of the cultic personnel to use the money properly is curtailed in the Chronistic narrative;[2] the money suffices for the supplying of Temple vessels according to Chronicles;[3] finally, the Chronistic account concludes with a statement of the restoration of regular sacrifices, denoting that the Mosaic cultus has been restored in the renewed Temple, albeit only for the lifetime of Jehoiada.[4] After the death of the priest, in a narrative unparalleled in the Deuteronomistic History, Joash and the princes of Judah abandon the Temple in favour of idolatry (2 Chron. 24.19) and the Temple court becomes the scene for the royal assassination of Jehoiada's son, the prophet Zechariah (2 Chron. 24.21). The Chronistic narrative therefore conveys a picture of a reign in which the Temple is first restored, but then its fortunes decline at the hands of the very king who restored it.

The monarchical history continues to include threats and offences against the Temple and its cultus. Amaziah's devotion to the Edomite

---

priest with his action on behalf of the Temple.

    1.   2 Chron. 24.6, 9; cf. Neh. 10.32-33. The change is effected, not only by the mention of Moses, but also by the proclamation of the tax throughout the realm in 2 Chron. 24.5 and 9, as opposed to offerings by pilgrims to the Temple in 2 Kgs 12.4. See Cazelles, *Les livres des Chroniques*, pp. 192-93; Myers, *II Chronicles*, pp. 137-38; Williamson, *1 and 2 Chronicles*, p. 319.

    2.   2 Kgs 12.7-8. A slighter reproach is still to be found at 2 Chron. 24.6, but it is for the non-collection of the money rather than the failure to apply it to its proper use.

    3.   2 Chron. 24.14a. This conflicts with the account of the Deuteronomistic History at 2 Kgs 12.13-14 which excludes such an application for the money.

    4.   2 Chron. 24.14b, for which there is no parallel in the *Vorlage*. Cf. Michaeli, *Les livres des Chroniques, d'Esdras et de Néhémie*, p. 208; Becker, *2 Chronik*, pp. 79-80.

idols whom he had set up as his gods (implicitly in Jerusalem)[1] brings defeat at the hands of the Northern Kingdom with the accompanying loss to the Temple of its vessels and treasures.[2] Uzziah threatens to infringe upon the priestly prerogative of burning incense in the Temple.[3] Jotham, despite his general faithfulness, does not give due attention to the Temple.[4] The Temple's fortunes fall to their nadir under Ahaz, who strips the Temple to send its wealth to the king of Assyria[5] and who also destroys the Temple vessels and shuts the Temple doors.[6]

The narrative pertaining to Hezekiah includes two distinct liturgical actions: the liturgy of reform and the Passover liturgy.[7] Both of these liturgies contain elements of progress for the Jerusalem Temple. The liturgy of reform, which contains a description of the low estate of the Temple and the disastrous consequences for Judah,[8] reverses some of

---

1.   Cf. 2 Chron. 25.14, for which there is no parallel in the *Vorlage*.

2.   2 Chron. 25.24; cf. 2 Kgs 14.14.

3.   2 Chron. 26.16-22, for which there is no parallel in the *Vorlage*.

4.   ויעש הישר בעיני יהוה ככל אשר־עשה עזיהו אביו רק לא־בא אל־היכל יהוה ועוד העם משחיתים (2 Chron. 27.2). The qualifying phrase (unparalleled in the *Vorlage*) is ambiguous, and is sometimes taken to identify Uzziah's sin as entering the Temple. This is unlikely, given the function of רק when used as a conjunction, i.e., to limit what has been expressed in the previous statement; see BDB, p. 956. This would produce a translation such as 'And he did what was right in the eyes of Yahweh according to everything which his father Uzziah did, only he did not go to the Temple of Yahweh and the people still were acting ruinously'. Cf. Cazelles, *Les livres des Chroniques*, p. 203; Myers, *II Chronicles*, p. 156. The Chronicler, following 2 Kgs 15.35, notes in 2 Chron. 27.3 that Jotham built the Upper Gate.

5.   2 Chron. 28.21; although this verse is Chronistic, the episode is also reported in 2 Kgs 16.8.

6.   2 Chron. 28.24; the Chronicler has heightened considerably the offences of Ahaz noted in 2 Kgs 16.17.

7.   2 Chron. 29.3-36 and 2 Chron. 30.1-31.1 respectively; these passages owe virtually nothing to the *Vorlage* where the direct narration of Hezekiah's cultic activity is limited to a single verse (2 Kgs 18.4).

8.   2 Chron. 29.6-9. This passage gives the impression that Hezekiah is about to launch upon an act of restoration for the entire range of infidelities committed by the ancestors of the nation—especially the kings—and not just those of Ahaz. Since the reform of Jehoiada and Joash, the Chronicler has made mention of the infidelities of Joash, of Amaziah and of Ahaz. P.R. Ackroyd, 'The Biblical Interpretation of the Reigns of Ahaz and Hezekiah', p. 253, makes the point that the statement of the infidelities of Ahaz in 2 Chron. 28.24-25 is framed in such a way as to prepare the

the recent negative elements of the Temple's fortunes: the doors are opened (2 Chron. 29.3), the vessels are restored,[1] the cultic personnel are organized at the king's behest according to the Davidic arrangements,[2] and sacrifices resume (2 Chron. 29.31-36). The inclusion of rubrical detail[3] and the precise grouping of the cultic personnel and the distinction of their function[4] give the impression that the narrative stems from actual liturgical experience, undoubtedly to be situated more in the Chronicler's day than in the time of Hezekiah.[5]

The reform of Hezekiah in Chronicles makes it possible for Israel to celebrate the Passover as a national liturgical action at the centralized cultic site. If historical, the centralized terms of Hezekiah's celebration (more in accord with the prescriptions of Deut. 16.1-8 that the more family-centred celebration envisaged in Exod. 12.1-20) would no longer constitute an act of restoration but of innovation. The Chronicler himself might be indicating at least a limited awareness of this fact in his narrative.[6] Whether in terms of restoration or of

stage for Hezekiah's reform; it would be more accurate to say that Ahaz was simply the last and most unfaithful of those whose sins necessitated the reform.

1. 2 Chron. 29.18-19. P.R. Ackroyd, 'The Temple Vessels—A Continuity Theme', pp. 166-81, has demonstrated the importance of the vessels in tracing the continuous religious tradition of the community, not least in Chronicles.

2. 2 Chron. 29.25-30. 2 Chron 29.12-14 lists Levites who are identified as descendants of David's liturgical musicians before the Ark and the Tent (cf. 1 Chron. 6.1-33; 15.16-24; 16.4-6, 37-42) among the functionaries at Hezekiah's reform. Two other references to the liturgical music (2 Chron. 29.25, 30) are an evocative reference to the hymn appointed by David for use by Asaph and his kinsmen in 1 Chronicles 16. Thus the liturgical personnel and the liturgical music provide an explicit connection with the origin of the Jerusalem cultus under David.

3. For example, the manipulation of blood in 2 Chron. 29.22, the imposition of hands upon the sin offering in 2 Chron. 29.23 and the prostrations in 2 Chron. 29.28, 30.

4. 2 Chron. 29.12-16, 21-22.

5. Randellini, *Il libro delle Cronache*, p. 442; Ackroyd, *I & II Chronicles, Ezra, Nehemiah*, p. 183; Willi, *Die Chronik als Auslegung*, pp. 199-200; D.L. Petersen, *Late Israelite Prophecy: Studies in Deutero-Prophetic Literature and in Chronicles*, p. 83.

6. 2 Chron. 30.5, 26; cf. H.H. Rowley, *Worship in Israel: Its Forms and Meaning*, p. 118; Dillard, *2 Chronicles*, p. 244. It is possible, of course, that the Chronicler is not referring to the innovation of a centralized celebration but to other distinctive features of Hezekiah's Passover, such as the participation of the Northern tribes; cf. Williamson, *Israel in the Books of Chronicles*, pp. 120-21; Halpern,

innovation, the Chronicler has shown that the story of the Temple and its cultus has advanced through the cultic activity of Hezekiah. However, by unambiguously stating that the Passover was celebrated in the second month rather than in the first[1] and that many of the participants were unclean,[2] the author prepares the narrative ground for a further stage of development in the cultic story, the highest it had reached since the days of Solomon (2 Chron. 30.26).

The Chronistic Hezekiah also advances the Temple's fortunes outside of the episodes which describe his liturgies in passages unparalleled in the Deuteronomistic History. He appoints the courses for the cultic personnel, makes provisions for the regular sacrifices and also provides for the upkeep of the cultic personnel and their families, enabling them to keep תורה more firmly (2 Chron. 31.2-4). The donations for the upkeep of the priests and Levites necessitates the building of chambers by Hezekiah in the Temple (2 Chron. 31.11) and the royal assignation of officials to distribute the donations (2 Chron. 31.13-19). In these matters, the Chronistic Hezekiah has gone beyond the task of mere restoration of Davidic provisions and has innovated in cultic matters on his own authority, as Welch correctly observes;[3]

'Sacred History and Ideology: Chronicles' Thematic Structure—Indications of an Earlier Source', p. 46.

1.   2 Chron. 30.2-3, 13, 15. This time note may reflect a vestige of historical fact and be related to a historical invitation to the Northern tribes. S. Talmon, 'Divergences in Calendar-Reckoning in Ephraim and Judah', pp. 60-61, suggests that Hezekiah was conceding a month's delay in his celebration in order to comply with a Northern cultic calendar which lagged a month behind that of Judah; cf. 1 Kgs 12.32.

2.   2 Chron. 30.17-20. This uncleanness of participants is a justification in the Chronicler's eyes for the slaying of the Passover victims by the Levites rather than by the heads of households as would be expected by the obvious meaning of Exod. 12.6. This rubric in the Chronistic account of Hezekiah's Passover (read together with the corresponding slaughter of the victim at Josiah's Passover in 2 Chron. 35.6-11) leads to the conclusion that the Chronicler is here reflecting his own experience of the Passover rituals wherein the slaughter of the victims belonged no longer to the heads of families, but to the Levites. Cf. Welch, *The Work of the Chronicler: Its Purpose and Date*, pp. 139-42; J.C. Rylaarsdam, 'Passover and the Feast of Unleavened Bread', pp. 667-68; M. Haran, 'The Passover Sacrifice', p. 91. The Mishnah indicates that the practice later reverted to slaughter by the heads of family; cf. *m. Pes.* 5.6.

3.   *The Work of the Chronicler: Its Purpose and Date*, p. 114.

the effect is that the origins of the post-exilic provisions for the cultic personnel are shown to have their origin in the royal authority of Hezekiah.[1]

Although some of the Chronicler's themes disappear after the Hezekiah narratives,[2] the concern with the Temple's fortunes continues in the Chronistic narrative. The degeneration at the beginning of Manasseh's reign included the building of altars for illicit cults in the Temple[3] and even the setting up of an idol there.[4] However, Manasseh himself corrects these specific desecrations of the Temple after his personal exile.[5] The portrayal of a positive period to Manasseh—proper to the Chronistic work—also shows him restoring מזבח יהוה and offering sacrifices on it.[6]

While the brief and negative narrative concerning Amon contains no specific reference to the Temple, the Temple becomes very prominent in the Chronistic narrative of Josiah's reign (2 Chron. 34.1–35.27), as it already is in the Deuteronomistic account (cf. 2 Kgs 22–23). The cultic concern of Josiah is evident early in the narrative as he purges and repairs the Temple (2 Chron. 34.8-13), during which activity the Book of the Law is discovered (2 Chron. 34.14-19).

1. *The Work of the Chronicler: Its Purpose and Date*, p. 120.

2. Halpern, 'Sacred History and Ideology: Chronicles' Thematic Structure—Indications of an Earlier Source', pp. 39-41, notes the cessation of the themes of rest, prosperity and salvation, and postulates a source which was originally concerned with Hezekiah.

3. 2 Chron. 33.4-5 (∥ 2 Kgs 21.4-5).

4. 2 Chron. 33.7-8 (∥ 2 Kgs 21.7-8). The Chronicler, following his *Vorlage* at 2 Kgs 21.7-8, marks this act by referring in vv. 7-8 to the conditionality of the promise to David concerning Israel's possession of the land and the placing of his שם in the Temple; it seems that the Chronicler has strengthened the emphasis on the condition by adding והחקים והמשפטים in v. 8 after the simpler phrase ולכל־התורה taken from 2 Kgs 21.8.

5. 2 Chron. 33.15. 2 Chron. 33.22 implies that there were other idols which Manasseh had erected but which he did not eradicate. Jerusalem itself still needs to be purged of illicit cultic images and sites in 2 Chron. 34.3, and 2 Chron. 34.8 mentions that the Temple also had to be purged; cf. Dillard, *2 Chronicles*, p. 269.

6. 2 Chron. 33.16. Noordtzij, 'Les intentions du Chroniste', p. 162, notes that the Chronicler has included Manasseh with David and Solomon as the kings who specifically offer sacrifice; this certainly serves to indicate that the Chronicler has portrayed Manasseh in total cultic faithfulness after his exile.

However, it is in the narrative of Josiah's Passover that true progression in the story of the Temple and its cultus can be charted. The progression is firstly given a sound foundation in tradition through several references to the figures of Israel's formative past.[1] These have the effect of linking the celebration of Josiah with the foundations of Israel's worship, portraying Josiah's Passover as their ideal implementation, similar to the way in which the Chronicler used links with past figures to portray Hezekiah's Passover as the grand restoration.

The concluding statement which summarizes the achievement of Josiah also harkens back to Israel's formative history, although in a different manner, and reinforces the overall impression that Josiah's Passover is a perfect expression of Israel's normative worship:

> And Passover was not celebrated like this in Jerusalem since the days of Samuel the prophet, nor did any of the kings of Israel celebrate like the Passover which Josiah celebrated with the priests, the Levites, all Judah, Israel (as it survived)[2] and the inhabitants of Jerusalem (2 Chron. 35.18).

By altering this verse from the original reference in the *Vorlage* at 2 Kgs 23.22 to the days of the Judges, the Chronicler has effectively brought the reader back, not to the time of the conquest, but to the beginning of monarchy and to the figure who was, for the Chronicler, the one who foretold the Davidic kingship (1 Chron. 11.3), who shared responsibility with David for the arrangements concerning the gatekeepers at the Tent (1 Chron. 9.22), and who dedicated spoil apportioned in the days of David for the care of the future Temple (1 Chron. 26.28). The Chronicler is also forming an even wider narrative bracket than he had constructed with the similar comparison

---

1. Thus there are two references to David as one who has established the arrangements for the cultic personnel (2 Chron. 35.4, 15), one to Solomon as temple builder (2 Chron. 35.3) and one to him as an arranger of cultic personnel (2 Chron. 35.4), two to Moses as the one through whom the precepts for the Passover have been communicated (2 Chron. 35.6, 12, although the latter is problematic since the Chronicler seems to have extended the provisions for removing portions of communion sacrifices in Lev. 3 to the Passover sacrifice), and one to Asaph, Heman and Jeduthun as co-arrangers with David of the Levitical singers (2 Chron. 35.15).

2. Although the meaning for the *niphal* participle here suggested in BDB, p. 594, is 'be present', the meaning 'be left after war, violence, etc.' is also given for the *niphal* and seems possible in this context, especially given the phrase ומכל שארית ישראל which occurs in 2 Chron. 34.9.

of Hezekiah's Passover to the days of Solomon (2 Chron. 30.26); these
two comparisons taken together have the effect of ensuring that the
audience perceives Hezekiah's Passover (and reform) as a restoration
of the cultus of the days of the United Monarchy and Josiah's
celebration as a progression upon it. In Josiah's Passover, therefore,
the Chronicler sees that kingship has reached at least one cultic height
that it had never reached before.

The Chronicler employs a curious phrase in 2 Chron. 35.20 to
effect the transition from the liturgical scene to the death of Josiah:
אחרי כל־זאת אשר הכין יאשיהו את־הבית. Although it occurs outside the
specifically cultic section of the Josiah narrative, the phrase represents
the Chronicler's summary of the liturgical scenes: through his cultic
activity, Josiah has established the Temple.[1] Read together with the
statement of 2 Chron. 35.18, this transitional phrase points the interpreter to investigate those aspects which distinguish the liturgies of
Josiah from all that preceded them in the Chronistic monarchical
history.

Josiah's liturgies, and especially his Passover, mark a true progression for the Chronicler because of two important factors: the availability of the Book of the Law and the liturgical authority of Josiah.
The discovery of the Book of the Law has certain implications for
understanding his picture of Josiah's liturgies. It means that the
covenant that Josiah enters into in 2 Chron. 34.29-32 entails a commitment to the Law of Yahweh as it had not been known in previous
generations; the covenant ceremony therefore marked the occasion
when king and people entered into the fullest possible covenant relationship according to the Mosaic Law. The discovery of the Book of
the Law also enables the Passover ceremony to take place according to
its provisions for the first time in the Chronistic narrative;[2] this alone

1.   Although the *hiphil* of כון is often translated as 'to prepare', such an interpretation would be unintelligible for 2 Chron. 35.20. Here, as elsewhere in the work,
the Chronicler seems to have taken the sense of the verb as it applies to God's action
on behalf of the dynastic rule of the Davidides ('to establish') and to have applied it
to the Davidides' action on behalf of the Temple cultus. Cf. 2 Chron. 8.16; 29.35;
35.16.

2.   This is according to the Chronicler's understanding of the Law rather than
according to a modern critical understanding, as is evident from the references to
Moses in 2 Chron. 35.6 and 12, neither of which relates directly to the Pentateuchal
provisions for the Passover. Even though reference is made to the Law of Moses in

would justify the Chronicler's praise of Josiah's Passover as a celebration unknown since the days of Samuel.

The second major factor that contributes to the liturgical progression evident in the Josiah narratives is the liturgical authority of Josiah.[1] Although Josiah is portrayed as one who enforces the Mosaic, Davidic and Solomonic ordering of the cultus, he also takes his place in their ranks as one who contributes to the full provisions of the Jerusalem ritual. This is clearest with regard to the Levites and their role in slaughtering the Paschal victim: what was an emergency measure in the celebration of Hezekiah (2 Chron. 30.17) has become normative in Josiah's Passover through the arrangements made by royal decree.[2]

In the speech of 2 Chron. 35.3-6, Josiah—assuming the mantle of David—makes a definitive change in the role of the Levites by ending their function of carrying the Ark of Yahweh and giving them new duties in the Passover celebration. By doing so, the Chronistic Josiah echoes David, who had expanded the Levitical function after declaring that the Levites no longer needed to carry the Tent and its vessels (1 Chron. 23.26-32). The presumption underlying this verse is that the Ark pales in significance beside the House containing it, an important point for the post-exilic situation which needed a theology in which it could not be essential to move, see or even have the Ark.

Hezekiah's Passover was praiseworthy, but Josiah's exceeds it; gone are the imperfections of celebration in the second month and the emergency role of the Levites. But not only does Josiah surpass

the narrative of Hezekiah's Passover (2 Chron. 30.16), the phrase ביד־משה in 2 Chron. 35.6, echoing the same phrase in 2 Chron. 34.14, reminds the reader that Josiah's Passover will reach a ritual perfection, made possible only through the discovery of the Book of the Law. Myers, 'The Kerygma of the Chronicler: History and Theology in the Service of Religion', p. 272, perceives a generally cultic understanding of the discovery of the Book of the Law in Chronicles in comparison to Kings: 'While mention of the book occurs an equal number of times in each story, accentuating its importance for both accounts, one has the distinct impression of an amplification of cult relationship and functions, especially of personnel and observances'.

1.   Cf. Japhet, *The Ideology of the Book of Chronicles and its Place in Biblical Thought*, pp. 440-41.

2.   2 Chron. 35.6. Through this decree, the Chronicler seems to have given the reason for the Passover practice known to him which was at variance with the family-centred celebration envisaged in Exod. 12.1-20.

Hezekiah in ritual perfection; 2 Chron. 35.18 implies that progress has even been made on the days of David and Solomon through this celebration. Such progress brings the Temple ritual to a new height which it had not even seen in its *Urzeit*, perfected by the faithfulness to the ritual provisions of David and Solomon, by full implementation of the Book of the Law, and by the new arrangements dictated by King Josiah himself which bring about the final stage of the cult centralization in the Chronicler's narrative.[1]

This brief survey indicates that the Chronicler has kept the ancient Near Eastern association of king and temple to the fore in his presentation of the post-Solomonic kings. Not only do they bear the responsibility for the Temple's maintenance, but they also enjoy some of the same cultic privileges as their forebears David and Solomon in authorizing the arrangements for the Temple and its cultus and even once in the offering of sacrifice. This latter picture emerges much more strongly in the Chronistic History than in its Deuteronomistic forebear. However, concerned as he is to trace the development of the Temple cultus in his work, the Chronicler seems to show that the arrangements for the Temple, its cultic personnel and its celebrations have all been completed by the end of Josiah's Passover celebration.

In this context it is noteworthy that Josiah goes to the scene of his death immediately after the narration of his Passover celebration. The scene begins with a significant phrase which calls attention to Josiah's contribution to the Temple (2 Chron. 35.20) and contains the shocking attribution of his death to the fact that he did not listen to God speaking through the Egyptian king Neco;[2] both of these features are proper to the Chronistic account of Josiah's death. The Chronicler has thus portrayed the death of Josiah as an act of divine retribution,[3] and linked it to the fate of the Northern Ahab in 2 Chron. 18.29-33.[4] While the Chronicler has bestowed the reward of a glorious burial

1. Welch, *The Work of the Chronicler: Its Purpose and Date*, pp. 139-42.

2. 2 Chron. 35.22. The unexpected and unequivocal nature of this statement undermines the suggestion of H.G.M. Williamson, 'Reliving the Death of Josiah: A Reply to C.T. Begg', pp. 9-10, that the death of Josiah is not important to the Chronicler's theology.

3. North, 'Theology of the Chronicler', *JBL* 82 (1963), p. 272; Michaeli, *Les livres des Chroniques, d'Esdras et de Néhémie*, p. 247.

4. Willi, *Die Chronik als Auslegung*, pp. 159-60; Dillard, *2 Chronicles*, p. 292.

upon Josiah (2 Chron. 35.24-25), this last good king has also been given a share with many other good kings who, in the last analysis, are a disappointment since they depart from their commitment to Yahweh and his ways in the latter part of their reigns.[1]

In bringing Josiah to an ignominious death, the Chronicler has shown Neco to be enunciating the authentic word of God. In this, the Chronicler may be indicating that there has been a transfer of Yahweh's election away from the Davidic dynasty, since God is now with Neco rather than with the Davidic dynasty.[2] This is substantiated by the Chronicler's use of elements from the Saul paradigm: Josiah is not only killed during a threat by foreigners,[3] he also dies for failure with regard to the word of God.[4]

It may be a mistake to see the episode of Josiah's death purely in terms of individual retribution upon Josiah himself. Rather, in a manner reminiscent of the Saul paradigm, the death of Josiah may be a Chronistic note of judgment for the dynasty itself.[5] The fact that this possible transfer of kingship occurs after the completion of the

1. For example Jehoshaphat in 2 Chron. 20.35-37, Joash in 2 Chron. 24.17-22, and perhaps even Hezekiah in 2 Chron. 32.31. Cf. C.T. Begg, 'The Death of Josiah in Chronicles: Another View', pp. 2-3.

2. Cf. 2 Chron. 13.12. See Cazelles, *Les livres des Chroniques,* p. 239; Begg, 'The Death of Josiah in Chronicles: Another View', p. 3. Begg also argues that the Chronistic placing of a divine warning in the mouth of Neco shows the Egyptian king performing a function formerly performed by Davidic kings (p. 5).

3. Becker, *2 Chronik*, p. 124.

4. 2 Chron. 35.22; 1 Chron. 10.13. Both of these passages are proper to the Chronicler.

5. If this possibility is admitted, then the ambiguity of Neco's statement can be interpreted as permitting a dual reading of Neco's 'oracle'. Neco's warning to Josiah in 2 Chron. 35.21 states לא־עליך אתה היום כי אל־בית מלחמתי; the phrase אל־בית מלחמתי is admitted to be enigmatic (cf. Williamson, *1 and 2 Chronicles*, p. 411). The suggestion of Rudolph, *Chronikbücher*, p. 331, that the phrase should be understood to apply to the House of Assyria which Neco intends to assist, seems valid; however, it does not account for the lack of specific reference in the Chronicler's text, and may therefore apply to only one of two levels of meaning intended in the phrase. Rudolph makes much of the distinction between על and אל, taking the latter to refer to assistance rather than attack; however, this does not fit the evidence cited in BDB, p. 40, for those places where אל represents a hostile relationship. The Chronicler may have intended to indicate that the action of Neco was primarily against the dynasty (בית) rather than against Josiah, thereby softening the negative judgment on Josiah implicit in the manner of his death.

arrangements for the Temple and its cultus is hardly accidental; rather, it may be serving as an indication that the dynasty has fulfilled its function in the plan of Yahweh once the Temple cultus is complete. If such a transfer of kingship away from the Davidic dynasty has been portrayed by the Chronicler, it should be particularly evident in the final episodes of his narrative.

From the Post-Josian Kings to the Edict of Cyrus

After the lengthy narrative concerned with Josiah, the audience's first impression of the 21 verses given to the era of the post-Josian kings must be that the Chronicler has nearly passed over these monarchs without comment. Thus Cancik characterizes the Chronicler's material on these four kings as 'a sharp staccato',[1] and Begg suggests that the Chronicler has chosen either to compress or to pass over the material concerning these kings in his *Vorlage* so that he might move all the more quickly to the beginning of the restoration in the Persian period.[2] However, the beginning of the Persian period reflected in 2 Chron. 36.22-23 is itself problematic, linked as it is with the scholarly debate over the relationship between Chronicles and Ezra–Nehemiah.

This section of the final form study of the Chronistic narrative will firstly consider the treatment that the Chronicler affords to the successors of Josiah, the last ruling members of the Davidic dynasty; in this consideration, it will emerge that the treatment of these kings in the Chronistic history forms an essential part of that work. This will permit the Edict of Cyrus to be seen in its proper role—not as a late addition to the Chronicler's work, but as an important part of the Chronistic re-presentation of the monarchical history in its final form.

From the Post-Josian Kings to the Exile (2 Chronicles 36.1-21)

While the brevity of the Chronistic treatment of the post-Josian kings may give the impression that the Chronicler has assigned little significance to these narratives, his earlier narrative technique suggests an alternative reason. It has already been demonstrated that the brief narrative concerned with Saul in 1 Chronicles 10 has provided

1.   'Das judische Fest: Ein Versuch zu Form und Religion des chronistischen Geschichtswerkes', p. 339.
2.   C.T. Begg, 'The Classical Prophets in the Chronistic History', p. 104.

the Chronistic history with a significant, if negative, beginning to the monarchical narrative; if the Chronistic treatment of Saul were longer, the paradigmatic quality of the narrative would have been jeopardized. Similarly, the narratives of the post-Josian monarchs may have been compressed in order to highlight those very aspects that are important to the Chronicler's purposes.[1] As well as being brief, the post-Josian section is notably similar to the Saul narrative in its negativity, giving the impression that, after the death of Josiah, the road to destruction and to the exile was inevitable.[2]

The narrative concerning the post-Josian monarchs can best be viewed through an analysis in terms of the three concerns considered in the above section relating to the kings from Rehoboam to Josiah. The first of these, the concern with divine retribution in relation to the cultus, is implied in the negative terms employed in the text when these terms are read against the background of the theme's explication in the accounts of preceding kings; this is true even though the cultic nature of the failure of the post-Josian kings is not emphasized in specific terms. Thus, Jehoiakim, Jehoiachin and Zedekiah are all condemned as having done what is evil בעיני יהוה,[3] with the further notes that Jehoiakim was guilty of abominations[4] and that Zedekiah refused to humble himself before Jeremiah (2 Chron. 36.12) while in his reign all the people followed the abominations of the nations.[5] The sentence of retribution is far more explicit, since each king suffers a truncated reign and none receives the burial with the fathers in the City of David which often characterizes the Chronicler's positive judgment upon a monarch. Instead, Jehoahaz is carried off to Egypt, Jehoiakim and Jehoiachin to Babylon, and even an implied reference to the death and burial of Zedekiah is lacking in the Chronistic work.[6]

1.   Mosis, *Untersuchungen zur Theologie des chronistischen Geschichtswerkes*, p. 205.

2.   Galling, *Die Bücher der Chronik, Esra, Nehemia*, pp. 182-83; Coggins, *The First and Second Books of the Chronicles*, p. 304.

3.   2 Chron. 36.5, 9, 12.

4.   2 Chron. 36.8. These abominations could well be a reference to the idolatry mentioned in Jer. 7.17-18, 30-31 in the view of Randellini, *Il libro delle Cronache*, p. 500. Cf. also Slotki, *Chronicles*, p. 342.

5.   2 Chron. 36.14. The same word, תעבות, is used here as for Jehoiakim in 2 Chron. 36.8.

6.   2 Chron. 36.4, 6, 10. 2 Kgs 24.6 implies that Jehoiakim died and was buried

The second concern, that of the dynastic promise, is also treated more by implication than through direct statement; in this case, however, the implications of the narrative seem more pointed. Like Saul, each king suffers a termination of his reign in the face of foreign invasions and the dynastic principle of the crown passing from father to son no longer maintains its consistency. Hence when the kingdom passes directly to a son, the son reigns for three months,[1] while the longer reigns are held when a lateral transfer has been made to the former king's brother.[2] Since the basic historical data have been set by the historical traditions (as found particularly in the Deuteronomistic *Vorlage*), the Chronicler is not responsible for determining either the comparative lengths of these reigns or the manner of their interruption, with the notable exception of the truncation of the reign of Jehoiakim (2 Chron. 36.6); the author has, however, framed these narratives to bring out a common message: by denying the post-Josian kings such royal literary trappings as the statement of their deaths and burials,[3] and, to a lesser extent, the naming of the queen mother,[4] the Chronicler seems to undermine their full legitimate status within the

in Jerusalem. It would seem that the Chronicler has adjusted the ultimate fate of Jehoiakim so that his theological interpretation of these reigns be strengthened; see Becker, *2 Chronik*, pp. 123-24. While the text of Chronicles does not state that Jehoiakim died in Babylon, this fate is implied by the fact that the binding of Jehoiakim in order to bring him to Babylon is the last episode concerning him in the narrative; on this and other possible interpretations of 2 Chron. 36.6, see Williamson, *1 and 2 Chronicles*, pp. 413-14.

1.   This is the case with Jehoahaz and Jehoiachin; 2 Chron. 36.2, 9. The same lengths for these reigns are to be found in the *Vorlage*.

2.   Jehoiakim and Zedekiah each reign for eleven years, the same length of time as stated in the *Vorlage*; 2 Chron. 36.5, 11. However, while 2 Kgs 24.17 describes Zedekiah as the uncle of Jehoiachin, 2 Chron. 36.10 describes him as the brother of Jehoiachin, perhaps taking אח as kinsman; cf. Slotki, *Chronicles*, p. 343.

3.   Compare 2 Chron. 12.16; 13.23; 16.13-14; 21.1, 20; 22.9; 24.25; 25.27-28; 26.23; 27.9; 28.27; 32.33; 33.20, 24; 35.24-25. Cf. Mosis, *Untersuchungen zur Theologie des chronistischen Geschichtswerkes*, pp. 205-208.

4.   Compare 2 Chron. 13.2; 15.16; 20.31; 22.2; 24.1; 25.1; 26.3; 27.1; 29.1. This literary feature is not consistent in the Chronicler's work and is absent after the Hezekiah narrative. However, the naming of the queen mother is a feature of the *Vorlage* for these monarchs in 2 Kgs 23.31, 36 and 24.8, 18; cf. Galling, *Die Bücher der Chronik, Esra, Nehemia*, pp. 183-84.

Davidic dynasty.[1] In the face of all that has been omitted from the *Vorlage* in regard to these monarchs by the Chronicler, it may be significant that he has retained the notices that Jehoiakim was made king by Neco and that Zedekiah was made king by Nebuchadnezzar.[2] These king-making actions demonstrate that the Israelite monarchy is, in practical terms, no longer in vassalage to Yahweh but to the dominating foreign power; that Yahweh has allowed this state of affairs to emerge in the Chronicler's view can be seen by his reference to the divinely sanctioned oath which bound Zedekiah to Nebuchadnezzar.[3]

The third concern, the fortunes of the Jerusalem Temple and its cultus, is treated more explicitly in the post-Josian narratives than is the case with the two previous concerns; the story of the fortunes of the Temple in this section is framed so as to form a downwards spiral. Thus, some Temple vessels are brought to Babylon by Nebuchadnezzar at the end of Jehoiachim's reign (2 Chron. 36.7), more are brought there at the end of Jehoiakin's reign (2 Chron. 36.10), and the rest are either taken or destroyed in the destruction of Jerusalem together with the Temple itself (2 Chron. 36.18-19). This progressive loss of the Temple vessels removes the utensils necessary for legitimate worship, indicating a diminuation of the Temple and its liturgy and pointing to the eventual destruction of the Temple edifice.[4]

The Chronicler gives explicit reasons, both historical and theological, for the Temple's destruction:

1.   There are some similarities between the Chronistic narratives of the post-Josian kings and the Chronistic treatment of Amon in 2 Chron. 33.21-25; Amon, too, is given a brief negative narrative which omits specific mention of burial (although it mentions his death by assassination). Perhaps the Amon narrative proleptically reflects a type of dynastic failure brought about by the sins of Manasseh which are perpetuated by Amon. In this case, the post-Josian kings would perform the same function for the monarchical narrative as a whole that Amon does for the Manasseh narrative, i.e., indicate the failure of the dynasty to satisfy the conditions for perpetuation and the endangerment of the dynastic promise. Cf. Mosis, *Untersuchungen zur Theologie des chronistischen Geschichtswerkes*, p. 205.
2.   2 Chron. 36.4, 10 (|| 2 Kgs 23.34; 24.17).
3.   2 Chron. 36.12. 2 Kgs 24.20, while mentioning Zedekiah's rebellion, makes no reference to Nebuchadnezzar's having made Zedekiah swear by God.
4.   Ackroyd, 'The Temple Vessels—A Continuity Theme', p. 178. This loss of Temple vessels has occurred before in the narrative, both under Amaziah in 2 Chron. 25.24 and under Ahaz in 2 Chron. 28.24.

And he [Zedekiah] even rebelled against the king Nebuchadnezzar who had made him swear by God; he stiffened his neck and hardened his heart from turning to Yahweh the God of Israel. Even all the princes of the priests and the people multiplied faithlessness treacherously according to all the abominations of the nations, and they desecrated the House of Yahweh which he had sanctified in Jerusalem. And Yahweh, the God of their fathers, sent to them by the hand of his messengers, sending early and often, for he had pity on his people and on his habitation. But they were makers of jest against the messengers of God and scorners of his words and mockers against his prophets until the wrath of Yahweh rose up against his people, until there was no healing (2 Chron. 36.13-16).

The Chronicler's reasons for the catastrophe, therefore, include the historico-theological cause of Zedekiah's offence against the divinely sanctioned oath made to Nebuchadnezzar,[1] his lack of repentance, the treachery of the priestly leaders and people in polluting the Temple,[2] and the rejection of the divine message and its messengers; the Deuteronomistic *Vorlage*, by comparison, mentions only the evil of Zedekiah (in continuance with the evil of Jehoiakim) and his rebellion against the king of Babylon (2 Kgs 24.19-20), although, earlier in the Deuteronomistic narrative, the sins of Manasseh were shown to be the cause of the catastrophe (cf. 2 Kgs 21.10-15).

The prophetic word through Jeremiah provides the narrative of the catastrophe with an *inclusio* which should not be overlooked: the account of Zedekiah's reign begins with his refusal to humble himself before Jeremiah[3] just as it concludes with the fulfilment of Jeremiah's word in the Sabbath rest afforded the land through the depopulation during the exile.[4] Although the Chronicler's concern with royal

1. This expansion of 2 Kgs 24.20 may depend upon Ezek. 17.11-21; cf. Williamson, *1 and 2 Chronicles*, p. 416; Becker, *2 Chronik*, p. 127.

2. Ezek. 8.3-18 may be echoed here. Cf. Harvey-Jellie, *Chronicles*, p. 324; Rudolph, *Chronikbücher*, p. 337; Cazelles, *Les livres des Chroniques*, p. 242.

3. 2 Chron. 36.12. There are several possible sections of the book of Jeremiah in the author's mind (as well as the possibility of traditions familiar to him but unknown to us). Among the passages in the prophetic book, Jer. 22.1-9 is of particular interest, since it reminds Zedekiah of the conditional nature of the Davidic covenant as well as stating the possible destruction of the city.

4. 2 Chron. 36.21. Cf. Jer. 25.11-12; 29.10. Jeremiah does speak of 70 years, but not in terms of allowing the land its Sabbath years. This Chronistic interpretation seems to come from Lev. 26.31-35; cf. Ackroyd, *I & II Chronicles, Ezra, Nehemiah*, p. 210; Virgulin, *Libri delle Cronache*, pp. 453-54.

failure to observe the prophetic word itself constitutes an identifiable theme in the Chronistic work,[1] this need not be seen in complete isolation from the author's cultic concerns, since prophecy for the Chronicler is a function of the cultic personnel[2] and can occur within the liturgical action (2 Chron. 20.15-17).

Into the prophetic *inclusio* of 2 Chron. 36.12-21, which shows that the word was fulfilled despite its having been previously ignored, the defilement of the Temple emerges as a major cause of the final tragedy in Chronicles. This can be clearly seen from the fact that the downfall of the nation begins in the sanctuary,[3] continuing with the destruction of the Temple itself and ending with the evacuation of the land:

> And he [Yahweh] brought up against them the king of the Chaldeans, and he slew their young warriors with the sword in the House of their sanctuary and he had no pity on youth or maiden, aged or grey-haired—all he gave into his hand. And all the vessels—great or small—of the House of God, and the treasures of the House of Yahweh and the treasures of the king and his princes, everything he brought to Babylon. And they burnt the House of God and they broke down the wall of Jerusalem, and its palaces they burnt with fire, and destroyed all its precious vessels. And those who survived the sword he brought into exile to Babylon, and they were slaves to him and to his sons until the rule of the kingdom of Persia, (this was to fulfil the word of Yahweh [spoken] by the mouth of Jeremiah) until the land had received its sabbaths. All the days of desolation, [the land] rested to complete seventy years (2 Chron. 36.17-21).

This account of the destruction, especially in the light of the preceding statement that there could be no remedy,[4] immediately brings the audience back to the highly conditioned statement of Yahweh in 2 Chron. 7.17-22, which promises a continuance of the Davidic dynasty in return for obedience and which threatens the destruction of the

---

1. It is identified as such by Mosis, *Untersuchungen zur Theologie des chronistischen Geschichtswerkes*, pp. 33-39.
2. 1 Chron. 25.1-3. Cf. Petersen, *Late Israelite Prophecy: Studies in Deutero-Prophetic Literature and in Chronicles*, pp. 8 and 87.
3. This same starting-point is to be observed in Ezek. 9.6-8, and some of the vocabulary of 2 Chron. 36.13-20 seems to be drawn from that passage in Ezekiel; see Curtis and Madsen, *A Critical and Exegetical Commentary on the Books of Chronicles*, p. 523.
4. 2 Chron. 36.16; Dillard, *2 Chronicles*, p. 300.

Temple and the evacuation of the people in return for unfaithfulness. The specific mention of the worship of foreign gods in 2 Chron. 7.19-22, itself programmatic for this penultimate episode, indicates that the audience is to view the cause of the catastrophe in the context of the infidelities of several post-Solomonic members of the Davidic dynasty and not of the infidelities of the post-Josian kings alone.[1] This reinforces the impression already given by the description of God's action and the people's response in 2 Chron. 36.15-16 which, while sometimes interpreted by commentators as applying to the reign of Zedekiah alone,[2] is better viewed as a summary reflection on events throughout the post-Solomonic era.[3]

The Chronicler has included a further indication that the destruction of the Temple and the exile were the result of a long history of sin by his very description of the exile in 2 Chron. 36.21. The span of 70 years for the exile during which the land could recover its lost Sabbaths indicates that the provisions of תורה had not been observed for the entire monarchical period (or at least the greater part of it);[4] the accumulation of neglect which is the cause of the destruction of the Temple and the nation is thus shown to lie in the larger monarchical period by this designation of 70 years required for reparation.[5] Of interest also is the fact that the reference to the lost Sabbaths itself might have been intended to contain a link with the Temple; while many exegetes note that 2 Chron. 36.21 necessarily results from a mixing of Jeremiah with the Priestly traditions,[6] the link that exists in

1.   Thus the seeking of foreign gods in the Chronistic work can be seen in the reigns of Jehoram (2 Chron. 21.6; cf. 2 Chron. 17.3-4), Ahaziah (2 Chron. 22.3-5), Joash (2 Chron. 24.18), Amaziah (2 Chron. 25.14-16), Ahaz (2 Chron. 28.2-4, 23-25), Manasseh (2 Chron. 33.2-9) and Amon (2 Chron. 33.22). 2 Chron. 36.14 also contains a reference to foreign cults practised by the priests and people in the reign of Zedekiah.

2.   See Barnes, *The Books of Chronicles*, p. 294; Mangan, *1–2 Chronicles, Ezra, Nehemiah*, p. 144.

3.   Cf. Ackroyd, *I & II Chronicles, Ezra, Nehemiah*, p. 208; Willi, *Die Chronik als Auslegung*, p. 222; McKenzie, *The Chronicler's Use of the Deuteronomistic History*, p. 182.

4.   Curtis and Madsen, *A Critical and Exegetical Commentary on the Books of Chronicles*, p. 524; Elmslie, *The Books of Chronicles*, p. 351; Slotki, *Chronicles*, p. 346.

5.   Williamson, *1 and 2 Chronicles*, p. 418.

6.   Specifically, Jer. 25.11 and 29.10 have been read by the Chronicler in the

the Priestly tradition between the observance of the Sabbath and the reverencing of the sanctuary has been largely ignored[1] (although it has sometimes been noted that the period of 70 years corresponds to the historical length of time best if the *terminus a quo* is marked by the destruction of the Temple and the *terminus ad quem* of the exile is equated with its restoration).[2] Thus, the length of time needed to compensate for the lost Sabbaths might have been intended to indicate a cultic indictment of the monarchy as a whole.

In both negativity and brevity, the similarities between the Chronistic treatment of the post-Josian kings and the treatment of Saul cannot be denied. Consideration of the Saul narrative resulted in a formulation of the following paradigm linked to ancient Near Eastern ideals of kingship: the Chronistic Saul is a king whose failure to seek Yahweh in the cultus amounts to מעל; the effect of this cultic מעל is to endanger Israel's security in the land and to provoke the anger of Yahweh; in turn, Saul and his dynasty are terminated and the kingship is turned elsewhere.

While it is obviously possible to apply the Saul paradigm to the post-Josian narrative, the process soon reveals that the Chronicler has not constructed a point-by-point correspondence between 1 Chronicles 10 and 2 Chronicles 36. It is true, for instance, that the post-Josian kings demonstrate cultic unfaithfulness, and that this unfaith-fulness endangers the nation's security in the land; however, explicit use of the characteristic root מעל is only found as a description of the actions of the priests and people, although these acts of unfaithfulness are

light of Lev. 26.34-39. Cf. Rudolph, *Chronikbücher*, pp. 337-38; Galling, *Die Bücher der Chronik, Esra, Nehemiah*, p. 185; Cazelles, *Les livres des Chroniques*, p. 243; Ackroyd, *I & II Chronicles, Ezra, Nehemiah*, pp. 209-10; Virgulin, *Libri delle Cronache*, pp. 453-54.

1. Cf. Lev. 26.2: את־שבתתי תשמרו ומקדשי תיראו אני יהוה. It should also be noted that Lev. 26.40-45 provides a way of understanding the return from exile as a divine action done in response to repentance and for the sake of the covenant with Abraham, Isaac and Jacob.

2. Virgulin, *Libri delle Cronache*, p. 454; Coggins, *The First and Second Books of the Chronicles*, p. 308; Williamson, *1 and 2 Chronicles*, p. 418; Mangan, *1-2 Chronicles, Ezra, Nehemiah*, p. 145. The possibility that the period of 70 years is intended to refer to no other span of time apart from that indicated in the prophetic oracle (as suggested by Noth, *The Chronicler's History*, p. 77) also exists.

clearly intended to be in continuity with the actions of the kings (2 Chron. 36.14).

The Saul paradigm has its application to the post-Josian monarchs, but it applies to them principally as the last act of the post-Solomonic drama. This is indicated in part by the use of the root מעל in the post-Solomonic narratives, a usage which signals cultic offence and which has often been used in conjunction with a diminishment of the nation's security in the land.[1] The Saul paradigm contains the note that Saul's death was the result of Yahweh's action (1 Chron. 10.14), just as a similar lethal action of Yahweh is noted in the account of the final catastrophe,[2] and previously in the account of the death of Josiah.[3] Seen against the pattern of the Saul paradigm, these notices of lethal divine action are a strong indication that the Davidic dynasty has been terminated by Yahweh.[4]

When the Chronistic account of the destruction of Jerusalem is viewed in terms of ancient Near Eastern temple ideology, a further indication that Yahweh has ended the dynasty emerges. Meyers expresses the principle succinctly in the statement, 'Temples were the structures par excellence for communicating to a wide audience the authoritative rule of the regime responsible for erecting them',[5] and the Chronicler has demonstrated his awareness of this principle through the close associations he has portrayed between the Temple and the dynastic promise.[6] Therefore, the destruction of the Temple meant that the visible sign of the relationship between the Davidic dynasty and Yahweh (and the place where it was celebrated) was also

1. Cf. 2 Chron. 26.16, 18; 28.19, 22; 29.6, 19; 33.22.

2. 2 Chron. 36.17. Many translations attribute the actual slaying to the king of the Chaldeans, but a more obvious reading of the text would apply the slaying to Yahweh, who הכל נתן בידו. Cf. Rudolph, *Chronikbücher*, p. 336.

3. This divine action is given in the proleptic statement of Neco in 2 Chron. 35.21 when he warns Josiah חדל־לך מאלהים אשר־עמי ואל־ישחיתך.

4. As has been seen, this may be implied also in 2 Chron. 35.20-24.

5. 'David as Temple Builder', p. 364.

6. For example, one might refer in this regard to the choice of Solomon, not just as king but as temple-builder (1 Chron. 22.7-10; 28.2-7, 20; 29.1; 2 Chron. 2.10-11) and the role of the Temple and its personnel in the restoration of Davidic rule under Joash (2 Chron. 23.1-21). Cf. D. Sesboué, 'Ruine temporaire de Jérusalem: 2 Chron. 36:14-16.19-23', pp. 31-32; Flanagan, *David's Social Drama: A Hologram of Israel's Early Iron Age*, p. 224.

destroyed, implying that the relationship itself was terminated.

The final element of the Saul paradigm involves the transfer of kingship from the terminated dynasty. Indications of such a transfer are present, though not overwhelmingly, in the text from the conclusion of Josiah's Passover in 2 Chron. 35.20 up to the exile in 2 Chron. 36.21. The Chronicler hints at this when he portrays Neco speaking authentically in the name of God, for Neco is then exercising a kingly function, indicating that the king of Egypt (and not the Davidic king) is in possession of that particular royal prerogative.[1] A transfer of legitimate kingship may also be indicated by the role of foreign monarchs in enthroning and deposing the Davidic kings after Josiah.[2] However, the clearest indication that kingship has been transferred from the Davidic dynasty to another monarch is given after the narratives of the Jerusalem monarchy have been completed, as shall be seen.

The Edict of Cyrus (2 Chronicles 36.22-23)
The present ending of the Chronistic work corresponds almost exactly to the opening words of the book of Ezra.[3] Those scholars who see a single work in the books of Chronicles, Ezra and Nehemiah often suggest that these verses are an indication of that unity.[4] Some

---

1.   2 Chron. 35.21; Begg, 'The Death of Josiah in Chronicles: Another View', p. 5.

2.   2 Chron. 36.3, 4, 6, 10.

3.   2 Chron. 36.22-23 ‖ Ezra 1.1-3. The final word of Chronicles (ויעל) represents, not the ending, but the beginning of a clause in Ezra; apart from this truncation, the differences are slight. The spellings of the names כורש and ירמיהו in Chronicles seem to be simple orthographic variations (the former also to be found written *plene* in Ezra, however, and the latter following the general pattern in Chronicles for this form of theophoric name), and the only true variants are בפי in 2 Chron. 36.22 (where Ezra reads מפי) and יהוה in 2 Chron. 36.23 (where Ezra reads יהי).

4.   Curtis and Madsen, *A Critical and Exegetical Commentary on the Books of Chronicles*, p. 525; Rudolph, *Chronikbücher*, p. 338; Michaeli, *Les livres des Chroniques, d'Esdras et de Néhémie*, p. 250; Virgulin, *Libri delle Cronache*, p. 454; Becker, *2 Chronik*, p. 129. It is interesting that North, while accepting the literary unity of Chronicles–Ezra–Nehemiah, finds the inclusion of 2 Chron. 36.22-23 to be evidence against that position 'since an author does not normally quote himself, at least without mention of the extenuating circumstances'; R. North, *Israel's Chronicle*, p. 281.

commentators see these final verses as a note to the reader to turn to the book of Ezra to continue the story,[1] while it is also suggested that a reason for the inclusion of these verses is to supply a more optimistic ending to Chronicles[2] and perhaps to the Hebrew Bible as a whole.[3] Many commentators, including some who find no literary unity between Chronicles and Ezra–Nehemiah, suggest that these verses were added to the Chronistic work by a hand other than the Chronicler's with the effect that the original ending at 2 Chron. 36.21 has assumed a penultimate position.[4]

The oft noted function of these verses in supplying a positive ending to Chronicles provides the key to their assessment. While it is true that an ending of the work with 2 Chron. 36.21 would have contained its own note of hope in the limitation of 70 years placed on the servitude and in the land receiving its Sabbaths,[5] the force of the verse would be very understated when compared to the dark narrative of 2 Chron. 36.1-20. Since such an ending would not even state that the nation did in fact return, the content of the hopeful ending would be limited to an implied restoration to the land. If the work had in fact ended at

1. Randellini, *Il libro delle Cronache*, p. 504; Myers, *II Chronicles*, p. 224; McConville, *Chronicles*, p. 270; Williamson, *1 and 2 Chronicles*, p. 419; Dillard, *2 Chronicles*, p. 302.

2. Harvey-Jellie, *Chronicles*, p. 326; Slotki, *Chronicles*, p. 347; Brunet, 'Le Chroniste et ses sources', p. 386; Galling, *Die Bücher der Chronik, Esra, Nehemia*, p. 185; Rudolph, *Chronikbücher*, p. 338; Cazelles, *Les livres des Chroniques*, p. 243; Virgulin, *Libri delle Cronache*, pp. 454-55; Coggins, *The First and Second Books of the Chronicles*, p. 309; Dillard, *2 Chronicles*, p. 302.

3. Michaeli, *Les livres des Chroniques, d'Esdras et de Néhémie*, p. 250; Ackroyd, *I & II Chronicles, Ezra, Nehemiah*, p. 210.

4. Curtis and Madsen, *A Critical and Exegetical Commentary on the Books of Chronicles*, p. 525; Rudolph, *Chronikbücher*, p. 338; Randellini, *Il libro delle Cronache*, p. 504; Virgulin, *Libri delle Cronache*, p. 454. Galling, *Die Bücher der Chronik, Esra, Nehemia*, p. 185, assigns it to his Second Chronicler. Both Williamson, *1 and 2 Chronicles*, p. 418, and Dillard, *2 Chronicles*, p. 302, hold that Chronicles and Ezra–Nehemiah are separate works yet treat these verses as a secondary addition to the Chronicler's work which has the effect of stitching the two works together.

5. Cf. Galling, *Die Bücher der Chronik, Esra, Nehemia*, p. 185; Williamson, *Israel in the Books of Chronicles*, pp. 9-10; R.B. Dillard, *2 Chronicles*, p. 302; De Vries, *1 and 2 Chronicles*, p. 423.

36.21, the overall effect would be more one of gloom than of assurance.

The function of 2 Chron. 36.22-23 in the final form of the Chronistic work can be more clearly seen when compared to the conclusion of the Deuteronomistic *Vorlage* at 2 Kgs 25.27-30.[1] The former work terminates with the release of the Davidic king Jehoiachin from prison and the benevolent provision for him at the Babylonian court, striking a final note of hope after the events of desolation and depopulation narrated in 2 Kgs 25.1-26; these final verses indicate a redaction of the Deuteronomistic History during the exilic period.[2] Davidic overtones, either in terms of a restoration of the Davidide Jehoiachin or in terms of a more general Davidic hope, have often been observed within this ending.[3]

In contrast, the canonical ending of Chronicles makes no mention of the fate of the Davidides; specific concern with the Davidides vanishes completely from the text with the note of Zedekiah's rebellion and refusal to turn to Yahweh in 2 Chron. 36.13. Since mention of the Davidides is lacking, the hopeful emphasis in the concluding verses falls elsewhere:

> In the first year of Cyrus, king of Persia, to complete the word of Yahweh [spoken] by the mouth of Jeremiah, Yahweh roused the spirit of Cyrus, king of Perisa, and he made a proclamation go out through all his kingdom (it was even in writing) to say: 'Thus says Cyrus, king of Persia: "All the kingdoms of the earth Yahweh, God of the heavens, has given to me and he has entrusted to me the building of a House for him in

---

1.   McKenzie has hardly established a case for his theory that the Chronicler's *Vorlage* was an edition of the Deuteronomistic History which lacked the material from the death of Josiah to the exile; cf. *The Chronicler's Use of the Deuteronomistic History*, p. 187. The question is somewhat peripheral, as pointed out by Ackroyd, 'History and Theology in the Writings of the Chronicler', p. 514, since the Chronicler would have been aware of Jehoiachin's later fortunes and could have incorporated the story had he so desired.

2.   Eissfeldt, *The Old Testament: An Introduction*, p. 285; Noth, *The Deuteronomistic History*, p. 12; Gray, *I & II Kings*, p. 773.

3.   For example von Rad, *Old Testament Theology 1: The Theology of Israel's Historical Traditions*, p. 343; Becker, *Messiaserwartung im Alten Testament*, pp. 51-52; P.R. Ackroyd, 'The History of Israel in the Exilic and Post-Exilic Periods', pp. 320, 331; Conroy, *1-2 Samuel, 1-2 Kings*, pp. 253-54. For a contrary position, cf. Noth, *The Deuteronomistic History*, p. 98.

Jerusalem, which is in Judah. Whoever among you of all his people,
Yahweh his God [is] with him, and let him go up"' (2 Chron. 36.22-23).

Although these concluding verses of Chronicles form an undeniable
part of the Chronicler's work in the final form under consideration
here, the question of their originality to the work might be considered
on the basis of their overall integration into the Chronicler's thought.
In the context of a final form reading, the question can be phrased in
terms of the contribution made by 2 Chron. 36.22-23 as a conclusion
to the work.

First, it must be acknowledged that these verses belong originally to
the book of Ezra rather than to Chronicles; this is indicated by the
truncated form in which the passage appears in Chronicles and by its
closer connection with the subject matter of Ezra.[1] However, this need
be no more than a statement that here the Chronicler has utilized a
source, that is, the (earlier) book of Ezra;[2] such an observation places
the contribution of 2 Chron. 36.22-23 to the Chronicler's work no
lower than that of the scores of verses which are clearly drawn from
the Deuteronomistic History. Even the abrupt ending of 2 Chron.
36.23, sometimes taken as problematic in Chronicles,[3] has been
accounted for as an ending which encourages the community toward
action in response to the narrative.[4]

1. Cf. Curtis and Madsen, *A Critical and Exegetical Commentary on the Books
of Chronicles*, p. 525; Elmslie, *The Books of Chronicles*, p. 351; Rudolph,
Chronikbücher, p. 338; Williamson, *Israel in the Books of Chronicles*, p. 9-10;
Cazelles, *Les livres des Chroniques*, p. 243; J. Becker, *2 Chronik*, p. 129.

2. For those scholars who hold that Chronicles once existed as part of a unified
work Chronicles–Ezra–Nehemiah, the consideration of Ezra as a source for the
Chronicler does not really exist as a possibility; once Chronicles is considered a separate work from Ezra–Nehemiah, whether by the same author or by a different hand,
the question of the order of their respective dates arises. Several scholars have suggested that Ezra–Nehemiah is older or have noted instances where Ezra–Nehemiah
seems to serve as a source for the Chronicler; for example, Brunet, 'Le Chroniste et
ses sources', p. 484; Japhet, 'The Supposed Common Authorship of Chronicles
and Ezra–Nehemiah Investigated Anew', p. 371; Johnson, *The Purpose of the
Biblical Genealogies*, pp. 37-38, 42; Johnstone, 'Guilt and Atonement: The Theme
of 1 and 2 Chronicles', pp. 114-15; Dumbrell, 'The Purpose of the Books of
Chronicles', pp. 260, 265-66; Graham, 'A Connection Proposed between II Chr
24, 26 and Ezra 9–10', pp. 256-58.

3. Williamson, *Israel in the Books of Chronicles*, p. 9.

4. Eskenazi, 'The Chronicler and the Composition of 1 Esdras', pp. 56-57; cf.

There are linguistic indications that the use of Ezra 1.1-3 as a source for 2 Chron. 36.22-23 traces back to that person or those persons conventionally designated as the Chronicler. The first such indication is the close affinity of 2 Chron. 36.22 with the prophetic *inclusio* in 2 Chron. 36.12-21 already noted; the connection between these texts is provided by specific mention of Jeremiah, and the bridge between 2 Chron. 36.21 and 2 Chron. 36.22 has been further emphasized by the substitution of the preposition ב for the preposition מן in Ezra 1.1. A further indication can be seen in the use of the phrase יהוה אלהיו עמו in 2 Chron. 36.23, for the Chronicler has already made variations of this phrase familiar to his audience through their previous use, often in the very context of proposed Temple construction.[1] Thus, the only two significant variant readings in 2 Chron. 36.22-23 can be seen as an attempt to stress the connections between the concluding verses of Chronicles and the rest of the book by strengthening the links of vocabulary between the Ezra passage and the rest of the Chronistic work.

A major contribution that this conclusion makes to the meaning of the final form of Chronicles (and a further indication that it was originally included by the Chronicler in his work) can be seen in the post-Davidic nature of the hope that it presents to the audience. As an ending to the work, the passage does not look to shadowy indications of a Davidic restoration but to the firm promise of a restored Temple, thus identifying the Temple and its cultus as the permanent salvific contribution that the House of David has made to the nation.[2] This reinforces the strong impression left by the portrayal of the dynasty's ineffectiveness after Josiah had finished establishing the Temple

Elmslie, *The Books of Chronicles*, p. 352.

1.   Cf. 1 Chron. 17.2; 22.11, 16; 28.20. The change of יהי in Ezra 1.3 to יהוה in 2 Chron. 36.23 may have been intended to bring the Ezra passage into closer conformity with these and other occurrences of the phrase in Chronicles; on the intensified affirmation achieved through this change, see Johnstone, 'Guilt and Atonement: The Theme of 1 and 2 Chronicles', p. 115. The substitution of האלהים for the divine name in 1 Chron. 17.2 (where it had appeared in the *Vorlage* at 2 Sam. 7.3) may serve as an indication that David's proposal (in the terms implied by 1 Chron. 17.1) would not be realized.

2.   Caquot, 'Peut-on parler de messianisme dans l'oeuvre du Chroniste?', pp. 119-20; Ackroyd, 'History and Theology in the Writings of the Chronicler', p. 514.

(2 Chron. 35.20), and by the omission of all mention of members of the Davidic House after 2 Chron. 36.13.

A further recognition of the contribution of 2 Chron. 36.22-23 as the conclusion to the Chronistic work (and the final indication here cited that its inclusion should be attributed to the Chronicler's hand) emerges when the passage is considered in terms of the Saul paradigm. In the consideration of the application of the paradigm in light of the narratives of the post-Josian monarchs, it was noted that the final element in the paradigm, the termination of the dynasty and the turning of kingship elsewhere, lacks an explicit application in the narrative up to 2 Chron. 36.21. By the inclusion of the Edict of Cyrus, the Chronicler posits a hopeful conclusion to his work with the portrayal of a king for God's people, just as the book of Kings ends with a hopeful story involving a Judaean king; that the king in Chronicles is Cyrus and not a Davidide is surprising and seems to mark a notable departure from his *Vorlage* on the part of the Chronicler. The present conclusion stands as proof that the Davidic dynasty no longer possesses an exclusive right to legitimate kingship over Israel and may indicate that the political rule of the Davidides belongs finally and definitely to the past.[1]

That the rule of Cyrus signals the termination of the Davidic dynasty can be seen by the application to him of two of the same emphases which were once operative in the dynastic promise to David: that the king reigns only under Yahweh and that the task of temple-building is linked with divinely established kingship.[2] In receiving the commission to build the Temple, Cyrus inherits the chief symbol of the legitimacy of the Davidic dynasty according to the common ideo-logical language of the ancient Near East,[3] and according to the Chronistic narrative of the monarchy. In this way, the conclusion to the Chronicler's work demonstrates that the task entrusted to David's

1. Goldingay, 'The Chronicler as a Theologian', p. 114.

2. Cf. especially 1 Chron. 17.12, 14. Sesboué, 'Ruine temporaire de Jérusalem: 2 Chron. 6:14-16.19-23', p. 33; Braun, 'Chronicles, Ezra, and Nehemiah: Theology and Literary History', p. 62.

3. Cf. C.L. Meyers, 'Jachin and Boaz in Religious and Political Perspective', pp. 167-78; *idem*, 'David as Temple Builder', p. 364; K.W. Whitelam, 'The Symbols of Power: Aspects of Royal Propaganda in the United Monarchy', pp. 170-72; Flanagan, *David's Social Drama: A Hologram of Israel's Early Iron Age*, p. 224.

successors has passed outside the Davidic House; the question must arise for those who see a hope of Davidic restoration in the Chronicler's thought of what position or task the Chronicler has left in his conclusion for such a restored Davidide.

The hope enshrined in the conclusion is that Israel once again receives its security in the land, a security that centres on the Jerusalem Temple. However, the restoration has no connection with the rule of a Davidic king, but comes through the divinely appointed Cyrus whose Edict stands as the symbol of hope in a post-Davidic world.

Conclusion

The final form of the Chronicler's presentation of the monarchical history reveals an incorporation of elements from the common ancient Near Eastern temple ideology; the Jerusalem kings are shown to exercise the role of temple-builders and to bear the responsibility for the Temple's maintenance. The Chronicler has woven this ideology into different aspects of his work, notably in his *Urzeit* portrayal of the period of David and Solomon as well as in his concern with the dynastic promise and in the theme of divine retribution.

The ancient Near Eastern temple ideology supplies the Chronistic work with aspects of both endorsement and threat for the Davidic dynasty. The Chronicler's monarchical history opens with an encapsulation of the aspect of threat in the Saul narrative; this narrative acts as a paradigm which is applied both positively and negatively in the remainder of the work. The aspect of endorsement can be found most clearly in the portrayal of David and Solomon as the founders of the Jerusalem Temple. The work of David and Solomon is continued and completed by the cultic concern of some of the post-Solomonic monarchs who continue to care for the Temple and to regulate and provide for its cultus, until the Temple and its cultus are declared established in 2 Chron. 35.20. At the same time, the Saul paradigm is echoed in its negative aspect in other narratives of the post-Solomonic kings. This paradigm not only supplies a pattern which is invoked for individual monarchs; it also provides the Chronicler's audience with a way of interpreting the end of the Davidic dynasty and also with a post-Davidic vision of the nation's future consonant with that expressed in the Edict of Cyrus. The net result of the Chronistic intertwining of endorsement and threat centred on the cultus is that the cultus emerges as a principle reason for the monarchy's very existence and takes precedence over the Davidic monarchy as the real concern of the Chronicler. This priority of the cultus in the Chronicler's re-interpretation of the monarchical history has implications for his views on kingship, on the dynastic promise to David and on the role of the nation in the post-exilic world, and the next chapter will be devoted to the consideration of these implications.

Chapter 3

THE CULTIC REINTERPRETATION OF ISRAEL'S ROYAL HISTORY AND HERITAGE IN CHRONICLES

Introduction

The final form reading undertaken in the previous chapter shows the need for a synthesis of the Chronicler's message concerning the place of kingship in Israel's history; it also demonstrates that an attempt to find such a synthesis must take account of the close connection between king and cultus generally accepted in the ancient Near Eastern world. Although the institution of kingship does not constitute the sole concern of the Chronicler, it is sufficiently central to the narrative to indicate an essential aspect of his theology and to provide a backdrop against which much of his work can be interpreted.

Three aspects of the Chronicler's concern with kingship provide the foci for the synthesis attempted in this chapter: first, the relationship between the cultus and the election of the dynasty; secondly, the Chronistic perspective on the fulfilment of the promise to David; and finally, the Chronicler's presentation of the Davidic nation, task and promise as realities which endure into his own day.

Kingship as a Cultic Vocation

Although the Deuteronomistic History does not set out to delineate the royal ideology operative in monarchical Israel and allows itself at least one unequivocally anti-monarchical statement in 1 Sam. 8.11-18, it does afford its modern reader glimpses into the place of the monarchs in the workings of pre-exilic society. In this way, a number of functions are associated with the role of the king by the Deuteronomistic Historian. Among these might be listed the general

government of the nation according to right order,[1] the adjudication
of justice in individual cases,[2] the leadership of the nation's armies in
military exploits[3] and a responsibility for leadership in cultic matters.[4]
Thus the depiction of the functions of Israelite kingship in the
Deuteronomistic History is in broad agreement with the general picture of the functions of kingship in the ancient Near East;[5] such a
broad functional correspondence does not, of course, mean that other
aspects of the ancient Near Eastern concept of kingship also necessarily apply to Israelite kingship.[6]

1.   For example Judg. 17.6; 2 Sam. 21.1-9; 23.3; 1 Kgs 3.9. This function is
implied in the request for kingship to Samuel, as is indicated by the introduction to
the request which describes the unjust behaviour of Samuel's sons: 1 Sam. 8.3-5,
20.

2.   For example 2 Sam. 15.2-4; 1 Kgs 3.16-28.

3.   For example 2 Sam. 5.17-21; 10.17-18; 1 Kgs 22.1-4; 2 Kgs 3.4-8. The
Deuteronomistic author indicates that this is a prime concern in the introduction of
kingship into Israel: 1 Sam. 8.20. David's inconsistency in this matter receives an
excuse in 2 Sam. 21.15-17, and possibly a reprimand in 2 Sam. 11.1 (which gave
rise to the present textual confusion of that verse in the MT); cf. R.P. Gordon, *1 & 2
Samuel*, pp. 252-53 and the evidence given in *BHS ad loc.*

4.   For example 2 Sam. 6.1-19; 7.1-2; 24.18-25; 1 Kgs 6.2-38; 8.1-66; 2 Kgs
12.4-8; 18.3-4; 22.4-7; 23.1-23.

5.   Evidence for the ancient Near Eastern kings' responsibility for general government according to right order, as well as for their role in the adjudication of
individual cases, is given in K.W. Whitelam, *The Just King: Monarchical Judicial
Authority in Ancient Israel*, pp. 17-28, and some evidence for the responsibility of
non-Israelite monarchs in relation to the cultus is cited and discussed by Frankfort,
Kingship and the Gods, pp. 267-74 and by Keel, *The Symbolism of the Biblical
World*, pp. 269-80; further evidence for this cultic responsibility is referred to in ch.
2 above. The evidence for the kingly leadership of the army among non-Israelite
nations in the ancient Near East is so abundant that many examples can even be
found in the Hebrew Bible itself, as well as in multitudinous temple inscriptions in
Egypt and Mesopotamia; cf. Gen. 14.1-9; Exod. 14.5-18; Num. 20.21-23; 1 Kgs
14.25-26; 20.1; 2 Kgs 15.29; 16.9; 18.13; 23.29.

6.   The Israelite depiction of kingship does differ from that of Israel's neighbours in other respects. For instance, the Israelite kingship has an origin in history,
whereas elsewhere kingship had mythical origins as an action of the gods in the
Urzeit; cf. A.L. Oppenheim, 'The Sumerian King List', pp. 265-66, and
E.A. Speiser, 'Etana', p. 114. The Egyptian identification of the king with one or
more deities (as in J.A. Wilson, 'The Divine Attributes of Pharaoh', p. 431) stands
in contrast to the biblical portrayal of the king as one whose human condition and
responsibility before Yahweh brings limiting moral strictures upon his power.

The investigation of Chronicles contained in the earlier chapters of this study indicates that, among all possible functions of the Israelite king, the cultic function receives a certain priority in the Chronistic picture, even though other aspects of the kingly role in the pre-exilic nation are also portrayed in the work.[1] The priority of the cultic function might indicate that, for the Chronicler, the importance of kingship lies primarily in the king's role as facilitator of the cultus. This possibility will be considered first against the background of the ancient Near Eastern evidence and then in consideration of the evidence found in the Chronistic work itself.

The Cultus and Royal Election in the Ancient Near East

In the final form study of Chronicles undertaken in the preceding chapter, the role of the ancient Near Eastern king in the acts of temple building and temple maintenance has already been invoked. In synthesizing the Chronistic picture of king and cultus, a second consideration of the relationship between king and cultus as attested in the non-Israelite texts will help to focus the Chronistic portrayal in the light of the post-dynastic situation in which the Chronicler formulated his theology.

The ancient Near Eastern temple ideology embodied a mutual relationship between king and cultus: just as the monarch assumed a responsibility for the cultus, the cultus bestowed blessings upon the monarch, legitimacy not being the least of these. Expressed in this way, it might be argued that monarchies exploited the religious traditions of their nations for their own glorification. Without excluding that possibility in individual regimes, the texts reveal a different perspective: the kingship existed, at least in part, for the sake of the cultus and the cultic responsibility lay near the centre of the very concept of king. To take but two brief examples to illustrate this general observation, the cultic reason for having a king is indicated in the prayer for a king by Ethiopians who ask 'that thou might give [to] us a lord, to revive us, to build the temples of the gods of Upper and Lower

---

1.   Mention might be made, in addition to the general categories identified in the Deuteronomistic History, of the king's role in the military sphere, including the construction of fortifications, which activities are discussed by Welten, *Geschichte und Geschichtsdarstellung in den Chronikbüchern*, pp. 9-172.

Egypt, and to present divine offerings'.[1] In the second illustration, although the text is fragmentary, it is clear from the context of a Babylonian text (extant in a copy from the Persian or Seleucid periods) that the king and his office were created for the sake of services that he would render to the cultus.[2]

The accession to the throne was also an accession to the priesthood, and the ancient Near Eastern texts show that ancient monarchs used references to their priesthood to speak of their accession.[3] Texts dealing with the accession of a king sometimes make the cultus a consideration in the divine choice of a person as king, especially when the cultus had been neglected in earlier regimes. Thus an Egyptian stela laments that, during the reign of Akh-en-Aton,

> the temples of the gods and goddesses from Elephantine [down] to the marshes of the Delta [had...and] gone to pieces. Their shrines had become desolate, had become *mounds* overgrown with [*weeds*]. Their sanctuaries were as if they had never been. Their halls were a footpath...[4]

and concludes its description of the restoration of the cultus under Tut-ankh-Amon with a declaration that Amon fashioned the king for the very purpose of reinstating the cultus.[5] The same sequence is present in the Theban Great Papyrus Harris which proceeds from the cultic disarray under a Syrian overlord to the divinely willed accession of Set-nakht before continuing to catalogue the cultic accomplishments of Set-nakht's son, Ramses III, thus implicitly indicating

---

1.   Wilson, 'The Divine Nomination of an Ethiopian King', p. 448.

2.   A. Sachs, 'Ritual for the Repair of a Temple', pp. 341-42.

3.   For example Oppenheim, 'Adad-Nirari III (810–783): Expedition to Palestine', p. 281; C. Kühne, 'Hittite Texts: Prayers', p. 171.

4.   J.A. Wilson, 'Tut-ankh-Amon's Restoration after the Amarna Revolution', p. 251.

5.   '... all life and satisfaction are with them for the nose of the Horus who repeats births, the beloved son [of Amon]... for He fashioned him in order that He (Himself) might be fashioned' (Wilson, 'Tut-ankh-Amon's Restoration after the Amarna Revolution', p. 252). Although the text might seem at first to be obscure, the reference to fashioning refers to the making of bejewelled golden images of Amon by Tut-ankh-Amon which has been described earlier in the text; Wilson suggests that the conclusion might refer to the general advancement of Amon's cult under Tut-ankh-Amon. The title 'the Horus who repeats births' is an unequivocal reference to the king in whom the god Horus is incarnate; see Frankfort, *Kingship and the Gods*, pp. 36-40.

the cultic factor in the choice of the dynasty.[1] The Babylonian Nabonidus asserts that his call to kingship came for the express purpose of restoring the cultus of the god Sin which had been hitherto neglected.[2] However, the devotion of Nabonidus to his deity entailed the neglect of the more official Babylonian cultus;[3] therefore Cyrus can present his own rise to kingship over Babylon as an act of Marduk on behalf of both the cultus and the people after the cultic atrocities of Nabonidus.[4]

The ancient Near Eastern ideology was thus capable of speaking of the cultic function of kings as a reason for the election of individual monarchs and dynasties, as well as a reason for the institution of kingship itself. From this perspective, kings are chosen to establish and maintain the cultus. Disregard for the cultic aspect of the royal vocation could be interpreted as the reason for a king's removal (as in the case of Nabonidus), just as the cultic accomplishments of a monarch or dynasty could stand as implicit proof of the wise choice of the gods.

While the ancient Near Eastern ideology could comprehend the removal of a monarch or dynasty, it did not seem to have either the need or the capacity to contemplate the ending of the institution of kingship. Kingship was an essential part of the social order which traced its origins back to the *Urzeit* and which reflected a reality that existed with the gods before it ever functioned in human realms.[5]

The situation of the Chronicler was different, however. For him, the national kingship was no longer a present reality as it once had been. The historical perspective on the origins of Israelite kingship,[6] lacking to his non-Israelite contemporaries, may have enabled the Chronicler to envisage an end to his national monarchy in a way that

1.   Cf. the texts given from the Great Papyrus Harris by J.A. Wilson, 'A Syrian Interregnum', p. 260, and 'From the Lists of Ramses III', pp. 260-62.

2.   Oppenheim, 'Nabonidus and his God', p. 562.

3.   Cf. Oppenheim, 'Nabonidus (555–539): Nabonidus and the Clergy of Babylon', pp. 312-15.

4.   Oppenheim, 'Cyrus (557–529)', pp. 315-16.

5.   See J.A. Wilson, 'Another Version of the Creation by Atum', pp. 3-4; Speiser, 'The Creation Epic', pp. 68-69; Oppenheim, 'The Sumerian King List', pp. 265-66; Speiser, 'Etana', p. 114.

6.   1 Sam. 8.4-22. An awareness that kingship in Israel had its origins in the sphere of human history is also attested by 1 Chron. 1.43.

would have been nearly impossible for those of other nations in the ancient Near East. However, the historical perspectives on Israelite kingship's origin and cessation would still leave unanswered the major question of why kingship formed part of God's plan for Israel in the first place.

Embodied in the ancient Near Eastern ideology which was available to the Chronicler (even if only in the cultic and historical traditions of Israel to which he was heir) lay a possible approach to this question of the phenomenon of kingship in Israel: one reason for the deity to bring kings and dynasties to power was to advance the cultus. The Saul paradigm established in 1 Chronicles 10 indicates that the Chronicler uses this cultic aspect of the kingly vocation negatively to explain how a king and his dynasty could vanish from power, and the author seems to have utilized the Saul paradigm and cultic failure to explain the disappearance of Davidides from the throne as well.[1] The Chronicler may have applied the cultic aspect of royal election positively in order to account for the appearance of a national kingship in Israel, thus adding into his consideration of the Israelite monarchy a new historical dimension to the perception of kingship common to the ancient Near East; this positive identification of a reason for the establishment of Israel's monarchy would allow the Chronicler to account for its non-permanency, once he could show that the reason for its existence had passed.

Such an application of the ancient Near Eastern ideology by the Chronicler should have two effects on his historical presentation: the first would be to intertwine the monarchical history with a history of the cultus in such a way that the cultic aspect assumes priority; the second would be that the Chronicler must show that the dynastic promise to David which was enshrined in his historical and liturgical traditions was never intended to be an unconditional guarantee of political rule for an unending line of Davidic kings. The first of these possible effects will now be explored, and the second will be investigated in the next section of this chapter.

---

1. See the discussion of the post-Josian kings and the Edict of Cyrus in the preceding chapter.

The Institution of the Cultus as the Task
of the Monarchy in Chronicles

The Chronicler viewed the liturgical life of Israel as having been divinely ordained since the days of Moses, and, in his outlook, the Mosaic provisions for worship still obtained.[1] However, the Mosaic cultus was not complete in the Chronicler's eyes since it lacked the Temple which was the central locus in the Chronicler's experience of worship. Even though other cultic sites existed in post-exilic Judah,[2] the Chronicler displays an unwavering loyalty to the Temple of Yahweh established in Jerusalem. As a child of an ancient Near Eastern culture, the Chronicler realized that the progression from the non-temple cultus of Moses to the Second Temple liturgy familiar to himself, and in which he was possibly a functionary, required a king since temple building was the business of kings or their equivalents. Therefore, to narrate the story of the Temple necessarily involved re-telling at least part of the history of the monarchy, just as, conversely, it would have been inconceivable in the ancient world to trace the history of the Jerusalem kings without giving the Temple some degree of prominence.

The Chronicler demonstrates his awareness that the task of temple-building required a king by affording the king a unique place in the process, not only in the construction of the edifice but also in the continuing cultic responsibility. Even though Moses is honoured as the original cult founder in various parts of the work,[3] David is also portrayed at times as a cult founder, a type of new Moses, especially through the granting to David of the תבנית from the hand of Yahweh in 1 Chron. 28.19;[4] the portrayal of David in Mosaic terms with its

1. 2 Chron. 8.13; 23.18; 24.6, 9; 30.16; 35.6, 12.
2. For example Rolla, 'La Palestina Postesilica alla luce dell'archeologia', pp. 117-18, speaks of a temple and two hundred altars for burning incense excavated at Lachish alone.
3. 1 Chron. 6.34; 15.15; 21.29; 2 Chron. 1.3; 5.10; 8.13; 30.16; 35.6. The Chronicler's reverence for Moses is attested to by Wellhausen, *Prolegomena to the History of Ancient Israel*, p. 203, who expresses the view that there is no real progression in the Chronistic portrayal of the cultus (with particular reference to the reforms of Hezekiah and Josiah), but that a rigid adherence to Mosaism is exhibited. It would seem that Wellhausen has failed to notice the real cultic authority which the Chronicler has predicated of the Davidic monarchs.
4. Cf. Poulssen, 'Rex et Templum in Israel', p. 268; Coppens, *Le messianisme*

overtones of cult founder is further enhanced by the correspondences, already discussed, which the Chronicler establishes between Solomon and Joshua. The regal authority in the cultus continues to be demonstrated in the Chronicler's work as the Temple is constructed under Solomon and as further provisions are made for it by later monarchs, all presuming implicitly the cult-founding authority of the Davidic dynasty.[1]

The fundamental nature of the kingly vocation as a cultic vocation can also be discerned in Chronicles by the correlation that the Chronicler makes between a successful reign and the cultic faithfulness of the monarch. Contrasting examples for this can be found in the Chronistic portrayal of the reigns of Abijah and Ahaz. Although the great speech of Abijah in 2 Chron. 13.4-12 may seem to be an unequivocal warning to the forces of the Northern Kingdom that to fight against the Davidic king is to wage war on God,[2] a closer reading reveals that the heart of the speech is a warning to the Northern troops that Judah has the cultus and cultic faithfulness on its side (2 Chron. 13.9-12). If it were simply a question of constant divine support for the Davidic king when facing a Northern threat, then Ahaz, who was faithless towards the cultus but unquestionably a Davidide, would also have prevailed over the Northern forces led by Pekah.[3] Instead, Ahaz is defeated in the narrative of that conflict, and the infidelity of the South is cited as the reason.[4] Since Ahaz fails in his cultic vocation, he fails in other aspects of his kingly vocation, and the comparison between Abijah and Ahaz shows that the cultic

royal, p. 107; De Vries, 'Moses and David as Cult Founders in Chronicles', p. 626.

  1. De Vries, 'Moses and David as Cult Founders in Chronicles', p. 635.

  2. Cf. 2 Chron. 13.5, 8, 12.

  3. The conflict with Israel is heightened in 2 Chron. 28.5-6 through the treatment of Aram and Israel as separate forces mounting separate attacks instead of the combined Syro-Ephraimite forces spoken of in Isa. 7.1-2 and 2 Kgs 16.5. Cf. Mosis, *Untersuchungen zur Theologie des chronistischen Geschichtswerkes*, p. 187.

  4. 2 Chron. 28.5-8. The Chronistic account of Ahaz's defeat is contrary— although not contradictory—to the impression given by the Deuteronomistic History; 2 Kgs 16.5 states that Pekah (together with Rezin of Aram) besieged Ahaz without overcoming him, and no reference is made to the episode given in Chronicles; cf. Thompson, *Situation and Theology: Old Testament Interpretations of the Syro– Ephraimite War*, pp. 96-97.

criterion is stronger in the Chronistic narrative than even the Davidic considerations.[1]

It would be somewhat simplistic to suggest that Chronicles has become simply a history of the cultus, although Gottwald comes very close to just such an equation.[2] The principle as enunciated by Goldingay[3] to the effect that 'It is the temple theme which provides the criterion of inclusion or omission' is true only up to a point; the Chronicler has also exhibited a concern to portray the history of the monarchy, with some attention, however minimal, given to every king named in the tradition. Although the temple theme often exerts a great gravitational pull on the monarchical material, a pure history of the cultus would not necessarily have included all that the Chronistic work encompasses. For that reason it is preferable to speak of Chronicles as a combined history of the monarchy and history of the cultus, a blending which in itself shows great affinity to the combination of king and cultus already to be found in the ancient Near Eastern ideology.

Although it also possesses a negative aspect, the cultic thread in the Chronicler's History lends a distinct impetus and contributes to the shape to the work. The concern with the construction of the Temple edifice dominates the Davidic and Solomonic narratives and accounts for their centrality; the concern with temple-building effects a transformation in the portrayal of both kings, and especially affects the picture of David.[4] However, the Temple edifice does not comprise the

1. The same pattern stated here for Ahaz is present in the Chronistic treatment of Amaziah's unfaithful period. After his service of the gods of Seir (2 Chron. 25.14-16), Amaziah suffers defeat by the forces of the Northern Kingdom (2 Chron. 25.20-24).

2. In Gottwald's view, the Chronicler's work (which for him includes the books of Ezra and Nehemiah) is 'a history of the temple and cult community of Jerusalem. The kings of Judah, the Persian overlords, and political affairs in general, acquire meaning only insofar as they contribute to the founding, upbuilding, and rebuilding of the cult community centred on temple and law' (N.K. Gottwald, *The Hebrew Bible: A Socio-Literary Introduction*, p. 515).

3. 'The Chronicler as a Theologian', p. 101.

4. Contrasting the Chronistic and the Deuteronomistic portrayals of David, Wellhausen, *Prolegomena to the History of Ancient Israel*, p. 182, protests that David has been transformed from a dynamic political and military hero into a feeble religious figure. Brunet, 'Le Chroniste et ses sources', p. 508, refers to the resulting Chronistic David as '*saint* roi David, le modèle du roi théocratique'.

entire cultus, and so the Chronicler shows other aspects of the cultic life of (post-exilic) Israel taking form in his depiction of history. The Chronistic History goes beyond the purely Mosaic cultus to trace the evolution of the Temple festival rituals, always under monarchical control.[1] An extensive and detailed concern with the various arrangements for the cultic personnel in both liturgical and material considerations manifests itself in the Chronicler's depiction of these arrangements coming into existence and being enforced under the wise and authoritative guidance of the Davidic king;[2] thus the Chronicler constructs for his readers the structures and roles pertaining to the cultic personnel which are familiar to himself and his audience and bestows upon these arrangements the legitimacy of royal authority.[3] Finally, more than one exegete has noticed that the Israel over which the Davidic kings rule is at base a liturgical קהל;[4] although the קהל of Israel exists before the monarchy, the Chronicler underscores the connection between the king and the קהל by portraying the Davidic king as the convener of the קהל and by showing the role of the קהל in accompanying the king as the Jerusalem cultus progresses

---

1.   Cf. especially 1 Chronicles 16; 2 Chronicles 5–7; 8.12-13; 30; 35. Cancik, 'Das judische Fest: Ein Versuch zu Form und Religion des chronistischen Geschictswerkes', p. 339, suggests that the festival narratives act as target points for the Chronistic narrative as a whole and make the cultic history into the Chronicler's major theme.

2.   1 Chron. 6.16-17; 15.2-24; 16.4-7, 37-42; 23.2–26.32; 28.13; 2 Chron. 5.11-14; 8.14-15; 13.9-12; 17.7-9; 19.8-11; 29.15, 21-30; 30.15-17; 31.2-19; 35.2-6, 10-15. Although the canonical prophets are usually not considered cultic functionaries, the Chronicler obviously considers prophets to function in this way, and the frequent Chronistic mention of prophets is another aspect of his concern for the cultic personnel; cf. 1 Chron. 25.1; 2 Chron. 20.14.

3.   Cf. Welch, *The Work of the Chronicler: Its Purpose and Date*, pp. 57-80, 114-20, 139-42; Freedman, 'The Chronicler's Purpose', pp. 436-42; Williamson, 'The Origins of the Twenty-Four Priestly Courses: A Study of 1 Chronicles XXIII–XXVII', pp. 251-68; J.P. Weinberg, 'Der König im Weltbild des Chronisten', p. 427; Wright, 'The Legacy of David in Chronicles: The Narrative Function of 1 Chronicles 23–27', pp. 229-42.

4.   For example Noth, *The Chronicler's History*, p. 92; Galling, *Die Bücher der Chronik, Esra, Nehemia*, p. 7; Goldingay, 'The Chronicler as a Theologian', p. 118; Brueggemann, *David's Truth in Israel's Imagination and Memory*, pp. 100-108.

in the Chronistic History;[1] in this way, the development of the cultus becomes a component in the history of the liturgical קהל of the nation.

In every major aspect of the establishment and progression of the Temple cultus, the monarch is to the fore. Von Rad,[2] Newsome,[3] Virgulin[4] and Brueggemann[5] are among those who find this royal prominence to be evidence of the Chronicler's concern to establish a legitimation of the post-exilic cultus through portraying a monarchical involvement in its foundation; however, such a legitimation only becomes fully intelligible against the wider background of the relationship between king and cultus in the ancient Near Eastern understanding.

Once placed against that ideological background, a new possibility emerges for interpreting the role of the Chronistic kings in the cultus: although the Chronistic kings exercise many functions, the cultus may have been portrayed by the Chronicler as the royal task *par excellence*. And this is precisely what several exegetes have discerned in the Chronicler's work: thus, for example Freedman[6] observes that the historical and political achievements of the Davidic dynasty have been subordinated to its cultic accomplishments; Poulssen[7] describes the Chronicler's ideal king as exercising his office primarily in the ambit of the Temple; Braun[8] notes that the Chronicler speaks of the dynastic promise in direct relationship to the construction of the Temple so that temple-building becomes the sole task laid upon Solomon; Mosis notes that the only real interest displayed in the Chronistic treatment

---

1. 1 Chron. 13.1-5; 15.3-11; 23.2; 28.1, 8, 21; 29.1-9; 2 Chron. 1.3; 5.2-4; 6.3, 12; 30.1, 5-13, 23; 2 Chron. 34.29 might also be added to this list, since, even though it only mentions Judah and Jerusalem, 34.18 implies that the phrase refers to all Israel. The all-Israel concern may be based in the concept of a liturgical קהל in total integrity; for this reason, the genealogies and 1 Chronicles 27 may also reflect a concern with the people as a cultic unit. See Williamson, *1 and 2 Chronicles*, pp. 174-75.

2. *Das Geschichtsbild des chronistischen Werkes*, pp. 98-99.

3. 'Toward a New Understanding of the Chronicler and his Purposes', p. 215.

4. *Libri delle Cronache*, p. 47.

5. *David's Truth in Israel's Imagination and Memory*, pp. 100, 107.

6. 'The Chronicler's Purpose', p. 437.

7. 'Rex et Templum in Israel', p. 269.

8. 'Solomon, the Chosen Temple Builder: The Significance of 1 Chronicles 22, 28, and 29 for the Theology of Chronicles', p. 587; 'Chronicles, Ezra, and Nehemiah: Theology and Literary History', p. 61.

of David and Solomon concerns their Temple-building function;[1] and McCarthy[2] finds that even some of the slight changes that the Chronicler has made to his *Vorlage* bring about a new emphasis in Chronicles on the Temple and the royal responsibility for it.

It therefore emerges that there is considerable evidence to suggest that the Chronicler viewed royal election primarily as a call to a cultic task, drawing into the centre of his history something which was already inherent in the ancient Near Eastern ideology and in the historical traditions of Israel. This aspect of royal election is especially influential in the depiction of David as a founder of the cultus, in the election of Solomon for the task of building the Temple, and in the authority that post-Solomonic monarchs display in the progression of the Temple cultus. The cultic side of the royal vocation also manifests itself negatively especially in the Saul paradigm, as well as in the disasters that follow upon the cultic failures of various post-Solomonic kings. A consideration of the cultic purpose of royal election not only provides the Chronicler with a way of accounting for the emergence of kingship in Israel, but also with a way of interpreting the end of dynasties, as is evident from the Saul paradigm.

The Fulfilment of the Davidic Promise in Chronicles

The Chronicler's emphasis on the cultus in the royal task is drawn from the traditional picture of kingship in Israel, even though it imbues that picture with a different hierarchy of priorities. In connecting kingship with aspects of the cultus, Chronicles shares the common Old Testament outlook, already evident in the Deuteronomistic History[3] and Psalms,[4] even though the way in which the new emphasis in the Chronistic work emerges also constitutes a point of distinction from some of the other material in the Hebrew Bible.

The shift of emphasis towards the priority of the cultic role of kings must be considered to be at least a partial reinterpretation of the place

---

1. *Untersuchungen zur Theologie des chronistischen Geschichtswerkes*, pp. 162-63.
2. 'Covenant and Law in Chronicles–Nehemiah', p. 26.
3. For example 1 Sam. 6.1-5, 14-16; 24.25; 1 Kgs 6.1-38; 8.62-65.
4. For example Ps. 78.68-70; 110.4; 132.1-18.

of the monarchy in the life of Israel. A reinterpretation of the place of the monarchy does not necessarily entail the exclusion of any role for the monarchy in Israel's future; the book of Ezekiel, for instance, reduces the status of the monarchy while envisaging a role for the prince in the future Israel.[1] It is conceivable that the purpose of the Chronicler's new emphasis on the cultic role of the monarch is not unlike that of Ezekiel, giving to future monarchs a place in restored Israel while implicitly restricting their role so that the abuses of the past will not be repeated. While this is possible, its likelihood is diminished by the fact that the Chronicler gives the Davidic monarchs greater authority in cultic matters than does his Deuteronomistic predecessor.[2]

When considering the reinterpretation of the place of the monarchy to be found in Chronicles, it is important to note that the Chronicler's narrative displays an undeniable interest in the dynastic promise to David. This promise, which had been applied to a succession of Davidides while they actually reigned on the Davidic throne, must necessarily acquire a somewhat changed significance in the work of an author who wrote in an era in which no Davidide had reigned within living memory. In what follows, that changed significance will be considered, together with its implications for the Chronicler's theology.

The Question of Messianism in Chronicles

A fully Christian reading of the Hebrew Bible takes place in the light of the Christian's belief that the Scriptures bear witness to Jesus as messiah. As such, a Christian reading will always tend towards the messianic interpretation, especially in the liturgical and spiritual reading of these ancient Scriptures. However, the messianic reading that Christians give to these passages is not necessarily a statement of

---

1. Cf. Ezek. 43.7; 44.2-3; 45.7-17; 46.2, 4-8, 10, 12, 16-18; 48.21.

2. Thus, for example, David lays down the liturgy of thanksgiving before the Ark in 1 Chron. 16.4-7 and sets the courses of the liturgical personnel in 1 Chron. 23.6–26.32, Solomon confirms the appointments of the priests and Levites in 2 Chron. 8.14, the newly-crowned Jehoiada's first royal action is to arrange the liturgical personnel in 2 Chron. 23.18-19, Hezekiah makes arrangements for the Temple sacrifices and provision for the upkeep of the Temple personnel in 2 Chron. 31.2-19 and Josiah establishes the functions of the Levites in the Passover liturgy in 2 Chron. 35.3-6. None of these incidents are to be found in the *Vorlage*.

the intentions of the original author or of the primary meaning that such passages had in the minds of their original audiences.[1] The very nature of these works as inspired, as well as their continued use through the ages, means that they possess levels of meaning of which the original authors could not conceive.[2] However, even critical exegesis can be influenced by the messianic interpretation which has been given to texts in the Christian tradition, obscuring the distinction between the meaning of a text in a later situation and the significance of the text as it spoke in its original dialogue,[3] and even at times obscuring the distinction between messianism and eschatology, as well as the distinctions between various possible types of messianism.[4] It is therefore essential to make a rigid distinction between the significance of the promise to David in Chronicles in the context of its original composition, and the significance of that same promise in the same work for those who read it in the light of the fulfilment of the dynastic promise in God's messiah;[5] only the former is the concern of the present study.

Critical exegesis concerns itself primarily with the meaning of a canonical work in the context of its original composition; but even studies beginning from this common base have resulted in varying interpretations of the basic import of the dynastic promise in Chronicles. No consensus has emerged, and the various investigations of the Chronistic thought on the Davidic promise have left us facing 'a

1.   Among the many discussions concerned with this problem, especially with regard to use of the prophets and psalms, the following might be noted: W.S. La Sor, 'The *Sensus Plenior* and Biblical Interpretation', pp. 47-64; R.E. Brown and S.M. Schneiders, 'Hermeneutics', pp. 1157-58; J. Jensen, 'Prediction-Fulfillment in Bible and Liturgy', pp. 646-62.

2.   The recent study and consideration of texts, biblical and non-biblical, has led interpreters to see the limitations of strictly confining meaning to the supposed intention of the author. In this regard, see P. Ricoeur, *Interpretation Theory: Discourse and the Surplus of Meaning*, pp. 89-95; W. Riley, 'Situating Biblical Narrative: Poetics and the Transmission of Community Values', pp. 38-40; *idem*, 'On the Location of Meaning in a Sacred Text', pp. 7-23.

3.   Becker, *Messiaserwartung im Alten Testament*, p. 65.

4.   Saebø, 'Messianism in Chronicles? Some Remarks to the Old Testament Background of the New Testament Christology', pp. 85-87.

5.   Such a messianic use of 1 Chron. 17.1-15 is evident in the Liturgy of the Hours of the Roman Rite by the assignation of this reading for the Office of Readings of the Solemnity of the Annunciation of the Lord.

grotesque dilemma—[Chronicles] is either intensely messianic or entirely non-messianic'.[1]

It was seen in the initial chapter that scholarly opinion is widely divided on this issue, ranging across a number of possibilities. For the purposes of this section of the study, these opinions can be considered according to two possible basic positions: the dynastic promise in Chronicles either holds out the hope of a dynastic restoration (whether eschatological or not)[2] or it expresses no such hope.[3] The question of messianism[4] in Chronicles only arises if evidence for a hope of dynastic restoration can be established in the work.

Some Chronistic texts are often cited as an indicator that the Chronicler foresees a Davidic restoration and as his means of expressing this explicitly in his work; a consideration of such a set of texts should indicate whether the Davidic restoration does in fact constitute a major part of the Chronicler's outlook which he has carefully and unequivocally expressed.

1.   Becker, *Messiaserwartung im Alten Testament*, p. 75.
2.   Among those who hold to the eschatological interpretation of the perceived promise of Davidic restoration in Chronicles might be mentioned von Rad, *Das Geschichtsbild des chronistischen Werkes*; Noordtzij, 'Les intentions du Chroniste'; Galling, *Die Bücher der Chronik, Esra, Nehemia*; Botterweck, 'Zur Eigenart der chronistischen Davidsgeschichte'; Brunet, 'La théologie du chroniste: théocratie et messianisme'; Randellini, *Il libro delle Cronache*, and Williamson, 'Eschatology in Chronicles'. Among those who favour a less eschatological but still David-restoring interpretation are Noth, *The Chronicler's History*, Freedman, 'The Chronicler's Purpose', and Cross, 'A Reconstruction of the Judean Restoration'.
3.   Among those who do not find an explicit hope for a dynastic restoration in Chronicles are Rudolph, *Chronikbücher*; Plöger, *Theocracy and Eschatology*; Schumacher, 'The Chronicler's Theology of History'; Caquot, 'Peut-on parler de messianisme dans l'oeuvre du Chroniste?'; Japhet, *The Ideology of the Book of Chronicles and its Place in Biblical Thought*, and De Vries, 'Moses and David as Cult Founders in Chronicles'.
4.   In the context of Chronicles, messianism is generally taken to refer to the future divine fulfilment of the dynastic promise to David after the fall of the Davidic throne, in a manner which goes beyond the simple restoration of the Davidic dynasty to power and which ushers in the time of fulfilment of various promises; in other words, discussion concerning Chronicles uses the simple term 'messianism' to signify the more precise concept of royal eschatological messianism which is related to parts of the prophetic tradition. Cf. Saebø, 'Messianism in Chronicles? Some Remarks to the Old Testament Background of the New Testament Christology', pp. 92-96,102.

For the sake of this consideration, the texts suggested as indicators of the importance of the Davidic covenant in the Chronicler's work by von Rad[1] will serve as a representative selection of texts sometimes put forward as evidence of the Chronicler's David-restoring outlook. The suggested evidence consists of: the changes made to Nathan's oracle in 1 Chron. 17.1-15; the prayers for the (re-)establishment of the Davidic dynasty in 2 Chron. 1.9, 6.17 and 6.42; the change in 2 Chron. 7.18 to read כרתי instead of the דברתי of the *Vorlage*; the reading מושל בישראל in 2 Chron. 7.18 as a messianic allusion to Mic. 5.1 in place of the *Vorlage*'s מעל כסא ישראל; the reference to the covenant of salt by which Yahweh had given the kingdom to David and his sons in 2 Chron. 13.5; the Chronicler's explicit mention of the Davidic Covenant in 2 Chron. 21.7; the invocation by Jehoiada of the Word of Yahweh concerning the sons of David in 2 Chron. 23.3;[2] and the texts which identify the kingdom of David with the kingdom of Yahweh.[3]

Taken as a group, the above texts are a solid indication that the Chronicler has a concern with the Davidic covenant (which is precisely the claim that von Rad makes for the majority of them). What is not clear from these texts, however, is that the Chronicler is using any or all of them to indicate his hopes of a Davidic restoration (as von Rad implies by his repeated statements of the conviction that the Chronicler expects a messianic fulfilment of the divine promises).[4] Thus the changes in the Chronistic version of Nathan's oracle, rather than pointing to a future successor to a long-empty Davidic throne, seem to make the oracle apply primarily to Solomon and to effect the omission of the safety-valve of chastisement.[5] The reading כרתי in

---

1. *Das Geschichtsbild des chronistischen Werkes*, pp. 123-27.

2. There is a misprint in von Rad's work which gives this reference as 2 Chron. 21.3; *Das Geschichtsbild des chronistischen Werkes*, p. 124.

3. For example 1 Chron. 17.14; 28.5; 2 Chron. 13.8.

4. *Das Geschichtsbild des chronistischen Werkes*, pp. 122-23, 126, 135-36.

5. Von Rad produces an unusually strong eschatological interpretation of אשר יהיה מבניך in 1 Chron. 17.11: 'Die Gültigkeit der Verheißung ist sichtlich für eine viel fernere Zukunft ausgeweitet, sie gilt nunmehr der Nachkommenschaft der Söhne Davids'; *Das Geschichtsbild des chronistischen Werkes*, p. 124. Cf. also *Old Testament Theology 1: The Theology of Israel's Historical Traditions*, p. 351: 'The prophecy of Nathan spoke of the descendants "who shall come forth from your loins" (II Sam. VII. 12); but with the Chronicler it is the descendants "who shall

2 Chron. 7.18 may, in fact, indicate a stronger concern with the covenantal nature of the word to David,[1] but the restoration of the Davidic dynasty only follows if such a dynastic promise is interpreted by the Chronicler to apply even after the long interruption which began in the sixth century; it should also be noted that this word כרתי has been introduced into a conditioned context (2 Chron. 7.17-18). The prayers in 2 Chron. 1.9 and 6.17 for the establishment of the dynastic promise may pertain to the narrated past rather than the active prayer of the Chronicler himself; the prayer in 2 Chron. 6.42, while probably representing the Chronicler's own prayer, is capable of carrying an entirely different significance than that of a prayer for the restoration of the Davidic dynasty.[2] The evidence indicates that the Chronicler has not introduced the phrase מושל בישראל into 2 Chron. 7.18, least of all as a messianic allusion to Mic. 5.1.[3] Abijah's invocation of ברית מלח, far from representing an unequivocal statement of an unending and unconditioned dynastic promise, could allude to a covenant which was rooted in a cultic meal and which required repetition for its continuity. The heightening of covenant in 2 Chron. 21.7 may emphasize the need of the dynasty to continue until the Temple, the ניר promised to David, is established;[4] and Jehoiada's statement in 2 Chron. 23.3 might bear a similar import.[5] The identification of the kingdom as belonging to Yahweh rather than to the Davidides is far from an unequivocal elevation of the status of the dynasty, and may instead refer to the Davidic king's position as vassal to Yahweh who is the true king of Israel.[6]

come forth from thy sons" (I Chron. XVII. 11)'.

1.   It is also possible that this reading is due to a scribal error; cf. W. Rudolph, *Chronikbücher*, p. 217.

2.   This is especially true in light of the democratization of the Davidic Covenant in Isa. 55.3 which the Chronicler seems to invoke here.

3.   The Septuagintal evidence of 3 Kgdms 9.5 shows the possibility that the Chronicler was following his *Vorlage*; cf. Curtis and Madsen, *A Critical and Exegetical Commentary on the Books of Chronicles*, p. 351.

4.   Cf. Coppens, *Le messianisme royal*, p. 51; Gray, *I & II Kings*, p. 297.

5.   The statement only necessitates an interpretation which demands the restoration of the Davidic dynasty when the verse is removed from its narrative context. Viewed in that light it is possible that the role of the House of David—and therefore the necessity of a Davidide on the throne—continues until the Temple is fully established; after that point, the necessity inherent in Jehoiada's statement vanishes.

6.   This would be more in keeping with ancient Near Eastern thought concerning

It emerges, therefore, that the evidence from the text of Chronicles suggested by von Rad fails to necessitate a David-restoring interpretation of the work. This same evidence does, however, succeed in indicating the Chronicler's concern with Yahweh's promise to David, but such a concern need not necessarily point to a conviction that the Davidic dynasty would be restored. It may point to the promise as a theological problem for which a solution, or at least an approach to a solution, is offered through the Chronicler's narrative.

Given the Chronicler's dual concern with the guilt of individual monarchs and with retribution, his work would have to show either that the dynastic promise was unconditioned and unlimited or that all the conditions upon the dynasty were fulfilled if his narrative were to indicate a belief in Davidic restoration. However, the conditionality placed upon the dynastic promise is indicated by a number of texts, especially from the Davidic and Solomonic narratives,[1] and the Chronicler may even have indicated a *terminus ad quem* for the dynasty in 1 Chron. 28.20; the reiteration of conditionality after the completion of the Temple dedication indicates that even this action does not fulfil the conditions which governed the future of the dynasty (2 Chron. 7.17-22). Moreover, the Chronicler's frequent reference to Psalm 132 in the Davidic and Solomonic narratives[2] might be a further allusion to the conditionality of the dynastic promise as expressed in Ps. 132.12, just as his entire perspective of conditionality may be closely related to the same psalm text.[3]

The conditioned nature of the dynastic promise carries its own significance in a work written when the promise had not provided a Davidic king for many generations; it testifies to a concern with the dynastic promise after hope for Davidic restoration no longer seemed

the relationship of the king and the deity. Cf. R. de Vaux, 'The King of Israel, Vassal of Yahweh', pp. 152-66. The identification of the kingdom as primarily belonging to Yahweh will be discussed below with reference to some of the non-Israelite evidence.

1.   For example 1 Chron. 28.7, 9; 2 Chron. 6.16; 7.17-22.

2.   This reference is most explicit in the quotation of this psalm in 2 Chron. 6.41-42, but less explicit reference to the psalm has been detected in 1 Chronicles 28 and in the whole framework of the narratives concerning these two kings. Cf. Welten, 'Lade–Tempel–Jerusalem: Zur Theologie der Chronikbücher', pp. 169-83; J.G. McConville, 'I Chronicles 28:9: Yahweh "Seeks Out" Solomon', pp. 106-107.

3.   McConville, 'I Chronicles 28:9: Yahweh "Seeks Out" Solomon', pp. 106-107.

a sustainable option in the mind of the author. By drawing out the conditionality of the dynastic promise and by portraying the unfaithfulness of many post-Solomonic kings, the Chronicler has shown that the members of the dynasty had failed to fulfil the conditions required for its continuance. The Chronicler thus explains the lack of a Davidic monarch as the result of the performance of the dynasty in the light of the conditionality of the promise to David, not as a defect in the dynastic promise itself. Since the Chronicler has thus shown the promise of a reigning dynasty to have been voided by the Davidic kings, the messianism that some exegetes have detected in Chronicles would seem to be largely a reflection of their own faith rather than of the Chronicler's message.[1]

Because the Chronicler has indicated his concern with the dynastic promise and yet has not demonstrated a hope for Davidic restoration, his interpretation must indicate a different function in the history of Israel for both the promise and the dynasty that it generated. Such a Chronistic interpretation would have to allow for the Davidic House to relinquish its function as the reigning dynasty in Jerusalem without endangering the enduring nature of the חסדי דויד referred to in 2 Chron. 6.42.

Bringing the Dynasty to an End
Von Rad puts forward the identification of the kingdom of David with the kingdom of Yahweh as one indication of the Chronicler's messianic concern with the dynastic promise.[2] This identification has been viewed in a similar light by Brunet,[3] Botterweck[4] and Saebø.[5] However, other exegetes find somewhat different significances in this

---

1. De Vries, 'Moses and David as Cult Founders in Chronicles', p. 637, makes the impassioned plea: 'Is it not time for scholars to give up the phantasm of a (quasi-) eschatological David?' However, De Vries himself seems to have held a David-restoring interpretation in his 'The Schema of Dynastic Endangerment in Chronicles', p. 73, thus illustrating the tenacity of the interpreter's own messianism in reading texts from the Hebrew Bible concerned with the monarchy.

2. *Das Geschichtsbild des chronistischen Werkes*, pp. 125-26. Von Rad mentions, in particular, 1 Chron. 17.14; 28.5; 29.23; 2 Chron. 9.8; 13.8.

3. 'Le Chroniste et ses sources', p. 505.

4. 'Zur Eigenart der chronistischen Davidsgeschichte', p. 433.

5. 'Messianism in Chronicles? Some Remarks to the Old Testament Background of the New Testament Christology', pp. 90-91

Chronistic portrayal of the kingdom as belonging properly to Yahweh: for example, Michaeli[1] and Schumacher[2] suggest that the Chronicler has related the kingdom of David to his greater concern, which is the theocracy; Myers[3] interprets the shift in emphasis away from the earthly ruler as a way of lessening the political role of David and his dynasty; Caquot[4] and Becker[5] suggest that, while the Davidic dynasty participates in the kingship of Yahweh, the emphasis on the kingdom belonging to Yahweh frees the divine kingship from absolute association with the earthly representatives; De Vries[6] finds that the Chronicler has shown that kingship belongs properly to Yahweh and is held by the Davidides on trust.

The Chronistic identification of the kingdom as belonging primarily to Yahweh immediately invokes the notion of theocracy which itself has been applied in contrasting ways to the Chronicler's thought. Thus while Rudolph[7] and Plöger[8] believe that the theocratic approach of the Chronicler excludes messianism, others, such as Brunet,[9] Galbiati[10] and Saebø[11] find that the Chronicler has displayed theocratic thought while retaining a place for the Davidide.

The proper analysis of this aspect of the Chronicler's presentation of the monarchical history should take the ancient Near Eastern evidence into account. Throughout the ancient Near East, the title of king is used for the deity and the relationship of earthly kingship to divine kingship is manifest in different ways. In Babylon, earthly kingship is conferred by the gods who bestow the insignia of kingship upon the earthly king[12] and the kingship can be spoken of as something

1. *Les livres des Chroniques, d'Esdras et de Néhémie*, p. 32.
2. 'The Chronicler's Theology of History', p. 15.
3. *I Chronicles*, pp. lxxxi-lxxxii.
4. 'Peut-on parler de messianisme dans l'oeuvre du Chroniste?', p. 119.
5. *Messiaserwartung im Alten Testament*, p. 77.
6. 'The Schema of Dynastic Endangerment in Chronicles', pp. 62,64.
7. *Chronikbücher*, p. xxiii.
8. *Theocracy and Eschatology*, pp. 34-44.
9. 'Le Chroniste et ses sources', pp. 484, 508, p. 349.
10. 'Il carattere sacro della regalità nell'antico Israele', p. 93.
11. 'Messianism in Chronicles? Some Remarks to the Old Testament Background of the New Testament Christology', p. 102.
12. Oppenheim, 'Nabonidus (555–539): Nabonidus' Rise to Power', p. 310; Sachs, 'Temple Program for the New Year's Festivals at Babylon', pp. 332, 334.

entrusted to the earthly king by the gods.[1] The Persian king Xerxes can acknowledge that his kingship has been granted by Ahuramazda under whose shadow the earthly king reigns.[2] Even though the identification of the Egyptian king as the living Horus makes the distinction between earthly kingship and divine kingship less precise, close correspondences to the language of Chronicles are also to be found in the Egyptian texts. Thus Amon-Re is hailed as the 'King of Upper and Lower Egypt'[3] and the throne of Egypt is designated as the throne of Amon[4] or of the gods;[5] the same outlook on the relationship between earthly kingship and divine kingship is reflected in the frequently occurring designation of Amon-Re as 'Lord of the Thrones of the Two Lands'.[6]

The evidence shows that the Chronicler has not devised a new and startling perspective through his theocratic emphasis, but has incorporated a view of the deity as the true ruler of the kingdom which was widespread in the ancient Near East. If the statement of the kingship of Yahweh can be taken as an indicator, then this theocratic outlook was already present to the Chronicler through the Psalms, as noted by Saebø who especially associates the Chronicler's viewpoint with Ps. 110.1.[7] However, an even closer association between the Chronicler and the Psalms on this point is incorporated into the Chronicler's work through the quotation of Ps. 96.10 at 1 Chron. 16.31; there the pronouncement to be made among the nations is יהוה מלך, the message of Yahweh's universal kingship.[8]

1.   A.L. Oppenheim, 'The Mother of Nabonidus', p. 561.
2.   A.L. Oppenheim, 'Xerxes (485–465)', pp. 316-17.
3.   J.A. Wilson, 'A Hymn to Amon-Re', p. 365.
4.   J.A. Wilson, 'The Asiatic Campaigning of Amen-hotep II', p. 245; 'Joy at the Accession of Ramses IV', p. 379; *idem*, 'The Divine Nomination of Thut-Mose III', p. 446.
5.   Wilson, 'A Syrian Interregnum', p. 260.
6.   Occurrences of this title may be seen in J.A. Wilson, 'The War against the Hyksos', p. 232; *idem*, 'A Hymn to Amon-Re', p. 365; M. Lichtheim, *Ancient Egyptian Literature 2: The New Kingdom*, pp. 26, 35, 43-46.
7.   'Messianism in Chronicles? Some Remarks to the Old Testament Background of the New Testament Christology', pp. 100-101.
8.   T.C. Butler, 'A Forgotten Passage from a Forgotten Era (1 Chron. 16:8-36)', p. 144.

The non-Israelite evidence bears out the opinion of those scholars who find no necessary conflict between the existence of a divine king and that of an earthly king or between theocracy and messianism. One could go further and suggest that the portrayal of the deity as king or as the giver of kingship presupposes that there is an earthly king who acts as the human representative of the divine authority; however, such a presupposition cannot be identified with the presumption of an eternal dynasty. In fact, the rights over kingship exercised by the deity allow for dramatic changes of power and may, in part, act as a means of affirming the kingdom's basic continuity in the face of apparent regal discontinuity.[1]

For this reason, it is significant that the Chronicler has ended his work with the positive portrayal of a non-Davidic king reigning over Israel in 2 Chron. 36.22-23. The reign of Cyrus is no interregnum unwilled by Yahweh; instead, the kingdoms of the earth, including Judah, have been given to Cyrus who further demonstrates his legitimacy by decreeing that the Temple is to be rebuilt. At the end of the history, even though active kingship has passed from the Davidides, the kingship of Yahweh remains intact and acknowledged, and Cyrus, his earthly representative, reigns for the benefit of Israel.[2]

Interpreters from both sides of the messianic question have no difficulty in seeing that the Davidic kingdom has come to an end (be that end temporary or otherwise) because of the sin of the Davidides, albeit compounded by the sin of the nation;[3] this is also the perspective

1. Cf. Wilson, 'The War against the Hyksos', p. 232; *idem*, 'A Syrian Interregnum', p. 260; Oppenheim, 'Cyrus (557–529)', pp. 315-16.

2. The canonical conclusion of Chronicles seems to run contrary to the logic of Williamson, *1 and 2 Chronicles*, p. 29: 'It is certainly true that [the Chronicler's] selection of material for the reigns of David and Solomon is largely governed by its relevance to the theme of temple building... but that does not therefore make their role dispensable thereafter... the Chronicler believed that a Davidic king was necessary for the successful maintenance of the temple cult even after the period of the united monarchy'. The Chronicler has indeed shown the place of a king in the construction of the Second Temple, but it is not a Davidic king.

3. Welch, *The Work of the Chronicler: Its Purpose and Date*, p. 29; van den Busshe, 'Le Texte de la prophétie de Nathan sur la Dynastie Davidique (II Sam.,VII–I Chron., XVII)', p. 389; Rudolph, 'Problems of the Books of Chronicles', p. 404; Sesboué, 'Ruine temporaire de Jérusalem: 2 Chron. 36:14-16.19-23', p. 30; Caquot, 'Peut-on parler de messianisme dans l'oeuvre du Chroniste?', p. 119.

that the Saul paradigm gives to the narrative. The question remains of why the end of the Davidic rule occurred when it did, and not (for example) during the reign of someone as faithless as Ahaz. The answer to this question can be found in the cultic task which gave David and his dynasty the royal vocation: the dynasty did not come to an end until it had completed the establishment of the Temple and its cultus;[1] once that task was accomplished, the accumulated and continuing unfaithfulness of the Davidides had its effect in the termination of their privileged position in Yahweh's kingdom.

With the completion of the cultus, the need for a Davidic dynasty had passed; the Chronicler shows no awareness of a specific role for the Davidides after that accomplishment, as some commentators note.[2] Indicators that the completion of the Temple cultus is a factor in the timing of the dynasty's cessation are not lacking in the text: at his commissioning, Solomon is assured by David that Yahweh will not abandon him עד־לכלות כל־מלאכת עבודת בית־יהוה (1 Chron. 28.20); Yahweh would not allow the extinction of the Davidic line at the time of Jehoram since God had promised David to give לו ניר ולבניו;[3] and the account of Josiah's death, which marks the beginning of the end of the dynastic reign for the Chronicler, is prefaced by the significant phrase אחרי כל־זאת אשר הכין יאשיהו את־הבית (2 Chron. 35.20), thus linking the ending of the dynasty with the completion of the cultic task.

The Chronicler has produced a close synthesis of elements from his tradition, all of which are related to the wider ancient Near Eastern outlook. The Chronicler accounts for the rise of kingship in Israel (and of the Davidic dynasty in particular) by emphasizing the cultic aspect of the royal vocation; his conditioned presentation of the dynastic promise, as well as his opening paradigmatic Saul narrative, allows for the possibility that the Davidic dynasty would lose power; the cultic task given to the Davidic dynasty accounts for the delay in termination of that dynasty in the face of much unfaithfulness; and the

---

1. Welch, *The Work of the Chronicler: Its Purpose and Date*, p. 53.
2. Becker, *Messiaserwartung im Alten Testament,* pp. 69-70; Petersen, *Late Israelite Prophecy: Studies in Deutero-Prophetic Literature and in Chronicles*, p. 56; De Vries, 'Moses and David as Cult Founders in Chronicles', p. 637.
3. 2 Chron. 21.7. The ניר in question is best interpreted as the Jerusalem Temple (and its cultus).

theocratic emphasis allows for the transfer of power, even to Cyrus, without endangering the essential nature of Israel as the people of Yahweh who works out his purposes in their history. Thus the Chronicler has shown that Yahweh has been faithful to his promise, while the Davidides have failed to be faithful. Even though this accounts for the termination of the dynasty, the Chronicler has a further concern. The reference to the Davidic promise in the traditions of Israel, and particularly the continued celebration of that promise in the Temple cultus,[1] necessitate that the Chronicler show that the promise to David still retains meaning for the nation, even in a post-Davidic age.

The Temple as Israel's Davidic Heritage
The Chronicler has carefully demonstrated in his narrative that the Temple and its cultus came into being through the accomplishments of the House of David: David himself conceived the project, established the site, made the preparations and received the תבנית; Solomon constructed and dedicated the edifice; and every arrangement for the cultic personnel and for the festivals was established by order of the Davidic kings. The Chronistic emphasis on the Temple as the lasting legacy of David and his House to the nation has been noted by several exegetes.[2] In what way the Chronicler could see the continuance of the promises to David in terms of the existence of the Temple and its cultus raises a somewhat different problem.

A clue to the Chronicler's method may be given by another element in his narrative. Within the larger history, the lesser story of the Ark can be traced, and the author displays a respect for the Ark as an essential element in the pre-exilic cultus. Concern for the Ark not only serves as a symbol of David's cultic faithfulness,[3] it also acts as a sign of Saul's unfaithfulness (1 Chron. 13.3). The Ark is brought to the Temple as a central act in the dedication,[4] and the residency of the

1. Cf. P.R. Ackroyd, 'Continuity and Discontinuity: Rehabilitation and Authentication', pp. 228-29.
2. For example, cf. Welch, *The Work of the Chronicler: Its Purpose and Date*, p. 53; Rudolph, *Chronikbücher*, p. xxiii; Caquot, 'Peut-on parler de messianisme dans l'oeuvre du Chroniste?', p. 120; Ackroyd, *The Age of the Chronicler*, p. 50; Mangan, *1–2 Chronicles, Ezra, Nehemiah*, pp. 4-5.
3. 1 Chron. 13.1-14; 15.1–17.1.
4. 2 Chron. 5.2-10; 6.11; cf. 1 Chron. 6.16.

Ark sanctified every place to which it had come (2 Chron. 8.11). Thereafter, the Ark is only mentioned again in 2 Chron. 35.3 in the command of Josiah by which the Ark is permanently deposited in the Temple.

The contrast in the Chronicler's treatment of the Ark—from the centre of cultic attention in the Davidic narrative to a single reference in the post-Solomonic narratives (and that only to deposit the Ark permanently in the Temple)—is so marked that Welch calls attention to this contrast when he postulates two strands of opposing viewpoints involved in the composition of the work.[1] However, it is possible to see the Chronicler's consideration of the Ark in a more integrated way once it is remembered that the Chronicler wrote in an age without the Ark; the Chronicler does not demonstrate an anxiety for the Ark's restoration, but uses the Ark as a way of considering the meaning of the cultus of his own age.[2] Thus, while the narrative begins with a presumption of the Ark's importance, it ends with a presumption of its unimportance in comparison with the other aspects of the Temple cultus. The Ark which had become unavailable to the cultus no longer forms a focus of interest or of legitimacy; the holiness and importance of the Ark has transferred itself to the Jerusalem Temple,[3] and therefore the loss of the Ark has not endangered the religious integrity of the Jerusalem cultus, even though the traditions of its worship still embody the memory of the Ark.

The Chronicler's historical situation with regard to the Ark was similar to his situation with regard to the Davidic king: both were once undeniably important in the history of his nation, and both were

---

1. *The Work of the Chronicler: Its Purpose and Date*, p. 154.
2. Welten, 'Lade–Tempel–Jerusalem: Zur Theologie der Chronikbücher', p. 170.
3. Welch, *The Work of the Chronicler: Its Purpose and Date*, pp. 40-41. M. Noth, 'Jerusalem and the Israelite Tradition', pp. 142-43, notes a similar transfer from the Ark to the city of Zion and calls attention to the fact that there seems to have been no lamentation over the loss of the Ark; this line of thought is most explicit in Jer. 3.16-17. Naturally, a certain fascination with the fate of the Ark is evident in later literature, and *m. Šeq.* 6.1-2 states that the tradition located its hiding place near the wood-store of the Temple. Despite Jer. 3.16-17, the Ark did become the object of an eschatological restoration to some; cf. 2 Macc. 2.4-8 and the later *Liv. Proph.* 2.11-18 (in both of which it is Jeremiah himself who hides the Ark!).

absent in his own era;[1] in the light of this, it may be significant that
the Chronicler has brought David and the Ark into conjunction in the
solemn conclusion to Solomon's prayer of dedication.[2] If the
Chronicler's approach to the Ark is typical of his approach to discontinuity, then the Davidic promise retains significance for the author's
own time insofar as that promise has been embodied by the Temple
and its cultus, just as for the Chronicler all the important aspects of
the Ark have been applied to the Temple.[3]

Although it is not difficult to see how the Chronicler has merged the
two tangible cultic realities of Ark and Temple, the incorporation of
the Davidic promise into the Temple of the Davidic covenant seems to
present greater problems. If the promise to David is viewed primarily
in terms of the dynasty, then it is especially difficult to see how the
Chronicler could have conceived of its continuance in the Temple and
its cultus. However, there is another aspect of Nathan's oracle which
also constitutes an important part of the promise to David:

> I will establish a place for my people Israel and I will plant them[4] and they
> will dwell in that place. They will not be perturbed again and the children
> of wickedness will not consume them any more as in preceding [times],
> from the days when I commanded judges over my people Israel; and I will
> humble all your enemies. And I tell you: a House Yahweh will build for
> you (1 Chron. 17.9-10).

1.   Welten, 'Lade–Tempel–Jerusalem: Zur Theologie der Chronikbücher',
p. 170; Ackroyd, 'History and Theology in the Writings of the Chronicler', p. 512.
   2.   2 Chron. 6.41-42. Both David and the Ark are already present in Ps. 132.8-
10 from which the Chronicler takes his conclusion, but he has altered the Davidic
reference in a way that seems to depend upon Isa. 55.3; presumably, the reference to
the Ark could also have been altered if its absence had posed a difficulty for the
Chronicler.
   3.   Among those aspects of the Ark that have been embodied by the Temple for
the Chronicler might be mentioned, for example, the Ark as the locus for seeking
Yahweh (1 Chron. 13.3), the association of the Ark with the name of God (1 Chron.
13.6), physical concern with the Ark and ministry before it as the function of the cultic personnel (1 Chron. 15.2, 13, 16-24; 16.4-6), and the place of the Ark as a locus
of sacrificial liturgy (1 Chron. 16.1-3).
   4.   The Hebrew treats 'Israel' as a singular term, and therefore uses the third
person masculine singular forms in this passage where the antecedent is יִשְׂרָאֵל.

This aspect of the promise to David, which is derived from the *Vorlage*,[1] resonates with ancient temple ideology as well: through the temple, the land receives blessings such as fertility and security.[2] This connection between land and Temple also entered Israelite thought, as Jer. 7.4-7 indicates.[3] There is perhaps a further connection between Temple and security in Nathan's oracle if the possibility is entertained that the Chronicler saw בית in 1 Chron. 17.10 to pertain to the Temple even more than to the dynasty.[4]

The Chronicler has indicated elsewhere that there is a relationship between the cultus (often symbolized by the Temple) and security in the land, governed by adherence to the commandments. This relationship opens the monarchical narrative in the form of the Saul paradigm in 1 Chronicles 10, although the genealogies are not without allusion to it.[5] The three elements of cultus, commandments and security again combine in the context of Temple building in 1 Chron. 28.6-8 where both Solomon and Israel are addressed. Solomon's prayer of dedication requests that many blessings come through the Temple cultus in 2 Chron. 6.19-39, many of which are concerned with matters of

---

1.   2 Sam. 7.10-11. Although it is sometimes suggested that the מקום of 2 Samuel 7 refers to the Temple, D.F. Murray, '*mqwm* and the Future of Israel in 2 Samuel VII 10', pp. 298-320, demonstrates that the term refers to the land with special reference to Israel's permanence and security.

2.   Cf. the hymn to Baal given in K.-H. Bernhardt, 'Ugaritic Texts: Myths', pp. 220-21, and the Sumerian hymn to the temple of Zababa given in Schmökel, 'Mesopotamian Texts: Hymns, Prayers and Laments', p. 106. Promises of blessings of fertility and security through the temple often occur in Mesopotamian texts related to the king; see Kramer, 'Gilgamesh and Agga', p. 46, and 'Inanna and the King', p. 641.

3.   It is interesting to note that Jeremiah 7 can refer to the expected blessing coming from the Temple without making explicit reference to the king as part of the process.

4.   Cf. McCarthy, 'Covenant and Law in Chronicles–Nehemiah', p. 26. The Chronicler exhibits a certain fondness for the possibility of more than one meaning in a word or phrase, and there is no reason to restrict בית to alternation between two mutually exclusive significances, both of which are obviously at work in the passage. This also helps in the understanding of passages such as 2 Chron. 6.10 where the building of the Temple is seen as a fulfilment of God's promise to David rather than the gift of David to God.

5.   Cf. 1 Chron. 2.7 (understood as a reference to Josh. 6.19 and Josh. 7.1-26); 1 Chron. 5.25-26; 9.1.

fertility and security;[1] Yahweh's acceptance of this prayer specifically promises precisely those blessings that apply to fertility and security,[2] and the connection between Temple and security in the land emerges once more in Yahweh's warning to Solomon that both will be removed if there be not observance of the commandments (2 Chron. 7.19-22).

In the post-Solomonic kings, the relation between Temple cultus and security in the land is established through the workings of the retribution theme in relation to the cultus. In addition to the presence of this general pattern, the Temple prayer of Jehoshaphat, which echoes the dedication prayer of Solomon, makes the connection between Temple and security in the land explicit (2 Chron. 20.6-12), as does the invitation from Hezekiah to the inhabitants of the North, in which they are encouraged to worship in the Jerusalem Temple so that the Northern exiles might be returned (2 Chron. 30.6-9). The narration of Manasseh's cultic atrocities contains a brief digression which demonstrates how closely the Chronicler viewed the connections between Temple, security and commandment:

> And [Manasseh] set up the carved image which he had made in the House of God, of which God had said to David and to Solomon his son: In this House and in Jerusalem which I have chosen from all the tribes of Israel will I place my Name forever. And I will not remove the foot of Israel again from the land where I have appointed for your ancestors, if only you take care to do all that I have commanded them, all the Law and decrees and ordinances in the hand of Moses (2 Chron. 33.7-8).

The final allusion to both Temple and security in the land is to be found in the closing verses of the canonical book, in which Cyrus simultaneously orders the rehabitation of the land and the rebuilding of the Jerusalem Temple (2 Chron. 36.22-23). Just as this passage signals the final passing of Davidic rule, it also signals the continuation of the promise to David concerning the nation's security in the existence of the Second Temple as the lasting Davidic heritage.

Although the Chronicler shows a wide range of appreciation for the

---

1.   2 Chron. 6.24-31, 34-39.

2.   2 Chron. 7.13-14. Although the Chronicler has taken the dedication prayer from his *Vorlage* (with the exception of the concluding verses), this passage is not paralleled by material in the Deuteronomistic History and seems to stem from the Chronicler himself; cf. McKenzie, *The Chronicler's Use of the Deuteronomistic History*, p. 89.

Temple and its blessings,[1] it seems that the security in the land promised in Nathan's oracle holds first place among the Temple blessings; this can be seen reflected in the rest enjoyed by some of David's faithful successors after the building of the Temple, which shows a connection between security and the cultus in the continuing narrative.[2] By drawing out the association of security in the land with Yahweh's promise to David, the Chronicler has found a means to show that the promise retains an importance and a validity which lives on in the Temple and its cultus after the Davidic kings have vanished from the throne.

McCarthy suggests in relation to the Chronistic form of Nathan's oracle that 'David's house is not so much his dynasty as the LORD's temple';[3] the present investigation leads to a similar conclusion in that, for the Chronicler, the House of the Temple has priority in the Davidic promise over the House of the Dynasty. David's dynasty was kept on the throne long enough to fully establish the Temple and its cultus which remains as the gift Yahweh has given to his people through the Davidic covenant[4] and through which that covenant continues to bring blessings to Israel. However, the post-dynastic and non-messianic vision of the Chronicler contains another important dimension, which shows how the Davidic heritage does remain valid and pertinent for the nation known to the Chronicler. This dimension forms the focus of the next and final section of this chapter.

Davidic Reality and the Post-Exilic Nation

The work of the Chronicler is manifestly not a work of scientific history in which the author attempts to produce a presentation of past

1. Other indications from the Chronicler that the Temple is a source of blessings for Israel include: the role of the Temple site in ending the plague in 1 Chron. 21.18–22.1; the identification of the Temple as the locus for Yahweh's earthly dwelling in 2 Chron. 5.13–6.2; the presence of Yahweh with his people (in battle) through faithfulness to the cultus in 2 Chron. 13.10-12; the role of the Temple cultus in the reinstatement of the Davidic line in 2 Chron. 23.1-11; and the abundance given the land in the fulfilling of the cultic demands in 2 Chron. 31.10.

2. Cf. 2 Chron. 13.23; 14.6; 15.15; 20.30; 23.21.

3. 'Covenant and Law in Chronicles–Nehemiah', p. 26. Cf. especially 1 Chron. 17.14: והעמדתיהו בביתי.

4. T. Hannay, 'The Temple', pp. 282-83.

events as they actually occurred, described in terms of the factors that brought them into actuality and their subsequent effects. To demand of the Chronicler that his work reflect the principles of scientific historiography would seem to be a greater anachronism than any to be found in the Chronicler's own work. While the Chronicler shows a genuine concern with the past and attempts to construct his work with some reference to sources and historical factors, his history has rightly been described as a precritical history, largely because of the predominance in the Chronicler's work of an approach to the past as a way to present an understanding of the present.[1] For this reason, the interpreter may presume that the Chronicler intended his work to be received primarily in relation to his contemporary situation while, at the same time, he genuinely demonstrates a concern to understand the past and the flow of events it contains, albeit in a precritical manner.

The contemporary emphasis presumed by the Chronicler's historiographical method gives to his work a concern with continuity between the narrated past and the present of the author and his community. This concern with continuity has been noted and interpreted in slightly different ways by different exegetes: it is seen by Noth[2] and Gottwald,[3] for example, as a continuity between the Chronicler's own cultic community and the ancient Israel that the Chronicler describes; it shows a continuity between the contemporary Judaean community and the whole assembled Israel under David according to Plöger[4] and Brueggemann,[5] and continuity between the post-exilic community and the past kingdom under faithful kings according to Virgulin;[6] this concern with continuity is even reflected in the vocabulary applied to

---

1. Goldingay, 'The Chronicler as a Theologian', pp. 108-11. Goldingay is careful to indicate that the Chronicler was truly attempting to produce an historical work, albeit different in character from works produced in accordance with the conventions of modern historiography. Various scholarly opinions regarding the nature of the Chronistic history have already been noted.

2. *The Chronicler's History*, p. 100.

3. *The Hebrew Bible: A Socio-Literary Introduction*, p. 518.

4. 'Reden und Gebete im deuteronomistischen und chronistischen Geschichtswerk', p. 57.

5. *David's Truth in Israel's Imagination and Memory*, pp. 99-108.

6. *Libri delle Cronache*, p. 58.

the nation according to Williamson[1] and Ackroyd.[2]

The concern with continuity focuses the Chronicler's work on his own time in such a way that the lessons of the past—be they given in terms of encouragement, exhortation to action or insight into the workings of God with his people—are generally intended to have immediate application to the audience who first received the Chronistic History.[3] Even though the Chronicler's narratives are peopled with the great figures of Israel's monarchical period, the author's concern with continuity means that the Chronistic History remains essentially a story for and about the community that first received it.

In this section, the Chronicler's History will be viewed in relation to the post-exilic nation that he was addressing. First, the identity and place of the nation in the Chronistic outlook will be examined, and then the place of the Temple and its cultus in the ideal of the post-exilic nation will be considered.

Identifying the Davidic Nation after the Exile

The Chronicler's own use of terms creates a difficulty for anyone who wishes to name the post-exilic nation in relation to the Chronistic work. Thus, even after the schism, although the Chronicler employs the term יהודה with reference to the Southern Kingdom,[4] he also uses ישראל when it would seem that no necessary allusion to the people of the North has been made.[5] This alone indicates that the Chronicler

---

1.   *Israel in the Books of Chronicles*, p. 107.

2.   'The Chronicler as Exegete', pp. 11, 13.

3.   Cf. von Rad, 'The Levitical Sermon in I & II Chronicles', pp. 267-80.

4.   One might note some of the occurrences of יהודה in the post-Solomonic narratives which are not paralleled in the MT of the Deuteronomistic History: 2 Chron. 11.5, 10, 12, 14; 12.4, 12; 13.14; 14.3, 5, 6, 7; 15.2, 9, 15; 17.5, 6, 9, 12, 14, 19; 20.3, 4, 13, 15, 17, 18, 20, 22, 24; 21.3, 11, 13, 17; 23.2, 8; 24.9, 18, 23; 25.5 (twice), 10; 28.6, 9, 17, 18, 19 (twice), 25; 29.8, 21; 30.1, 6, 12, 25; 31.1, 20; 32.8, 9, 25, 33; 33.9, 14, 16; 34.3, 5, 9; 35.18, 24; 36.4, 10, 23. While some of these occurrences may be seen primarily in terms of the tribe or its territory (e.g., 2 Chron. 11.10, 12), others must be viewed as a reference to the kingdom (e.g., 2 Chron. 13.14; 32.8); some passages seem to use the term first in one sense and then in the other (e.g., 2 Chron. 14.6-7), an obvious indication that the Chronicler did not make a hard and fast distinction between a use of יהודה for the tribe and its use for the kingdom.

5.   The Chronicler often uses ישראל with reference to the Northern Kingdom,

conceived of the nation of Israel as truly continuing in the people of the South even after the schism and the devastation of the Northern Kingdom, and therefore either יהודה or ישראל could be used as its name. Placed in the context of the Chronicler's concern with continuity, this nomenclature for the pre-exilic Southern Kingdom implies that the name ישראל should also apply to the post-exilic nation resident in Judah and Jerusalem.[1]

The terminology used by the Chronicler in relation to the South raises the question of his attitude towards the North, especially towards the descendants of the Northern Kingdom in the author's own time. Those scholars who argue for the unity of the books of Chronicles, Ezra and Nehemiah often claim that the Chronicler exhibits an anti-Samaritan attitude as one of his principal characteristics.[2] While this would seem to be a valid judgment for the viewpoint of Ezra–Nehemiah,[3] the question must be reassessed once one admits the possibility that Chronicles is distinct from Ezra–Nehemiah.[4]

Viewed within the confines of Chronicles alone, the Chronicler allows that the Northern schism is from God (2 Chron. 11.4), yet he ultimately denies legitimacy to the Northern Kingdom as a separate reign, seemingly because of the unfaithful actions of the Northern kings. The unfaithfulness of the Northern kings is expressed in cultic terms early on in the post-Solomonic narratives when the Chronicler

even independently of his *Vorlage* (for example 2 Chron. 13.4, 12; 17.1; 21.13). However, Williamson, *Israel in the Books of Chronicles*, p. 102, lists eleven clear cases of the Chronicler's use of ישראל to refer to the Southern Kingdom: 2 Chron. 12.1, 6; 19.8; 21.2, 4; 23.2; 24.5, 16; 28.19, 23, 27. None of these occurrences suggested by Williamson has a parallel in the Deuteronomistic *Vorlage*.

1. This application seems to be made directly in 1 Chron. 9.1-2.

2. Cf. Wellhausen, *Prolegomena to the History of Ancient Israel*, pp. 187-88; Elmslie, *The Books of Chronicles*, pp. xxxviii-xlii; Noth, *The Chronicler's History*, p. 100; Rudolph, *Chronikbücher*, p. ix; Michaeli, *Les livres des Chroniques, d'Esdras et de Néhémie*, pp. 27, 34; Plöger, *Theocracy and Eschatology*, p. 40; Goldingay, 'The Chronicler as a Theologian', pp. 120-21.

3. Cf. Neh. 2.19-20; 4.1-5.

4. This does not mean that scholars who argue for the unity of Chronicles with Ezra–Nehemiah do not sometimes suggest that a concern for the unity of all Israel can be discerned in Chronicles. Cf. Botterweck, 'Zur Eigenart der chronistischen Davidsgeschichte', pp. 409, 433; Stinespring, 'Eschatology in Chronicles', p. 211; Myers, 'The Kerygma of the Chronicler: History and Theology in the Service of Religion', p. 265; Virgulin, *Libri delle Cronache*, pp. 43-46.

relates that Jeroboam instigated illegitimate shines and cultic personnel (2 Chron. 11.14-15), a point that he echoes again in Abijah's speech (2 Chron. 13.9). The illegitimacy of the North as a separate kingdom is also reflected in the statements of guilt predicated of the North in its last days as a kingdom (2 Chron. 28.10, 13).

However, the lack of legitimacy for the Chronicler pertains primarily to the North's existence as a separate political and cultic entity; the question of the legitimate claims of the Northern people to be part of Israel is a different matter. When considering this question, it may be significant that the Chronicler has not only omitted but has made no allusion to the Deuteronomistic Historian's account of the settlement of the Northern territory after the fall of Samaria (wherein the Deuteronomistic Historian indicates his view that the inhabitants of the former Northern Kingdom are impure in race and cult [2 Kgs 17.24-41]). Instead of this anti-Samaritan comment on the end of the Northern Kingdom, the Chronicler exhibits a concern to involve the people of the North in the cultus and in cultic reform after the fall of the North.[1] This new place in the Chronistic work for the people of the North after the end of the Northern Kingdom has sometimes been noted as an indicator of the Chronicler's openness towards the inhabitants of the North in his own day as authentic members of Israel.[2]

The benign consideration that the Chronicler affords the people of the North after the fall of Samaria is in keeping with a tendency detectable elsewhere in his work, from the start of David's kingship with the consensus of all Israel[3] and his initial cultic activity with the gathering of the complete nation,[4] through the strengthening of Rehoboam's kingdom by the immigration of Northern refugees[5] and the mention of faithful Northerners in the reign of Asa,[6] to the

---

1. Cf. 2 Chron. 30.1-12; 34.6-9, 21, 33; 35.18.
2. Welch, *The Work of the Chronicler: Its Purpose and Date*, p. 17; Williamson, *Israel in the Books of Chronicles*, pp. 119-26; Japhet, *The Ideology of the Book of Chronicles and its Place in Biblical Thought*, pp. 318-34; R.L. Braun, 'A Reconsideration of the Chronicler's Attitude toward the North', pp. 59-62; Knoppers, 'Reform and Regression: The Chronicler's Presentation of Jehoshaphat', pp. 523-24.
3. 1 Chron. 11.1-3. Cf. Japhet, 'Chronicles, Book of', cols. 522, 525.
4. 1 Chron. 13.1-5. Cf. Becker, *1 Chronik*, pp. 63-65.
5. 2 Chron. 11.16-17. Cf. Randellini, *Il libro delle Cronache*, pp. 356-57.
6. 2 Chron. 15.9. Cf. Williamson, *1 and 2 Chronicles*, p. 270.

kindness shown to the captured Judaeans by Northern people.[1] The same benign concern can be readily discerned in the inclusiveness of the genealogies which begin the work.[2] Although Braun may have gone beyond the evidence in suggesting that Chronicles is written as an appeal to the North to join the South in the cultus,[3] the Chronicler exhibits an openness towards the inhabitants of the North which exceeds the attitude evident in other post-exilic works.[4] In sum, the Chronistic view, while never doubting the legitimacy of the post-exilic Southern community as ישראל, is sensitive to the necessity for all Israelites, North and South, to comprise the fulness of the people.[5]

The tension between the reality of the author's view of his post-exilic Judaean community as the true Israel and his ideal of a united Israel is best viewed in the light of the Chronicler's perception of the covenant relationship between Yahweh and Israel. The Chronicler seems to have viewed the covenant relationship in a unified manner, seeing the Davidic covenant as a particular expression of the larger covenant reality.[6] Although the covenant with Abraham is mentioned

1.   2 Chron. 28.12-15. Cf. F.S. Spencer, '2 Chronicles 28:5-15 and the Parable of the Good Samaritan', pp. 343-49.
2.   1 Chron. 1-9. Cf. Johnson, *The Purpose of the Biblical Genealogies*, pp. 37-38, 47-49.
3.   'The Message of Chronicles: Rally 'Round the Temple', p. 512.
4.   Notably Ezra and Nehemiah. This is not to state that the openness of the Chronicler is necessarily exclusive to him; the eponymous character of the post-exilic book of Tobit belongs to the tribe of Naphtali and is numbered among those in exile as a result of the fall of the Northern Kingdom, although the book is careful to note that Tobit had always been faithful to the cultus of the Jerusalem Temple (cf. Tob. 1.1-14).
5.   Williamson, *Israel in the Books of Chronicles*, p. 96.
6.   This emerges from a consideration of the six occurrences of the word ברית in the covenant-making scenes of the post-Solomonic narratives (2 Chron. 15.12; 29.10; 34.30; 34.31 [twice]; 34.32). Although these scenes might be interpreted as covenant renewals invoking the covenant at Sinai (and this would be especially apt for the covenant made under Josiah in 2 Chron. 34), covenant-making has a reality and an immediacy for the Chronicler that seems to de-emphasize the historically past reality of covenant in favour of a lived, present reality. The Chronicler is aware that the covenant is associated with Abraham (1 Chron. 16.17) and Moses (2 Chron. 5.10), but explicit references to them do not predominate when the Chronicler speaks of covenant. No progression in the relationship between Yahweh and Israel is apparent as a result of the different acts of covenant-making in Chronicles, and the picture that emerges can be interpreted as that of a unified

explicitly only in the Ark liturgy of David,[1] the Chronicler's unified approach to covenant gives an added emphasis to this point of the origin of the covenant relationship, as noted by several exegetes,[2] with the result that all Israel (and not just post-exilic Judah) can be included. However, the continuation of the covenant relationship through the covenant with David means that loyalty to the covenant entails loyalty to the Temple which was a physical result and manifestation of the Davidic covenant; this continuity between the Temple and Abraham is indicated by the identification of the Temple mount with Mount Moriah in 2 Chron. 3.1,[3] as well as by the motif of security in the land.[4] Thus while all Israelites share in the covenant relationship with Yahweh, those who adhere to the Jerusalem cultus truly constitute Israel for the Chronicler, since they are the ones who have remained faithful to the covenant relationship begun with Abraham and who consequently inherit its promises; the cultic קהל constitutes Israel as the nation that is heir to the Davidic heritage, a nation where all the Israelite descendants of Abraham belong, even if they are not actually to be found there in the Chronicler's experience.[5]

covenant relationship which has particular manifestations in history.

1.   1 Chron. 16.13, 16-17. It should be noted that 1 Chron. 16.16-17 interprets the covenant with Abraham as continuing only with his descendants through Isaac and Jacob (as does its source in Ps. 105.9-10); cf. Slotki, *Chronicles*, p. 92.

2.   For example Noordtzij, 'Les intentions du Chroniste', p. 162; Brunet, 'Le Chroniste et ses sources', pp. 362-63, 369, 376; Poulssen, 'Rex et Templum in Israel', p. 268; Ackroyd, *The Age of the Chronicler*, p. 509.

3.   Although this name for the Temple mount suits the Chronicler's outlook and is only to be found in the Hebrew Bible in 2 Chron. 3.1, the identification does not seem to have originated with him. A graffito dated to c. 500 BCE had been rendered as 'For you yourself have blessed Moriah, the dwelling place of Yah, O Yahweh' by E. Lipinski, 'North Semitic Texts from the First Millennium BC: Graffiti', p. 251, but this rendering is no longer viewed as viable; cf. I. Kalimi, 'The Land of Moriah, Mount Moriah, and the Site of Solomon's Temple in Biblical Historiography', p. 347. However, Kalimi does find evidence in Genesis 22 to indicate that 'the Temple Mount was identified with the site of the Aqeda during the period of the First Temple', even though the name 'Mount Moriah' itself may have originated with the Chronicler (p. 350).

4.   For example 1 Chron. 16.15-18; 17.9-10, 21; 2 Chron. 6.24-31, 34-39; 7.19-22; 33.7-9.

5.   This identification of the post-exilic community as the Davidic nation carries with it the necessary implication that the Davidic covenant now belongs to the whole

As well as his concern with the descendants of the Northern Kingdom, the Chronicler exhibits a concern with the relationship of Israel to non-Israelites. Although the Chronicler often presents the threat to security in the land in terms of a threat from non-Israelite nations,[1] there is also a positive place for the non-Israelite in the history of Israel. Thus, for example, non-Israelites are shown to be involved in the work of constructing the Jerusalem Temple,[2] just as non-Israelites help to provide some of the materials for it.[3] Non-Israelites are even present in the list of David's officials,[4] and Solomon seeks the kindly reception of their prayers by Yahweh in his own prayer of dedication.[5] Although the Chronicler shows that many later foreign alliances[6] proved to be inimical to the faithfulness of the king who engaged in them (since the monarch's choice to depend upon foreign powers is seen as undermining his dependence upon Yahweh),[7] Solomon demonstrates an ability to engage in friendly relationships with non-Israelites without endangering his fidelity to

people of Israel, an implication that will be discussed below.

1. For example 1 Chron. 10.7; 2 Chron. 6.24, 34, 36; 12.2-9; 14.8-14; 20.1-12; 21.16-17; 24.23-24; 28.5-6, 17-18, 20; 32.1, 9-19; 36.17. The threat to Israel need not always arise from foreign peoples, however; cf. 1 Chron. 21.1-17; 2 Chron. 6.26, 28.

2. 1 Chron. 22.2; 2 Chron. 2.6, 13-15, 16-17.

3. 1 Chron. 22.4; 2 Chron. 2.2-15; cf. also 2 Chron. 9.10-11. The very site for the Temple is identified as ארן היבוסי גרן in 1 Chron. 21.15-28 and 2 Chron. 3.1, but the Chronicler does not seem to consider this prior possession an authentic non-Israelite contribution to the building of the Temple since the site has been duly purchased by David.

4. 1 Chron. 27.30-31. Although the Chronicler may here be dependent upon a source (no longer extant) that identifies these officials as non-Israelite (cf. Rudolph, *Chronikbücher*, pp. 183-84), the non-Israelite nature of the identification must have been apparent to him; the inclusion of these identifications in the work should be seen as more than accidental.

5. 2 Chron. 6.32-33.

6. The alliances spoken of here also include those made with the Northern Kingdom as a separate political entity.

7. Berg, 'After the Exile: God and History in the Book of Chronicles and Esther', pp. 113-14; Dillard, 'Reward and Punishment in Chronicles: The Theology of Immediate Retribution', p. 167. Cf. especially 2 Chron. 16.7-8 and 25.7-8; the attitude of faithful Hezekiah as expressed in 2 Chron. 32.7-8 stands in sharp contrast.

Yahweh,[1] and non-Israelite monarchs can even be shown in the Chronicler's work to be acting on behalf of Yahweh.[2] A basic openness to non-Israelites can be detected in the Chronistic History, together with the recognition that non-Israelites can also pose a threat and snare to the nation according to the circumstances; the Chronicler's openness seems to depend upon the presumed goodwill of the Gentiles involved towards Yahweh and his Temple.[3]

The highest place afforded in the book to a non-Israelite must undoubtedly go to Cyrus, the last Gentile mentioned; even though the treatment of Cyrus is confined to two verses (2 Chron. 36.22-23), this brief passage attributes Cyrus's action on behalf of the Jerusalem Temple to divine inspiration and his rule to the direct decision of Yahweh. The Chronicler does not stand alone in the Hebrew Bible in passing such a positive judgment on the accession of Cyrus,[4] but such a judgment has a particular effect in the Chronistic work: in his presentation of monarchical history, the Chronicler names a non-Israelite as the final legitimate monarch of his narrative. Kingship has passed from Israel, not as a diminuation of the divine plan, but as a new expression of the universal reign of Yahweh who possesses all the kingdoms of the earth and who therefore is free to bestow them upon Cyrus for the benefit of Israel and the Jerusalem Temple.[5] With the passing of the Jerusalem kingship, the political aspect of the nation's existence as a kingdom has also passed into the hands of Cyrus and his successors,[6] and the post-exilic nation could now be even more fully centred on the service of Yahweh. The Davidic nation in the period of the Chronicler has become essentially a liturgical nation existing

1.   Cf. 2 Chron. 2.2-15; 8.11, 17-18; 9.1-12, 14, 21, 23-24.

2.   For example 2 Chron. 35.21-22; 36.17.

3.   Rudolph, *Chronikbücher*, p. xxiv; Newsome, 'Toward a New Understanding of the Chronicler and his Purposes', p. 206.

4.   The same judgment is, of course, to be found in the parallel passage, Ezra 1.1-3; earlier evidence of the interpretation of Cyrus's accession as an act of Yahweh is present in Deutero-Isaiah (Isa. 44.28–45.4). The prophetic literature also portrays other non-Israelite kings as instruments of Yahweh, as in Isa. 10.5-15 and Jer. 25.9 (wherein Yahweh refers to Nebuchadrezzar as עבדי).

5.   2 Chron. 36.23. Cf. Coppens, *Le messianisme royal*, p. 106; Sesboué, 'Ruine temporaire de Jérusalem: 2 Chron. 36:14-16.19-23', p. 33; Becker, *Messiaserwartung im Alten Testament*, p. 47.

6.   Goldingay, 'The Chronicler as a Theologian', pp. 114-15.

among the nations with the providence secured by their covenant relationship with Yahweh and by fidelity to that cultus which was divinely instituted through the actions of the Davidic kings.[1]

It is noteworthy that several of these themes identifying the post-exilic Davidic nation and its place in the world are present in the thanksgiving hymn of 1 Chron. 16.8-36:[2] Israel is the nation descended from the patriarchs and bound in relationship to Yahweh by covenant since their day (1 Chron. 16.13, 15-17), found among the nations but under the protection of Yahweh himself (1 Chron. 16.20-22, 35); the non-Israelite nations themselves are to be brought to the knowledge of the kingship of Yahweh (1 Chron. 16.31) and to worship of him (1 Chron. 16.23, 28-29); Israel has been especially called to the praise of Yahweh (1 Chron. 16.8-12, 23, 34, 36) and to making him known among the nations of the world (1 Chron. 16.8, 24). Even as early in the narrative as the Jerusalem liturgy of David, the Chronicler has begun to build his picture of the universal kingship of Yahweh which encompasses the non-Israelite nations; but there is also an essential place for Israel, the nation that includes all of those descended from Abraham, Isaac and Jacob who are gathered in worship according to the cultic arrangements legitimized by David and his

---

1. Cf. Rudolph, *Chronikbücher*, p. xxiii; Schumacher, 'The Chronicler's Theology of History', pp. 19-21; Plöger, 'Reden und Gebete im deuteronomistichen und chronistischen Geschichtswerk', p. 64; Petersen, *Late Israelite Prophecy: Studies in Deutero-Prophetic Literature and in Chronicles*, p. 56; Gottwald, *The Hebrew Bible: A Socio-Literary Introduction*, p. 518; Brueggemann, *David's Truth in Israel's Imagination and Memory*, pp. 100, 107.

2. The thanksgiving hymn represented by this passage seems to be a conscious redaction of existing psalmic material which produces a new unity; Brunet, 'Le Chroniste et ses sources', p. 503, gives a typical analysis of the compilation: 'Il s'agit (xvi,8-36) d'un morceau composé d'extraits du *Ps.*, cv (1-15 = *Chron.*, 8-22), du *Ps.*, xcxvi (1-13 = *Chron.*, 23-33), et d'extraits du *Ps.*, cvi (1.47.48 = *Chron.*, 34-36), avec la doxologie finale du IVe livre des *Psalmes*'. Although some attribute the inclusion of the thanksgiving hymn to a later stratum of redaction than that responsible for the material surrounding it (as do Ruldolph, *Chronickbücher*, p. 127, and J.A. Loader, 'Redaction and Function of the Chronistic "Psalm of David"', p. 69), more recent studies concentrate on the hymn as an integral part of the Chronistic work; cf. Butler, 'A Forgotten Passage from a Forgotten Era (1 Chron. 16.8-36)', pp. 142-50; Japhet, 'Conquest and Settlement in Chronicles', pp. 205-18; A.E. Hill, 'Patchwork Poetry or Reasoned Verse? Connective Structure in 1 Chron. 16', pp. 97-101.

House and who must still look to Yahweh—and only to Yahweh—for deliverance from their enemies.[1] The concerns evident in this thanksgiving hymn attributed to David offer their own testimony to the Chronicler's identification of the post-exilic cultic community as the Davidic nation continuing into a new age, but carrying the same basic concerns, challenges and promises that have been with Israel since the beginning of the Davidic *Urzeit*.

The Post-Exilic Temple and Cultus:
The Davidic Task and the Davidic Blessing Continue
The identification of the motives behind the production of any literary work is necessarily an uncertain undertaking. In the case of the Chronicler, the raw materials for such an identification are limited basically to the existence of the earlier Deuteronomistic History, modern knowledge of the post-exilic period and the internal evidence of the Chronistic work itself. Such a limitation of raw materials means that only a general and partial identification of the Chronicler's motives can be achieved with any degree of demonstrable probability.

The availability of the Chronicler's major source in the Deuteronomistic History indicates that there was a shift in circumstances which required a new orientation to the older historical traditions of the nation.[2] The Chronicler's own concern with the traditions related to the monarchical period combined with the lack of monarchy in the post-exilic period has led several scholars to the conclusion that the Chronicler was, in some way, concerned especially with the meaning of the monarchy for his own non-monarchical period,[3] a conclusion with which the findings of this investigation are in general accord. Such an identification does not exclude a variety of other

1. Cf. 1 Chron. 16.35.
2. Von Rad, *Das Geschichtsbild des chronistischen Werkes*, pp. 120-21; Willi, *Die Chronik als Auslegung*, pp. 53-54; Japhet, 'Conquest and Settlement in Chronicles', p. 205.
3. This conclusion, in one particular manifestation, obviously lies behind the David-restoring interpretation of Chronicles advocated by some, including Cazelles, *Les livres des Chroniques*, pp. 22-25, Cross, 'A Reconstruction of the Judean Restoration', pp. 12-13, and Newsome, 'Toward a New Understanding of the Chronicler and his Purposes', pp. 213-16. For a similar perspective without Davidic restoration, cf. also Welten, 'Lade–Tempel–Jerusalem: Zur Theologie der Chronikbücher', p. 170, and Mangan, *1–2 Chronicles, Ezra, Nehemiah*, pp. 3-4.

possible motives from the Chronicler's effort, such as concern with the cultic personnel or a desire to compose a history containing appropriate edification and object lessons in its individual episodes. However, the Chronicler demonstrates a particular and indisputable interest in the monarchy and composes his narrative largely according to the parameters of the monarchical period. Since the Chronicler is led by the need to establish continuity, his interest in the monarchy is not restricted to developing an understanding of the monarchical past; he is also interested in presenting an appreciation of the monarchical aspect of his post-exilic present.

In the light of this, it is interesting to note that the two words in Chronicles which seem to have generated the most comment are חסדי דויד in 2 Chron. 6.42, for they occur in a conclusion to the prayer of Solomon which immediately draws the Davidic reality into a period past David himself. Although this expression occurs in a section that is largely a quotation from Ps. 132.8-10, the expression itself represents a divergence from the MT of that psalm and is generally conceded to be related to, and possibly dependent upon, the same expression in Isa. 55.3.[1] In the consideration of this phrase in the final form study of the Solomonic material, it was observed that the Chronicler may have incorporated here a dual reference to the faithful deeds of David and to the covenant promise made to him.

Although Solomon's prayer in Chronicles for Yahweh to be mindful of חסדי דויד is often viewed as a prayer for Davidic restoration,[2] the results of the present investigation indicate that this is improbable. When the expression is viewed in relation to Isa. 55.3, however,

---

1. For example Curtis and Madsen, *A Critical and Exegetical Commentary on the Books of Chronicles*, p. 345; von Rad, *Das Geschichtsbild des chronistischen Werkes*, pp. 126-28; Noth, *The Chronicler's History*, p. 105; Galling, *Die Bücher der Chronik, Esra, Nehemia*, p. 93; Rudolph, *Chronikbücher*, p. 215; Caquot, 'Peut-on parler de messianisme dans l'oeuvre du Chroniste?', pp. 118-19; Myers, *II Chronicles*, pp. 37-38; Goldingay, 'The Chronicler as a Theologian', p. 117; Becker, *2 Chronik*, p. 29. Some suggest that the Chronicler preserves an earlier version of the psalm; see Harvey-Jellie, *Chronicles*, p. 207 and Ackroyd, *I & II Chronicles, Ezra, Nehemia*, p. 113.

2. For example, cf. von Rad, *Das Geschichtsbild des chronistischen Werkes*, pp. 126-28; de Vaux, Review of *Chronikbücher* by W. Rudolf, p. 280; Brunet, 'La théologie du chroniste: théocratie et messianisme', p. 390; Williamson, *1 and 2 Chronicles*, pp. 220-21.

another possibility emerges. In the passage from Deutero-Isaiah, the phrase has been used to speak of the covenant with David applying to all the nation, and not just to the Davidic House.[1] The Davidic covenant was always intended for the welfare of the entire nation and not just for the welfare of the Davidides, so it would never have been entirely inappropriate to speak of the Davidic covenant, even in its dynastic aspect, with reference to its benefits for the nation.[2] However, Deutero-Isaiah effected a transfer of aspects of the role of the monarch and of the Davidic promises to the entire people through his application of חסדי דויד to the nation in Isa. 55.3 as well as by the context in which the expression occurs.[3] The Chronicler may well have taken this phrase from Deutero-Isaiah precisely because it had already been used in a way that was harmonious with his own outlook: after the political role of kingship was seen to apply to Cyrus,[4] the religious reality which once had pertained to the king could then be reapplied so that it would be seen to pertain to the entire Davidic nation.[5]

1. Westermann, *Isaiah 40–66*, pp. 281-84; R.N. Whybray, *Isaiah 40–66*, pp. 191-92.

2. In Ps. 78.68-72, for example, the choice of David is linked with the choice of Judah and the benefit of Israel; similarly, Ps. 132.11-16 speaks of the blessing of Zion and its people in the context of the Davidic covenant, and Ps. 144.10 acclaims the people under the Davidic monarch as a blessed people. The connection between the righteous rule of the ideal Davidide and God's blessing for the people is evident in a variety of texts (for example Isa. 9.2-9; Jer. 23.5-6; 33.15-26; Ezek. 37.24-25; Ps. 72.1-17). Even the false security associated with the Jerusalem Temple (cf. Jer. 7.4) can be considered a perverse perception of the benefits for the nation which derive from the Davidic covenant.

3. Becker, *Messiaserwartung im Alten Testament*, pp. 63-64; E. Schuller, *Post-Exilic Prophets*, pp. 110-11. The specific aspect of the monarchical role mentioned is that of witness to Yahweh's power among the nations (Isa. 55.4-5). This same role belongs to the nation in the Chronicler's outlook as is evident from the hymn of thanksgiving in 1 Chronicles 16 (cf. 1 Chron. 16.8, 24). It would seem that the expression חסדי דויד in Isa. 55.3 is intended to refer primarily to the Davidic covenant rather than to the achievements of David; cf. Williamson, '"The Sure Mercies of David": Subjective or Objective Genitive?', pp. 31-49. The dual meaning of the expression emerges in 2 Chron. 6.42 in part from the similar expressions found in 2 Chron. 32.32 and 2 Chron. 35.26.

4. Isa. 44.28–45.4; 2 Chron. 36.23.

5. Goldingay, 'The Chronicler as a Theologian', p. 114-15. The suggestion of Williamson, *1 and 2 Chronicles*, p. 221, is curious: '. . . his allusion to Isa. 55.3

The religious reality of David, evoked in the Dedication Prayer at 2 Chron. 6.42, finds its focus in the Temple being dedicated by Solomon's prayer. The post-exilic Temple provided the link with the Davidic past, and has even been described in itself as 'the messianic symbol'.[1] While such a statement would claim too much if applied to the Chronicler's thought, the Temple and its cultus provides a tangible expression in Chronicles of the two aspects of the Davidic reality contained in the dual meaning of the phrase חסדי דויד: the Davidic task of providing for the cultus and being faithful to it constitutes the first aspect, and the second is to be found in the Davidic promise which has not only brought the Temple and its cultus into being, but which continues to provide blessings for the nation. In this respect, the Temple can be termed a sign of the covenant with the people in the Chronicler's work.[2]

The author's concern with the appropriate role of the cultic personnel should not distract the audience from the fact that the Chronicler has carefully demonstrated throughout his work that the Davidic task of establishing the Temple and its cultus was always associated with the entire nation; in this way an emphasis on the place and function of the people is evident in the Chronicler's History.[3] Thus in the inaugural act of bringing the Ark to Jerusalem, David assembles all Israel to partake in the event both in the initial attempt[4] and in its

must be seen as an attempt to reassert the royalist interpretation of the promises to David, unlike Isa. 55.3 itself, which appears rather to transfer the promise to the people as a whole'. The quotation of an earlier source in the affirming context of the conclusion of Solomon's prayer hardly seems the most obvious method for refuting the viewpoint of the earlier source, especially when it depends upon a presumption of such familiarity with it that a two-word allusion would be sufficient to invoke it.

1. Hannay, 'The Temple', p. 284.

2. Sesboué, 'Ruine temporaire de Jérusalem: 2 Chron. 36:14-16.19-23', p. 31-32. In this context, the statement of Solomon regarding the Temple in 2 Chron. 6.11 should be noted: ואשים שם את־הארון אשר שם ברית יהוה אשר כרת עם־בני ישראל as well as the divergence from the *Vorlage* which begins 1 Kgs 8.21 with ואשם שם מקום לארון. Covenant is here used in the unified sense which seems to predominate in the Chronistic outlook; the covenant as signified by the Temple would especially represent that relationship in terms of the enrichment it received from the deeds of the faithful members of the Davidic House.

3. Japhet, 'Chronicles, Book of', col. 529.

4. 1 Chron. 13.2-5.

successful completion.[1] The revelation of the Temple site to David takes place in response to David's prayer on behalf of the nation when it had been endangered by pestilence (1 Chron. 21.17-18). The task of constructing the Temple is entrusted principally to Solomon, but it is also entrusted to the nation;[2] even the solemn act of giving the תבנית to Solomon takes place in the context of an assembly of princes and officials from all Israel[3] who also contribute generously and freely to the cost of construction.[4] An assembly of all the elders, leaders and princes of Israel brings the Ark to the completed Temple[5] and all Israel participates in the dedication of the Jerusalem Temple.[6] The cultic role of the entire nation, North and South, is also recognized in the Chronicler's post-Solomonic narratives: the covenant ceremony of Asa involves participants from Northern tribes as well as from the tribes of Judah and Benjamin;[7] Hezekiah invites participants from the North to his Passover, and some respond,[8] and these participants involve themselves in the cultic reform of Israel's territory, North and South, and contribute the tithe for the support of the cultic personnel;[9] the North contributes materially to the restoration of the Temple under Josiah (2 Chron. 34.8-9), and Northern participants are present at Josiah's Passover (2 Chron. 33.17-18). However, just as the people share in the royal activity on behalf of the cultus, they also share in the royal opprobrium for cultic unfaithfulness;[10] this aspect represents the darker side of the responsibility the people bear for the cultic task.

1.   1 Chron. 15.3, 28.
2.   1 Chron. 22.17-19; 28.21. The princes of the people are told directly: וקמו ובנו את־מקרש יהוה האלהים (1 Chron. 22.19).
3.   1 Chron. 28.1-2, 11, 19-21.
4.   1 Chron. 29.6-9, 16-17.
5.   2 Chron. 5.2, 4.
6.   2 Chron. 5.3; 6.3, 12-13; 7.3-4, 6, 8. The reference to כל־איש ישראל in 2 Chron. 5.3 indicates that an assembly of the leading figures mentioned in 2 Chron. 5.2 constitutes the assembly of all Israel. Cf. Dillard, *2 Chronicles*, p. 41.
7.   2 Chron. 15.9-10. Cf. also 2 Chron. 15.8 wherein the reform activity involves cities taken from the territory of Ephraim.
8.   2 Chron. 30.1-11, 18, 21, 25.
9.   2 Chron. 31.1, 4-6.
10.   Cf. 2 Chron. 24.17-19, 24; 29.6-9; 33.10; 36.14-16. In 2 Chron. 27.2, the corruption of the people is given in contrast to the king's general attitude of faithfulness.

The cultic task pertaining to the people of the Chronicler's day, to provide for the cultus and to be faithful to it, emerges clearly in the Chronicler's work as a task that they have borne since before the foundation of the Jerusalem Temple and one bestowed upon them by the founder of the Temple cultus, King David himself;[1] the overall impression left by the Chronistic picture of the people's involvement in the Temple-building task is that their contribution was essential for the success of the Davidic–Solomonic project.[2] The same material support of tithes and free-will offerings that had obtained in the past would also be forthcoming from the Davidic nation in the post-exilic age.[3] The congregation that belongs to the Chronicler's experience of worship is composed of a people descended from the congregation of all Israel in David's day, people who are also related to their ancient forebears by their cultic vocation and faithfulness.[4] The very response to Cyrus's edict would entail the people's assistance in the Temple-building activity, assuming the same role that they had once performed successfully under David and Solomon.[5] In this way, the Chronicler's Israel would continue the work begun by the חסדי דויד referred to in 2 Chron. 6.42 and echoed in 2 Chron. 32.32 and 2 Chron. 35.26.

The Chronicler's use of חסדי דויד has another aspect, that of the covenantal love and blessing that Yahweh had bestowed upon David. Considered in terms of its application to the entire nation, this covenant blessing, which flows from the presence of Yahweh and his name with Israel through the Temple,[6] has already been identified as the security that the nation would enjoy in its land rather than the dynastic promise. True to the notion of covenant blessing, the granting of this security depends upon the nation's faithfulness to the covenant demands which, in this case, centre upon the Jerusalem Temple and its cultus; by fulfilling the demands placed upon them, the

---

1. Cf. 1 Chron. 22.17-19; 28.21.
2. Japhet, *The Ideology of the Book of Chronicles and its Place in Biblical Thought*, p. 421.
3. Cf. Rudolph, 'Problems of the Books of Chronicles', p. 408.
4. Cf. Myers, *I Chronicles*, p. lxxv.
5. Cf. Schumacher, 'The Chronicler's Theology of History', pp. 19-20; Ackroyd, 'History and Theology in the Writings of the Chronicler', pp. 514-15; *idem*, 'Continuity and Discontinuity: Rehabilitation and Authentication', p. 225.
6. Cf. 2 Chron. 6.1-2; 7.16; 33.7-8.

people inherit that rest for which David could only hope and which he had made a possibility for those who had become heirs to the promise in his wake.

The Chronicler has thus portrayed the reality of David to be vibrant in the Chronicler's own time. The Davidic reality in his post-exilic vision received a solid expression in the Temple and cultus which came into being through David and his dynasty, but which continued through the faithfulness of the Davidic nation, who still gathered in worship and even constructed and maintained the post-exilic Temple. They were assured that, if they remained faithful to the covenant demands, they would enjoy everlasting rest in the land in accordance with the promise which Yahweh had made to David.

Conclusion

The Chronicler had composed his work in a time when the ancient Near Eastern royal ideology, still vibrant in the ancient world and still living in the post-exilic nation through the historical and liturgical traditions, posed problems for understanding the monarchical traditions of Israel; kingship had passed from Israel despite what might have been expected to proceed from Yahweh's promise to David. By concentrating on the cultic vocation which the ancient ideology attributed to kings, the Chronicler placed the dynastic promise into the larger context of the Temple as the major effect of the Davidic covenant, and thus demonstrated through his narrative that the days of the dynasty had ended while the covenant with David remained. The Davidic covenant persisted for the Chronicler and his audience in the task (which the people had from the days of David himself) to worship at the Temple and to provide for its needs and the needs of its cultus in utter faithfulness. The Davidic covenant could also be seen in the rest that the people enjoyed, for the covenant blessing (which traced back to the divine promise to Abraham) was none other than security in the land for a faithful and devoted people.

SUMMARY AND CONCLUSIONS

The foregoing study investigated the interplay of king and cultus in the Chronistic re-presentation of the monarchical history. In doing so, it delved into an aspect of the Chronicler's work which comparison with the Deuteronomistic *Vorlage* recommends to the modern reader of Chronicles.

The attempt to situate the Chronicler's History, undertaken in the first chapter of this investigation, resulted in an affirmation of the work of those scholars who see Chronicles as a separate composition from the books of Ezra and Nehemiah, even though both Chronicles and Ezra–Nehemiah reflect some common language and concerns. The author of Chronicles, be that author an individual or a school, should be located among the cultic personnel of the Second Temple and seems to have written in the late Persian period of Israel's history. It was postulated in the first chapter that the Chronicler's need to re-present the monarchical history arose from the non-monarchical state of the post-exilic nation; the meaning of David and his House would therefore be less political in emphasis and more theological for the Chronicler and his original audience. It was also postulated that the language and thought evident in the Psalms had exerted some influence on the author and on the resulting re-presentation.

The cultic concern of Chronicles was traced in a final form reading of the Chronistic monarchical history in the second chapter. This final form reading noted the paradigmatic nature of the Chronicler's Saul narrative, and the underlying motifs in this narrative of cultic unfaithfulness and the resultant insecurity in the land. David's portrayal in Chronicles makes him emerge as founder of the Temple cultus as well as of the dynasty. The intrinsic connection between the cultic portrayal of David and the gift of the dynasty was seen, not only in the Davidic narrative, but also in the Chronistic account of Solomon who, through his temple-building, completes what David had begun. The cultic theme was traced through the narratives of the post-Solomonic kings, noting that these monarchs are often rewarded or punished in direct consequence of their cultic faithfulness, as the reader would expect from the Saul paradigm; also in these episodes, a story of the Temple and its completion was found, and the significance of the climax reached in 2 Chron. 35.20 was noted. The consideration of the dynastic promise and its Chronistic treatment throughout the final form study of the second chapter led to the suggestion that the Saul paradigm was intended to apply to the whole of the Davidic dynasty, accounting for the disappearance of this dynasty's political rule in the reality of the post-exilic nation in accordance with the type of conditionality expressed in Psalm 132 and without compromising God's promise to David. In light of this, it could be seen that the Edict of Cyrus forms an integral part of the Chronicler's work and is given by the Chronicler as a clear indication that the Davidic rule, having finished its cultic task, had given way to a new regime with God's approval because of the dynasty's unfaithfulness.

The third chapter drew upon previous aspects of the investigation to produce a synthesis of the Chronicler's thought on king and cultus. It was first shown that, in line with thought to be found elsewhere in the ancient Near East, the Chronicler had seen that the primary role of the monarchy in Israel was the institution of the cultus and viewed royal election chiefly as a vocation to a cultic task. Secondly, it was shown how the Chronicler's presentations of the conditioned nature of the dynastic promise and of the greater kingship of Yahweh combine to explain how the dynasty no longer maintained political rule in Israel and how the Temple and its cultus endured as the Davidic heritage in the post-exilic nation. Finally, the Chronicler's concern to show the continuity between his own post-exilic nation and Davidic Israel was explored, together with the Chronicler's perception that it was upon the whole of the post-exilic people that the Davidic task and blessing devolved.

One result of the foregoing study was an indication of the vitality of the royal temple ideology in post-exilic Israel; its survival is due, at least in part, to the expression that the ideology had received in the cultic and historical traditions of Israel, both of which are influential in the Chronicler's work. The Chronicler gave an unusual application to this ideology, which had formerly been applied to give divine legitimacy to Davidic rule in pre-exilic Israel; he used such tenets to be found in it as the kingship of Yahweh and the cultic vocation of the king to demonstrate how Davidic rule could come to an end. A further and related result of this study has been to demonstrate that the David-restoring hope perceived by some commentators is, in fact, an illusion created by the isolation of certain passages from the total context of the Chronistic History and by viewing them in the light of the messianic faith of the interpreters themselves. The Chronicler is indeed interested in the promise to David, but sees that promise to have its enduring reality in the Temple and cultic community of God's post-exilic people.

Although the Chronicler's work lost much of its immediacy with the passing of the Temple cultus it celebrates, it is not difficult to suggest many rich and striking applications of his vision to the attention of his modern readers: the seeking of God, the need for wholeness of heart, the all-inclusiveness of God's concern for his people might be mentioned among these. However, none emerges from this study so powerfully as the centrality of an authentic worship of God which, because it celebrates the covenant relationship between God and his people, is a celebration of his promises and an acceptance of his demands. For the sake of that type of worship, even whole dynasties are made to rise and fall.

BIBLIOGRAPHY

Ackroyd, P.R., *I & II Chronicles, Ezra, Nehemiah* (TBC; London: SCM Press, 1973).
—*The Age of the Chronicler* (Auckland: Colloquium, 1970).
—'The Biblical Interpretation of the Reigns of Ahaz and Hezekiah', in W.B. Barrick
    and J.R. Spencer (eds.), *In the Shelter of Elyon: Essays on Ancient Palestinian
    Life and Literature* (JSOTSup, 31; Sheffield: JSOT Press, 1984), pp. 247-59.
—'Chronicles–Ezra–Nehemiah: The Concept of Unity', *ZAW* 100 (1988), pp. 189-
    201.
—'Continuity and Discontinuity: Rehabilitation and Authentication', in D.A. Knight
    (ed.), *Tradition and Theology in the Old Testament* (Philadelphia: Fortress Press,
    1977), pp. 215-34.
—'The Chronicler as Exegete', *JSOT* 2 (1977), pp. 2-32.
—'The Historical Literature', in D.A. Knight and G.M. Tucker (eds.), *The Hebrew
    Bible and its Modern Interpreters* (Philadelphia: Fortress Press, 1985), pp. 279-
    324.
—'History and Theology in the Writings of the Chronicler', *CTM* 38 (1967),
    pp. 501-15.
—'The History of Israel in the Exilic and Post-Exilic Periods', in G.W. Anderson (ed.),
    *Tradition and Interpretation: Essays by Members of the Society for Old Testament
    Study* (Oxford: Clarendon Press, 1979), pp. 320-50.
—'The Temple Vessels—A Continuity Theme', in J.A. Emerton *et al.* (eds.), *Studies in
    the Religion of Ancient Israel* (VTSup, 23; Leiden: Brill, 1972), pp. 166-81.
Adinolfi, M., 'Le "opere di pietà liturgica" di David in 2 Cron. 6,42', *BO* 8 (1966),
    pp. 31-36.
Albright, W.F., 'The Date and Personality of the Chronicler', *JBL* 40 (1921),
    pp. 104-24.
—'The Judicial Reform of Jehoshaphat', in D. Frankel (ed.), *The Alexander Marx
    Jubilee Volume* (New York: The Jewish Theological Seminary of America, 1950),
    pp. 61-82.
Allen, L.C., 'Kerygmatic Units in 1 & 2 Chronicles', *JSOT* 41 (1988), pp. 21-36.
Anderson, A.A., *Psalms* (NCB; 2 vols.; London: Marshall, Morgan & Scott, 1981).
Barnes, W.E., *The Books of Chronicles* (CBSC; Cambridge: Cambridge University Press,
    1899).
—'The Midrashic Element in Chronicles', *Expos* 5.4 (1896), pp. 426-39.
—'The Religious Standpoint of the Chronicler', *AJSL* 13 (1896–97), pp. 14-20.
Barr, J., *Biblical Words for Time* (SBT, 33; London: SCM Press, 2nd edn, 1969).
Bartlett, J.R., 'The Edomite King-List of Genesis XXXVI.31-39 and I Chron. I.43-50',
    JTS 16 (1965), pp. 301-14.

Bea, A., 'Neuere Arbeiten zum Problem der biblischen Chronikbücher', *Bib* 22 (1941), pp. 46-58.

Becker, J., *1 Chronik* (NEchtB; Würzburg: Echter, 1986).

—*2 Chronik* (NEchtB; Würzburg: Echter, 1988).

—*Messiaserwartung im Alten Testament* (SBS, 83; Stuttgart: Katholisches Bibelwerk, 1977).

Begg, C.T., 'The Classical Prophets in the Chronistic History', *BZ* 32 (1988), pp. 100-107.

—'The Death of Josiah in Chronicles: Another View', *VT* 37 (1987), pp. 1-8.

—' "Seeking Yahweh" and the Purpose of Chronicles', *LS* 9 (1982), pp. 128-41.

Bendavid, A., *Parallels in the Bible* (Jerusalem: Carta, 1972).

Berg, S.B., 'After the Exile: God and History in the Book of Chronicles and Esther', in J.L. Crenshaw and S. Sandmel (eds.), *The Divine Helmsman: Studies on God's Control of Human Events Presented to Louis H. Silberman* (New York: Ktav, 1980), pp. 107-27.

Bernhardt, K.-H., 'Ugaritic Texts: Myths', in W. Beyerlin (ed.), *Near Eastern Religious Texts Relating to the Old Testament* (trans. J. Bowden; OTL; London: SCM Press, 1978), pp. 190-221.

Botterweck, G.J., 'Zur Eigenart der chronistischen Davidsgeschichte', *TQ* 136 (1956), pp. 402-35.

Braun, R.L., 'Chronicles, Ezra, and Nehemiah: Theology and Literary History', in J.A. Emerton (ed.), *Studies in the Historical Books of the Old Testament* (VTSup, 30; Leiden: Brill, 1979), pp. 52-64.

—*1 Chronicles* (WBC, 14; Waco, TX: Word Books, 1986).

—'The Message of Chronicles: Rally 'Round the Temple', *CTM* 42 (1971), pp. 502-14.

—'A Reconsideration of the Chronicler's Attitude toward the North', *JBL* 96 (1977), pp. 59-62.

—'Solomon, the Chosen Temple Builder: The Significance of 1 Chronicles 22, 28, and 29 for the Theology of Chronicles', *JBL* 95 (1976), pp. 581-90.

Bright, J., *Covenant and Promise: The Prophetic Understanding of the Future in Pre-Exilic Israel* (Philadelphia: Westminster Press, 1976).

Brown, R.E., and S.M. Schneiders, 'Hermeneutics', in R.E. Brown, J.A. Fitzmeyer and R.E. Murphy (eds.), *The New Jerome Biblical Commentary* (London: Geoffrey Chapman, 1990), pp. 1146-65.

Brueggemann, W., *David's Truth in Israel's Imagination and Memory* (Philadelphia: Fortress Press, 1985).

Brunet, A.-M., 'Le Chroniste et ses sources', *RB* 60 (1953), pp. 481-508; 61 (1954), pp. 349-86.

—'La théologie du chroniste: théocratie et messianisme', in J. Coppens, A. Descamps and E. Massaux (eds.), *Sacra Pagina: Miscellanea Biblica Congressus Internationalis Catholici de Re Biblica*, I (Gembloux: Duculot, 1959), pp. 384-97.

Brunner, H., 'Egyptian Texts: Precepts for Life', in W. Beyerlin (ed.), *Near Eastern Religious Texts Relating to the Old Testament* (trans. J. Bowden; OTL; London: SCM Press, 1978), pp. 44-63.

—'Egyptian Texts: Royal Texts', in W. Beyerlin (ed.), *Near Eastern Religious Texts Relating to the Old Testament* (trans. J. Bowden; OTL; London: SCM Press, 1978), pp. 27-30.

Busshe, H. van den, 'Le Texte de la prophétie de Nathan sur la Dynastie Davidique (II Sam.,VII–I Chron., XVII)', *ETL* 24 (1948), pp. 388-91.

Butler, T.C., 'A Forgotten Passage from a Forgotten Era (1 Chron. 16:8-36)', *VT* 28 (1978), pp. 142-50.

Cancik, H., 'Das judische Fest: Ein Versuch zu Form und Religion des chronistischen Geschichtswerkes', *TQ* 150 (1970), pp. 333-48.

Caquot, A., 'Peut-on parler de messianisme dans l'oeuvre du Chroniste?', *RTP* 16 (1966), pp. 110-20.

Cazelles, H., *Les livres des Chroniques* (SB; Paris: Cerf, 2nd edn, 1961).

Charlesworth, J.H., *The Old Testament Pseudepigrapha* (2 vols.; London: Darton, Longman & Todd, 1983, 1985).

Clements, R.E., *God and Temple* (Oxford: Basil Blackwell, 1965).

Clifford, R.J., *The Cosmic Mountain in Canaan and the Old Testament* (HSM, 4; Cambridge, MA: Harvard University Press, 1972).

Coggins, R.J., *The First and Second Books of the Chronicles* (CBC; Cambridge: Cambridge University Press, 1976).

Conroy, C., *1–2 Samuel, 1–2 Kings* (OTM, 6; Wilmington, DE: Michael Glazier, 1983).

Cooke, G., 'The Israelite King as Son of God', *ZAW* 73 (1961), pp. 202-26.

Coppens, J., *Le messianisme royal* (LD, 54; Paris: Cerf, 1968).

Cross, F.M., 'A Reconstruction of the Judean Restoration', *JBL* 94 (1975), pp. 4-18.

Curtis, E.L., and A.A. Madsen, *A Critical and Exegetical Commentary on the Books of Chronicles* (ICC; Edinburgh: T. & T. Clark, 1976).

Danby, H., *The Mishnah* (Oxford: Oxford University Press, 1977).

Deboys, D.G., 'History and Theology in the Chronicler's Portrayal of Abijah', *Bib* 71 (1990), pp. 48-62.

De Vries, S.J., *1 and 2 Chronicles* (FOTL, 11; Grand Rapids: Eerdmans, 1989).

—'Moses and David as Cult Founders in Chronicles', *JBL* 107 (1988), pp. 619-39.

—'The Schema of Dynastic Endangerment in Chronicles', *PEGLMBS* 7 (1987), pp. 59-77.

Dillard, R.B., 'The Chronicler's Jehoshaphat', *TrinJ* 7 (1986), pp. 17-22.

—'The Literary Structure of the Chronicler's Solomon Narrative', *JSOT* 30 (1984), pp. 85-93.

—'The Reign of Asa (2 Chronicles 14–16): An Example of the Chronicler's Theological Method', *JETS* 23 (1980), pp. 207-19.

—*2 Chronicles* (WBC, 15; Waco, TX: Word Books, 1987).

—'Reward and Punishment in Chronicles: The Theology of Immediate Retribution', *WTJ* 46 (1984), pp. 164-72.

Driver, G.R., *Canaanite Myths and Legends* (OTS, 3; Edinburgh: T. & T. Clark, 1976).

Driver, S.R., *An Introduction to the Literature of the Old Testament* (Edinburgh: T. & T. Clark, 9th edn, 1961).

Duke, R.K., *The Persuasive Appeal of the Chronicler: A Rhetorical Analysis* (JSOTSup, 88; Sheffield: JSOT Press, 1990).

Dumbrell, W.J., 'The Purpose of the Books of Chronicles', *JETS* 27 (1984), pp. 257-66.

Durham, J.I., 'שלום and the Presence of God', in J.I. Durham and J.R. Porter (eds.), *Proclamation and Presence: Old Testament Essays in Honour of Gwynne Henton Davies* (London: SCM Press, 1970), pp. 272-93.

Edelman, D., 'The Manassite Genealogy in 1 Chronicles 7:14-19: Form and Source', *CBQ* 53 (1991), pp. 179-201.

Eissfeldt, O., *The Old Testament: An Introduction* (trans. P.R. Ackroyd; Oxford: Basil Blackwell, 1974).

Elmslie, W.A.L., *The Books of Chronicles* (CBSC; Cambridge: Cambridge University Press, 1916).

Epstein, I., *The Babylonian Talmud* (18 vols.; London: Soncino, 1952).

Eskenazi, T.C., 'The Chronicler and the Composition of 1 Esdras', *CBQ* 48 (1986), pp. 39-61.

Fishbane, M., *Biblical Interpretation in Ancient Israel* (Oxford: Clarendon Press, 1989 [1985]).

Flanagan, J.W., *David's Social Drama: A Hologram of Israel's Early Iron Age* (JSOTSup, 73; JSOT Press, 1988).

Frankfort, H., *Kingship and the Gods* (Chicago: University of Chicago Press, 1978 [1948]).

Freedman, D.N., 'The Chronicler's Purpose', *CBQ* 23 (1961), pp. 436-42.

Friedman, R.E., 'Sacred History/Sacred Literature', in R.E. Friedman (ed.), *The Creation of Sacred Literature: Composition and Redaction of the Biblical Text* (Berkeley: University of California Press, 1981), pp. 1-3.

Galbiati, E., 'Il carattere sacro della regalità nell'antico Israele', *BO* 19 (1977), pp. 89-100.

Galling, K., *Die Bücher der Chronik, Esra, Nehemia* (ATD, 12; Göttingen: Vandenhoeck & Ruprecht, 1954).

Garsiel, M., 'Puns upon Names as a Literary Device in 1 Kings 1–2', *Bib* 72 (1991), pp. 379-86.

Ginsberg, H.L., 'Poems about Baal and Anath', *ANET*, pp. 129-42.

Goetze, A. 'Daily Prayer of the King', *ANET*, pp. 396-97.

—'Ritual for the Erection of a House', *ANET*, pp. 356-57.

—'The Telepinus Myth', *ANET*, pp. 126-28.

Goldingay, J., 'The Chronicler as a Theologian', *BTB* 5 (1975), pp. 99-126.

Gordon, R.P., *1 & 2 Samuel* (Exeter: Paternoster Press, 1986).

Gottwald, N.K., *The Hebrew Bible: A Socio-Literary Introduction* (Philadelphia: Fortress Press, 1985).

Graham, M.P., 'A Connection Proposed between II Chr 24,26 and Ezra 9–10', *ZAW* 97 (1985), pp. 256-58.

Gray, J., *I & II Kings* (OTL; London: SCM Press, 1977).

Grayson, A.K., 'The Creation Epic: Additions to Tablets V-VII', *ANET*, pp. 501-503.

Gunkel, H., *Die Psalmen* (Göttingen: Vandenhoeck & Ruprecht, 6th edn, 1986).

Halpern, B., *The Constitution of the Monarchy in Israel* (HSM, 25; Chico, CA: Scholars Press, 1981).

—'Sacred History and Ideology: Chronicles' Thematic Structure--Indications of an Earlier Source', in R.E. Friedman (ed.), *The Creation of Sacred Literature:*

Composition and Redaction of the Biblical Text (Berkeley: University of California Press, 1981), pp. 35-54.

Hannay, T., 'The Temple', *SJT* 3 (1950), pp. 278-87.

Haran, M., 'The Passover Sacrifice', in J.A. Emerton *et al.* (eds.), *Studies in the Religion of Ancient Israel* (VTSup, 23; Leiden: Brill, 1972), pp. 86-116.

Harvey-Jellie, W.R., *Chronicles* (CB; Edinburgh: T.C. & E.C. Jack, 1906).

Hertzberg, H.W., *I & II Samuel* (trans. J.S. Bowden; OTL; London: SCM Press, 1976 [1960]).

Hill, A.E., 'Patchwork Poetry or Reasoned Verse? Connective Structure in 1 Chron. 16', *VT* 33 (1983), pp. 97-101.

Holladay, W.L., *A Concise Hebrew and Aramaic Lexicon of the Old Testament* (Leiden: Brill, 1971).

Japhet, S., 'Chronicles, Book of', *EncJud*, V, cols. 517-34.

—'Conquest and Settlement in Chronicles', *JBL* 98 (1979), pp. 205-18.

—'The Historical Reliability of Chronicles: The History of the Problem and its Place in Biblical Research', *JSOT* 33 (1985), pp. 83-107.

—'The Ideology of the Book of Chronicles and its Place in Biblical Thought', *Im* 4 (1974), pp. 24-27.

—*The Ideology of the Book of Chronicles and its Place in Biblical Thought* (trans. A. Barber; BEATAJ, 9; Frankfurt: Peter Lang, 1989).

—'The Supposed Common Authorship of Chronicles and Ezra–Nehemiah Investigated Anew', *VT* 18 (1968), pp. 330-71.

Jensen, J.S., 'Prediction-Fulfilment in Bible and Liturgy', *CBQ* 50 (1988), pp. 646-62.

Johnson, A.R., *Sacral Kingship in Ancient Israel* (Cardiff: University of Wales Press, 2nd edn, 1967).

Johnson, M.D., *The Purpose of the Biblical Genealogies* (SNTSMS, 8; Cambridge: Cambridge University Press, 1969).

Johnstone, W., 'Guilt and Atonement: The Theme of 1 and 2 Chronicles', in J.D. Martin and P.R. Davis (eds.), *A Word in Season: Essays in Honour of William McKane* (JSOTSup, 42; Sheffield: JSOT Press, 1986), pp. 113-38.

—'Reactivating the Chronicles Analogy in Pentateuchal Studies, with Special Reference to the Sinai Pericope in Exodus', *ZAW* 99 (1987), pp. 16-37.

Kalimi, I., 'The Land of Moriah, Mount Moriah, and the Site of Solomon's Temple in Biblical Historiography', *HTR* 83 (1990), pp. 345-62.

Kapelrud, A.S., 'Temple Building, a Task for Gods and Kings', *Or* 32 (1963), pp. 56-62.

—'Tradition and Worship: The Role of the Cult in Tradition Formation and Transmission', in D.A. Knight (ed.), *Tradition and Theology in the Old Testament* (Philadelphia: Fortress Press, 1977), pp. 101-24.

Keel, O., *The Symbolism of the Biblical World* (trans. T.J. Hallett; London: SPCK, 1978).

Klein, R.W., 'Abijah's Compaign against the North (II Chr 13)—What Were the Chronicler's Sources?', *ZAW* 95 (1983), pp. 210-17.

—*Textual Criticism of the Old Testament: The Septuagint after Qumran* (GBSOT; Philadelphia: Fortress Press, 1974).

Knoppers, G.N., 'Reform and Regression: The Chronicler's Presentation of Jehoshaphat', *Bib* 72 (1991), pp. 345-62.

Kramer, S.N., 'Gilgamesh and Agga', *ANET*, 1974, pp. 44-47.

—'Inanna and the King', *ANET*, pp. 640-41.

—'Ur-Nammu Hymn: Building of the Ekur and Blessing by Enlil', *ANET*, pp. 583-84.

Kraus, H.-J., *Psalmen* (BKAT, 15; 2 vols; Neukirchen–Vluyn: Neukirchener Verlag, 3rd edn, 1966).

Kühne, C., 'Hittite Texts: Prayers', in W. Beyerlin (ed.), *Near Eastern Religious Texts Relating to the Old Testament* (trans. J. Bowden; OTL; London: SCM Press, 1978), pp. 165-74.

La Sor, W.S., 'The *Sensus Plenior* and Biblical Interpretation' in D.K. McKim (ed.), *A Guide to Contemporary Hermeneutics: Major Trends in Biblical Interpretation* (Grand Rapids: Eerdmans, 1986).

Lemke, W.E., 'The Synoptic Problem in the Chronicler's History', *HTR* 58 (1965), pp. 349-63.

Lévi-Strauss, C., *Myth and Meaning* (London: Routledge & Kegan Paul, 1978).

Levin, C., *Der Sturz der Königin Atalja* (SBS, 105; Stuttgart: Katholisches Bibelwerk, 1982).

Lichtheim, M., *Ancient Egyptian Literature 2: The New Kingdom* (Berkeley: University of California Press, 1976).

Lipinski, E., 'North Semitic Texts from the First Millennium BC: Graffiti', in W. Beyerlin (ed.), *Near Eastern Religious Texts Relating to the Old Testament* (trans. J. Bowden; OTL; London: SCM Press, 1978), p. 251.

Lisowsky, G., *Konkordanz zum hebräischen Alten Testament* (Stuttgart: Deutsche Bibelgesellschaft, 2nd edn, 1981).

Loader, J.A., 'Redaction and Function of the Chronistic "Psalm of David"', *OTWSA* 19 (1976), pp. 69-75.

McCarthy, C., and W. Riley, *The Old Testament Short Story* (MBS, 7; Wilmington, DE: Michael Glazier, 1986).

McCarthy, D.J., 'Covenant and Law in Chronicles–Nehemiah', *CBQ* 44 (1982), pp. 25-44.

—*Old Testament Covenant: A Survey of Current Opinions* (GPT; Oxford: Basil Blackwell, 1973).

McConville, J.G., 'I Chronicles 28:9: Yahweh "Seeks Out" Solomon', *JTS* 37 (1986), pp. 105-108.

—*Chronicles* (DSB; Edinburgh: Saint Andrew Press, 1984).

McKenzie, S.L., *The Chronicler's Use of the Deuteronomistic History* (HSM, 33; Atlanta: Scholars Press, 1984).

Malamat, A., 'A Forerunner of Biblical Prophecy: The Mari Documents', in P.D. Miller, P.D. Hanson and S.D. McBride (eds.), *Ancient Israelite Religion: Essays in Honor of Frank Moore Cross* (Philadelphia: Fortress Press, 1987), pp. 33-52.

Mangan, C., *1–2 Chronicles, Ezra, Nehemiah* (OTM, 13; Wilmington, DE: Michael Glazier, 1982).

Mays, J.L., *Micah: A Commentary* (OTL; London: SCM Press, 1976).

Meyers, C.L., 'David as Temple Builder', in P.D. Miller, P.D. Hanson and S.D. McBride (eds.), *Ancient Israelite Religion: Essays in Honor of Frank Moore Cross* (Philadelphia: Fortress Press, 1987), pp. 357-76.

—'Jachin and Boaz in Religious and Political Perspective', *CBQ* 45 (1983), pp. 167-78.

Michaeli, F., *Les livres des Chroniques, d'Esdras et de Néhémie* (CAT, 16; Neuchâtel: Delachaux & Niestlé, 1967).

Moran, W.L., 'Divine Revelations', *ANET*, pp. 623-26.

Mosis, R., *Untersuchungen zur Theologie des chronistischen Geschichtswerkes* (FTS, 92; Freiburg: Herder, 1973).

Mowinckel, S., 'Erwägungen zum chronistischen Geschichtswerk', *TLZ* 85 (1960), cols. 1-8.

Murray, D.F., '*mqwm* and the Future of Israel in 2 Samuel VII 10', *VT* 40 (1990), pp. 298-320.

Myers, J.M., *I Chronicles* (AB, 12; Garden City, NY: Doubleday, 1979).

—*II Chronicles* (AB, 13; Garden City, NY: Doubleday, 1979).

—'The Kerygma of the Chronicler: History and Theology in the Service of Religion', *Int* 20 (1966), pp. 259-73.

Na'aman, N., 'Sources and Redaction in the Chronicler's Genealogies of Asher and Ephraim', *JSOT* 49 (1991), pp. 99-111.

Newsome, J.D., 'Toward a New Understanding of the Chronicler and his Purposes', *JBL* 94 (1975), pp. 201-17.

Noordtzij, A., 'Les intentions du Chroniste', *RB* 49 (1940), pp. 161-68.

North, R., 'The Chronicler: 1–2 Chronicles, Ezra, Nehemiah', in R. Brown, J.A. Fitzmyer and R.E. Murphy (eds.), *The Jerome Biblical Commentary* (London: Geoffrey Chapman, 1968), pp. 402-38.

—'The Chronicler: 1–2 Chronicles, Ezra, Nehemiah', in R. Brown, J.A. Fitzmyer and R.E. Murphy (eds.), *The New Jerome Biblical Commentary* (London: Geoffrey Chapman, 1989), pp. 362-98.

—'Does Archeology Prove Chronicles' Sources', in H.N. Bream, R.D. Heim and C.A. Moore (eds.), *Light unto My Path: Old Testament Studies in Honor of Jacob M. Myers* (Philadephia: Temple University Press, 1974), pp. 375-401.

—*Israel's Chronicle* (St Marys, KS: St Louis University School of Divinity, 1963).

—'Theology of the Chronicler', *JBL* 82 (1963), pp. 369-81.

Noth, M., *The Chronicler's History* (trans. H.G.M. Williamson; JSOTSup, 50; Sheffield: JSOT Press, 1987).

—*The Deuteronomistic History* (trans. J. Doull; JSOTSup, 15; Sheffield: JSOT Press, 1981).

—'Jerusalem and the Israelite Tradition', in *The Laws in the Pentateuch and Other Studies* (trans. D.R. Ap-Thomas; London: SCM Press, 1984), pp. 132-44.

—*Leviticus* (trans. J.E. Anderson; London: SCM Press, 2nd edn, 1981).

Oppenheim, A.L., 'Adad-Nirari III (810–783): Expedition to Palestine', *ANET*, pp. 281-82.

—'Antiochus Soter (280–262/1)', *ANET*, p. 317.

—'Ashurnasirpal II (883–859): Expedition to Carchemish and the Lebanon', *ANET*, pp. 275-76.

—'Cyrus (557–529)', *ANET*, pp. 315-16.

—'The Dedication of the Shamash Temple by Yahdun-Lim', *ANET*, pp. 556-57.

—'Gudea, Ensi of Lagash', *ANET*, pp. 268-69.

—'The Mother of Nabonidus', *ANET*, pp. 560-62.

—'Nabonidus (555–539): Nabonidus and the Clergy of Babylon', *ANET*, pp. 312-15.

—'Nabonidus (555–539): Nabonidus' Rise to Power', *ANET*, pp. 308-11.

—'Nabonidus and his God', *ANET*, pp. 562-63.

—'The Sumerian King List', *ANET*, pp. 265-66.

—'Tiglath-pileser I (1114–1076): Expeditions to Syria, the Lebanon, and the Mediterranean Sea', *ANET*, pp. 274-75.

—'Xerxes (485–465)', *ANET*, pp. 316-17.

Ottoson, M., 'הֵיכָל hêkal', *TDOT*, III, pp. 382-88.

Parrot, A., *Le temple de Jérusalem* (CAD, 5; Neuchâtel: Delachaux & Niestlé, 2nd edn, 1962).

Petersen, D.L., *Late Israelite Prophecy: Studies in Deutero-Prophetic Literature and in Chronicles* (SBLMS, 23; Missoula, MT: Scholars Press, 1977).

—'Portraits of David, Canonical and Otherwise', *Int* 40 (1986), pp. 130-42.

Plöger, O., 'Reden und Gebete im deuteronomistichen und chronistischen Geschichtswerk', in *Aus der Spätzeit des Alten Testaments* (Göttingen: Vandenhoeck & Ruprecht, 1971), pp. 50-66.

—*Theocracy and Eschatology* (trans. S. Rudman; Oxford: Basil Blackwell, 1968).

Poulssen, N., 'Rex et Templum in Israel', *VD* 40 (1962), pp. 264-69.

Porter, J.R., 'The Accession of Joshua', in J.I. Durham and J.R. Porter (eds.), *Proclamation and Presence: Old Testament Essays in Honour of Gwynne Henton Davies* (London: SCM Press, 1970), pp. 102-32.

—'Old Testament Historiography', in G.W. Anderson (ed.), *Tradition and Interpretation: Essays by Members of the Society for Old Testament Study* (Oxford: Clarendon Press, 1979), pp. 125-62.

Quellette, J., 'Temple of Solomon', *IDBSup*, pp. 872-74.

Rad, G. von, *Das Geschichtsbild des chronistischen Werkes* (BWANT, 54; Stuttgart: Kohlhammer, 1930).

—'The Levitical Sermon in I & II Chronicles', in *The Problem of the Hexateuch and Other Essays* (trans. E.W.T. Dicken; London: SCM Press, 1984), pp. 267-80.

—*Old Testament Theology 1: The Theology of Israel's Historical Traditions* (trans. D.G.M. Stalker; Edinburgh: Oliver & Boyd, 1968 [1957]).

—'The Royal Ritual in Judah', in *The Problem of the Hexateuch and Other Essays* (trans. E.W.T. Dicken; London: SCM Press, 1984), pp. 222-31.

Rahlfs, A., *Septuaginta* (Stuttgart: Deutsche Bibelgesellschaft, 1935).

Randellini, L., *Il libro delle Cronache* (SBibbia; Rome: Marietti, 1966).

—'Il libro delle Cronache nel decennio 1950–1960', *RivB* 10 (1962), pp. 136-55.

Ricoeur, P., *Interpretation Theory: Discourse and the Surplus of Meaning* (Fort Worth: Texas Christian University Press, 1976 [1973]).

Riley, W., 'On the Location of Meaning in a Sacred Text', *PIBA* 13 (1990), pp. 7-23.

—'Situating Biblical Narrative: Poetics and the Transmission of Community Values', *PIBA* 9 (1985), pp. 38-52.

Ringgren, H., *Religions of the Ancient Near East* (trans. J. Sturdy; London: SPCK, 1973).

Robert, A., and A. Feuillet, *Introduction to the Old Testament* (New York: Desclée, 1968).

Rolla, A., 'La Palestina Postesilica alla luce dell'archeologia', *RivB* 34 (1986), pp. 111-19.

Rowley, H.H., *Worship in Israel: Its Forms and Meaning* (London: SPCK, 1978 [1967]).

Rudolph, W., *Chronikbücher* (HAT; Tübingen: Mohr, 1955).

—'Problems of the Books of Chronicles', *VT* 4 (1954), pp. 401-409.

Runnalls, D., 'The King as Temple Builder: A Messianic Typology', in D.Y. Hadidian (ed.), *Spirit within Structure: Essays in Honour of George Johnston on the Occasion of his Seventieth Birthday* (PTMS NS 3; Allison Park, PA: Pickwick Publications, 1983), pp. 15-37.

Rylaarsdam, J.C., 'Passover and the Feast of Unleavened Bread', *IDB*, III, pp. 663-68.

Sachs, A., 'Ritual for the Repair of a Temple', *ANET*, pp. 339-42.

—'Temple Program for the New Year's Festivals at Babylon', *ANET*, pp. 331-34.

Saebø, M., 'Messianism in Chronicles? Some Remarks to the Old Testament Background of the New Testament Christology', *HBT* 2 (1980), pp. 85-109.

Sakenfield, K.D., *The Meaning of HESED in the Hebrew Bible: A New Inquiry* (HSM, 17; Missoula, MT: Scholars Press, 1978).

Schmökel, H., 'Mesopotamian Texts: Hymns, Prayers and Laments', in W. Beyerlin (ed.), *Near Eastern Religious Texts Relating to the Old Testament* (trans. J. Bowden; OTL; London: SCM Press, 1978), pp. 99-118.

Schniedewind, W.M., 'The Source Citations of Manasseh: King Manasseh in History and Homily', *VT* 41 (1991), pp. 450-61.

Schuller, E., *Post-Exilic Prophets* (MBS, 4; Wilmington, DE: Michael Glazier, 1988).

Schumacher, J.N., 'The Chronicler's Theology of History', *TTh* 13 (1957), pp. 11-21.

Sesboué, D., 'Ruine temporaire de Jérusalem: 2 Ch 36:14-16.19-23', *AsSeign* 17 (1970), pp. 28-33.

Slotki, I.W., *Chronicles* (SBB; London: Soncino, 1978 [1952]).

Smith, W.R., *Lectures on the Religion of the Semites* (London: A. & C. Black, rev. edn, 1894).

Snaith, N.H., *The Distinctive Ideas of the Old Testament* (London: Epworth Press, 1944).

Solomon, A.M., 'The Structure of the Chronicler's History: A Key to the Organization of the Pentateuch', *Semeia* 46 (1989), pp. 51-64.

Speiser, E.A., 'The Creation Epic', *ANET*, pp. 60-72.

—'Etana', *ANET*, pp. 114-18.

Spencer, F.S., '2 Chronicles 28:5-15 and the Parable of the Good Samaritan', *WTJ* 46 (1984), pp. 317-49.

Stinespring, W.F., 'Eschatology in Chronicles', *JBL* 80 (1961), pp. 209-19.

Stolz, F. 'נוּחַ *nûaḥ* ruhen', *THAT*, II, cols. 43-46.

Stuhlmueller, C., *Psalms 2* (OTM, 22; Wilmington, DE: Michael Glazier, 1983).

Talmon, S., 'Divergences in Calendar-Reckoning in Ephraim and Judah', *VT* 8 (1958), pp. 48-74.

Thompson, M.E.W., *Situation and Theology: Old Testament Interpretations of the Syro-Ephraimite War* (Sheffield: Almond Press, 1982).

Throntveit, M.A., 'Linguistic Analysis and the Question of Authorship in Chronicles, Ezra and Nehemiah', *VT* 32 (1982), pp. 201-16.

—*When Kings Speak: Royal Speech and Royal Prayer in Chronicles* (SBLDS, 93; Atlanta: Scholars Press, 1987).

Torrey, C.C., *The Chronicler's History of Israel* (New Haven: Yale University Press, 1954).

Trompf, G.W., 'Notions of Historical Recurrence in Classical Hebrew Historiography', in J.A. Emerton (ed.), *Studies in the Historical Books in the Old Testament* VTSup, 30; Leiden: Brill, 1979), pp. 213-29.

Tsevat, M., 'The House of David in Nathan's Prophecy', *Bib* 36 (1965), pp. 353-56.

Vannutelli, P., *Libri Synoptici Veteris Testamenti seu Librorum Regum et Chronicorum Loci Paralleli* (2 vols.; Rome: Pontifical Biblical Institute, 1931).

Vaux, R. de, 'The King of Israel, Vassal of Yahweh', in *The Bible and the Ancient Near East* (trans. D. McHugh; London: Darton, Longman & Todd, 1971), pp. 152-66.

—Review of *Chronikbücher*, by W. Rudolph, *RB* 64 (1957), pp. 278-81.

Virgulin, S., *Libri delle Cronache* (NVB, 10; Rome: Edizioni Paoline, 2nd edn, 1977).

Walters, S.D., 'Saul of Gibeon', *JSOT* 52 (1991), pp. 61-76.

Ward, J.M., 'The Literary Form and Liturgical Background of Psalm LXXXIX', *VT* 11 (1961), pp. 321-39.

Weber, R., *Biblia Sacra iuxta Vulgatam Versionem* (2 vols.; Stuttgart: Württemberg, 1969).

Weinberg, J.P., 'Das Eigengut in den Chronikbüchern', *OLP* 10 (1979), pp. 161-81.

—'Der König im Weltbild des Chronisten', *VT* 39 (1989), pp. 415-37.

—'Das Wegen und die funktionelle Bestimmung der Listen in I Chr 1–9', *ZAW* 93 (1981), pp. 91-114.

Weinfeld, M., 'Covenant, Davidic', *IDBSup*, pp. 188-92.

Weiser, A., *The Psalms* (trans. H. Hartwell; OTL; London: SCM Press, 1982).

Welch, A.C., *The Work of the Chronicler: Its Purpose and Date* (London: Oxford University Press, 1939).

Wellhausen, J., *Prolegomena to the History of Ancient Israel* (trans. Menzies and Black; Gloucester, MA: Peter Smith, 1983 [1878]).

Welten, P., *Geschichte und Geschichtsdarstellung in den Chronikbüchern* (WMANT, 42; Neukirchen–Vluyn: Neukirchener Verlag, 1973).

—'Lade–Tempel–Jerusalem: Zur Theologie der Chronikbücher', in A.H.J. Gunneweg and O. Kaiser (eds.), *Textgemäss: Aufsätze und Beitrage zur Hemeneutik des Alten Testament: Eine Festschrift für E. Würthwein* (Göttingen: Vandenhoeck & Ruprecht, 1979), pp. 169-83.

Westermann, C., *Isaiah 40–66* (trans. D.M.G. Stalker; OTL; London: SCM Press, 1976).

Whitelam, K.W., *The Just King: Monarchical Judicial Authority in Ancient Israel* (JSOTSup, 12; Sheffield: JSOT Press, 1979).

—'The Symbols of Power: Aspects of Royal Propaganda in the United Monarchy', *BA* 49 (1986), pp. 166-73.

Whybray, R.N., *The Second Isaiah* (OTG; Sheffield: JSOT Press, 1983).

—*Isaiah 40–66* (NCB; London: Marshall, Morgan and Scott, 1981).

—*The Succession Narrative: A Study of II Sam. 9–20 and I Kings 1 and 2* (SBT, 9; London: SCM Press, 1968).

Willi, T., *Die Chronik als Auslegung* (FRLANT, 106; Göttingen: Vandenhoeck & Ruprecht, 1972).

Williamson, H.G.M., *1 and 2 Chronicles* (NCB; London: Marshall, Morgan & Scott, 1982).

—'Eschatology in Chronicles', *TynBul* 28 (1977), pp. 115-54.

—*Israel in the Books of Chronicles* (Cambridge: Cambridge University Press, 1977).

—'The Origins of the Twenty-Four Priestly Courses: A Study of 1 Chronicles XXIII–XXVII', in J.A. Emerton (ed.), *Studies in the Historical Books of the Old Testament* (VTSup, 30; Leiden: Brill, 1979), pp. 251-68.

—'Reliving the Death of Josiah: A Reply to C.T. Begg', *VT* 37 (1987), pp. 9-15.

—'"The Sure Mercies of David": Subjective or Objective Genitive?', *JSS* 23 (1978), pp. 31-49.

Wilson, J.A., 'Another Version of the Creation by Atum', *ANET*, pp. 3-4.

—'The Asiatic Campaigning of Amen-hotep II', *ANET*, pp. 245-48.

—'The Divine Nomination of an Ethiopian King', *ANET*, pp. 447-48.

—'The Divine Nomination of Thut-mose III', *ANET*, pp. 446-47.

—'From Amen-hotep III's Building Inscription', *ANET*, pp. 375-76.

—'A Hymn to Amon-Re', *ANET*, pp. 365-67.

—'The Hymn of Victory of Thut-mose III', *ANET*, pp. 373-75.

—'Joy at the Accession of Ramses IV', *ANET*, pp. 378-79.

—'A Syrian Interregnum', *ANET*, p. 260.

—'Tut-ankh-Amon's Restoration after the Amarna Revolution', *ANET*, pp. 251-52.

—'The War against the Hyksos', *ANET*, pp. 232-33.

—'The Divine Attributes of Pharaoh', *ANET*, p. 431.

—'From the Lists of Ramses III', *ANET*, pp. 260-62.

Wright, G.E., 'Cult and History: A Study of a Current Problem in Old Testament Interpretation', *Int* 16 (1962), pp. 3-20.

Wright, J.W., 'The Legacy of David in Chronicles: The Narrative Function of 1 Chronicles 23–27', *JBL* 110 (1991), pp. 229-42.

Zalewski, S., 'The Purpose of the Story of the Death of Saul in 1 Chronicles X', *VT* 39 (1989), pp. 449-67.

Zerafa, P.P., 'Il sacerdozio nell'antico Testamento', *SD* 60 (1970), pp. 621-58.

INDEXES

INDEX OF REFERENCES

OLD TESTAMENT

JOURNAL FOR THE STUDY OF THE OLD TESTAMENT

Supplement Series